AF449534

Björn Rombach and Emma Ek Österberg (editors)

Leadership is the problem

– and therefore not the solution

Santérus
Academic Press
Sweden

www.santerus.se

© 2019 The authors and Santérus Academic Press Sweden
ISBN 978-91-7335-055-6
Cover art: "Development" by Wassily Kandinsky, 1926; Alten/Dessau-alten, Germany
Media: oil, panel, Location: Georges Pompidou Center, Paris, France
Cover profile: Sven Bylander
Typefaces used: Indigo Antiqua Pro by Fontanova Ström AB; Anziano Pro by Stefan Hattenbach, MAC Rhino Fonts
Santérus Academic Press is an imprint of
Santérus Förlag, Stockholm, Sweden
info@santerus.se
Printed by BOD, Germany 2019

Contents

Authors

REBECKA ARMAN, Ph.D., is a researcher and assistant professor at the Department of Business Administration, University of Gothenburg. Arman teaches leadership skills and has conducted research into what health-care managers do with their time, focusing on their activities and communications. In addition, Arman has explored the organisation of IVF clinics in Sweden as well as dismissals and changes in the pharmaceutical industry.

JOHAN BERGLUND is a researcher and teacher at the Stockholm School of Economics. He has previously examined issues of identity, knowledge, language, and power. In his dissertation, Berglund studied the difficulties faced by HR specialists in gaining full recognition and status in organisations. Berglund still retains an interest in these theoretical issues and in human resources management as a field of knowledge. The study of massively multiplayer online games (MMOGs) is a relatively new area of research in which he plans to increasingly immerse himself.

ERIC CARLSTRÖM is a professor of Health Care Sciences at the Sahlgrenska Academy, University of Gothenburg. He is also a trained specialist nurse with 30 years' experience in emergency ambulance services. Carlström earned his Ph.D. in Public Administration in 2005 and has researched the context of health and crisis management since then. His studies concentrate on collaboration, integration, teamwork, and organisational culture.

ANNA CREGÅRD is an associate professor in Business Administration and the Dean of the School of Business, Engineering and Science at Halmstad University. She conducts research into governance and leadership in public and non-profit organisations. Cregård is particularly interested in leadership that can be described as difficult, complex, or complicated, for example when employees would prefer to govern themselves or where there are changes and sudden dismissals. In addition, Cregård is also interested in innovation and organisational changes.

EMMA EK ÖSTERBERG is a lecturer in Public Administration at the School of Public Administration, University of Gothenburg. Her research considers the organisational dimensions of governance in the public sector. In this field, she has explored processes of marketisation in the transport sector as well as audit practices in the welfare sector.

STAFFAN FURUSTEN is the Director of the Stockholm Centre for Organizational Research (Score) and an associate professor at the Stockholm School of Economics. Furusten has published several books, book chapters, and articles on the production and distribution of management concepts and management consultancy. Other research interests include new forms of regulation (*e.g.* standards) as well as value conflicts in public and market organisations. A recently initiated research project concerns the practice of sustainability in organisations.

IRÉNE LIND NILSSON has a Ph.D. in Pedagogy. Her thesis, *Leadership in Crisis, Chaos, and Change,* is based on an empirical study of companies and the public sector. Nilsson worked for several years as a project manager at the IPF Institute at Uppsala University and has extensive experience of consultative work in employee and management training. Nilsson also has experience of working as a manager in the public sector. Currently a freelance writer and consultant, she has published books and book chapters about leadership, power, communication, and ethics.

ÖSTEN OHLSSON was a professor of management at the University of Gothenburg, School of Public Administration. His research was largely about how reforms and new ideas are transformed into development activities in private companies and public organisations. Over the last decade, his primary research interest was directed towards a general criticism of management discourse. Östen Ohlsson died during the work on this anthology.

BJÖRN ROMBACH has served as a professor at the School of Public Administration, University of Gothenburg, since 1995. Over the years, Rombach has written or contributed to a series of books and other publications treating financial management, leadership, quality, and organisation.

ROLF SOLLI is a professor of Business Administration at the University of Borås but maintains connections to the University of Gothenburg. His research interests lie in the field of the governance and management of political organisations, predominantly local authorities and regions. In recent years, this interest has concentrated on municipal leaders, civic involvement, film as empirical evidence, and contemporary accounting management.

CHAPTER 1

Is leadership really the solution?

Emma Ek Österberg, Björn Rombach, and Östen Ohlsson

This book about leadership targets all those seeking a better understanding of the mysterious phenomenon called leadership. Our readership includes scholars exploring leadership, leaders and those who want to become leaders, as well as all those who are led or would like to be led. Consequently, this book is aimed at practically everyone. We combine this broad ambition with a slightly narrower one, focusing particularly on those striving to develop and improve leadership in both theory and practice. We aim to be critical, but also to participate in the ongoing debate on what leadership is and should be, combining outsider and insider perspectives.

In this book, we expand our knowledge of leadership from two starting points, both of which are intended to turn things on their heads. The first starting point is analytical and is an implicit analytical assumption running throughout the book, *i.e.* that leadership constitutes a problem, not a solution. More precisely, we argue that the actual notion that leadership constitutes a solution is the main problem, because it limits leadership research. We will revisit this assumption later in this chapter. The second starting point is empirical and entails studies of leadership in contexts that are usually overlooked. We call these contexts extreme, and by that we mean extreme in one respect only, *i.e.* that they are not where most leadership research finds its empirical basis. Traditional businesses and public authorities are replaced with other settings, such as a monastery and polar expeditions, in order to see beyond the preconditions of modern bureaucracy. Our interest in leadership outside the usual narrow confines is based on two observations:

– *Leadership researchers are notably unanimous*. There seem to be no major battles right now, and scarcely any minor ones. Despite the constant flow of new studies and books on leadership, the actual body of relevant knowledge remains homogeneous. It would seem as though leadership research is completed and that we have all the theories we need.

– *Those who lecture about leadership and those taking leadership courses seem to agree on the topics a leadership course should cover*. The demand for leadership courses is still high but new questions are seldom asked. Perhaps there have simply been too many courses? Or perhaps some of us have repeated ourselves for too long?

This admittedly sweeping assessment of leadership science started by asking what leadership researchers actually agree on. When we searched for answers in the mainstream literature, many variants and alternatives were indeed found. After all, researchers have attempted to challenge the hegemony of the prevailing discourse in many ways. When consulting various literature reviews (*e.g.* Döös & Waldenström 2008) or leading textbooks (*e.g.* Yukl 2012), it becomes clear that one important distinction is between the formal and informal aspects of leadership, by some referred to as management versus leadership. A closely related variant is the popular distinction between transactional and transformational leadership, although the terms have changed over time. Being transformational seems to be much more desirable than being transactional, but this preference is also likely to have changed over the years together with the significance of the two terms. The dichotomy was described a long time ago by Max Weber (1922/1998), though he referred to it as bureaucratic versus charismatic authority.

When we search for an answer at the forefront of research, exemplified by the journal *The Leadership Quarterly*, a different picture emerges. We reviewed the titles and abstracts of every issue published in 2015 and 2016 (journals.elsevier.com/the-leadership-quarterly), finding a total of 71 articles (four special issues were excluded). One conclusion, based on this review, is that leadership scholars at the forefront of research seem to agree that leadership (and leaders) are of great importance, noticeable in the large majority of studies focusing on leaders' or leadership's effects on various outcomes. This applies to both leadership in general and specific forms of leadership. Four themes stand out as especially important in the reviewed articles: transformational leadership, ethical leadership, empowering leadership, and the personal traits of leaders. As in leading textbooks, the articles underline the distinction between transactional and transformational leadership, with the emphasis on exploring the latter. Of the articles reviewed, 18 concentrate on matters directly or indirectly relating to transformational leadership. Furthermore, 11 articles deal explicitly with questions of ethics and morality, usually leaders' ethical approach or ability to make ethical decisions. However, a few articles highlight unethical behaviour either by leaders themselves or by their employees. Empowering leadership is another recurring theme, focusing on the supportive role of leaders often in relation to effects on employee creativity or motivation. Eight articles have this as their topic, and additional articles on salient leadership could possibly fit in this category as well. The last theme that stood out in the review is an old acquaintance in the leadership literature, *i.e.* various traits of the leader. Eleven articles reported on studies of, for example, leaders' duration of service, age, gender – and even dopamine transporter genes – as well as employees' perceptions of traits such as attractiveness.

As to courses in leadership, they all seem very much the same. It is as though we agree on what there is to know and how it ought to be taught. Even our opposition to the mainstream is consistent: we set leaders against managers, authoritarian against democratic, and transformational against transactional leaders. We all highlight the feminine, charismatic, and transparent. We set post-postmodernism against anecdotes about the military, spiritual, imperial, and quite a few other historical forms of leadership. We often share the same basic beliefs and notions with, for example, the consultants and managers who take our courses. For example, we often all assume that leaders are important, that strong leadership is good leadership, and that leadership is a conscious activity and a profession.

Behind this book lies a fervent desire that the study of leadership in contexts not usually addressed in leadership research will spread some uncertainty as to whether the knowledge we hold is as universal as we believe it to be. We hope that examples from settings often neglected in the leadership literature will be instructive, since they shake up conventional notions. We argue that by studying the unconventional (here referred to as 'extreme'), one may also learn a thing or two about the conventional. We intend to contribute to the development of leadership theories that apply to extreme contexts, of course, but also to contexts that are not particularly extreme at all.

The perils of leadership

A basic element of the modernist dream of a rational life is the belief that the problem comes before the solution: a rational decision-maker analyses the problem before trying to find the best possible solution to it. However, we know that the situation is often the other way around, or at least not so straightforward, as we have known for long that we often find out solutions to problems that we did not even know existed (Cohen, March & Olsen 1972).

The same seems to be true of the leadership literature, which treats leadership as a solution to nearly every problem. Some parts of the literature bring nuance to the matter by claiming that certain types of leadership, such as weak or authoritarian leadership, constitute a problem that can be solved with other forms of leadership, such as strong or transformational leadership. But let us take this a step further: let us consider leadership in general as a problem and not a solution.

Many problems, such as production problems or lack of staff commitment, need not reasonably include a leadership component. But whatever the problem may be, it seems almost mandatory to solve it through the engagement of new and better leadership. This also means that a variety of problems are presented as leadership problems. When a party loses an election or performs badly in newspaper-generated political polls and surveys, or when a company performs worse than it did the previous quarter, it is usually suggested that a new and better leader ought to be appointed. This is extremely common in the sport industry.

Furthermore, not just any leadership but a certain type of leadership is often presented as the solution to the problems of our time. Long ago democratic leadership was in vogue (Lewin, Lippitt & White 1939). Perhaps we still would like to have transformational leadership (Burns 1978), but other types of leadership, such as 'fierce leadership' (Scott 2011), personal leadership (Törnblom 2011), sustainable leadership (Lange 2011), and ethical leadership (Brown, Treviño & Harrison 2005), are also on offer these days.

The claims made for various types of leadership like these are mostly rather sweeping, being said to apply in principle to all aspects of life. Admittedly, there are still those who follow Paul Hersey and Ken Blanchard (1969), who argued that leadership can be situation dependent, but it is more common for one type of leadership to be portrayed as applicable to all kinds of activities (Holmblad Brunsson 2007).

The general solution to most problems in life cannot be one single type of leadership. For example, those of us who would like to learn more about parenthood usually seek help and advice from sources quite different from those promising to develop skills by way of transformational leadership. We believe that specific forms of leadership might be beneficial in specific types of operations. Having extensive knowledge of how to run a railroad company, for example, is probably important if that is one's mission. However, it is unclear why one would need skills in 'clear leadership' (Bushe 2010) when a train has stalled between Stockholm and Copenhagen.

Although leadership is likely to provide a solution to many social and organisational problems, it should be equally clear that leadership in itself may constitute a problem. There are plenty of stories of new strong leadership in an entrepreneurial enterprise suddenly putting an end to the creativity that was the driver of growth and the objective in the first place. Similar examples of leaders who, through their exercise of leadership, have caused great harm can be found in the literature on the Second World War.

Considering leadership a problem, as in the above examples, is hardly controversial. Leaders throughout history have not exactly formed an unbroken line of positive progress. Leadership can be a problem for leaders themselves, just as it is for those who are led. Leadership can also be a problem for the operations to which leaders have been appointed, and to 'customers' who, throughout history, have had reason to complain of their exposure to the effects of leadership. The main problem treated in this book does not concern the difficulty of leading well or the various negative effects of leadership, but the actual notion that leadership constitutes a solution. It is the constant search for a better leader, or better leadership, that ought to be problematised. This includes the concept of leadership itself, all the questionable testimonies of strong leaders, the endeavour to lead, or the desire to be led, all of which contribute to the idea that leadership is the solution, not only to organisational problems, but to the problems of life in general.

Too much leadership?

In his book *On Becoming a Leader* (2003), the leadership guru Warren Bennis calls for more leadership. According to Bennis, the lack of morality in society, as well as being due to economic and social problems, is largely due to a shortage of leaders. Bennis is of course referring to a lack of *good* leaders, but for him and so many others there does not seem to be any distinction.

We find the ways in which the concepts 'leaders' and 'leadership' are used to be confusing. More leaders do not necessarily entail more leadership, and the two concepts should be analytically distinguished. Similarly confusing is the meaning of good leadership: good or better leadership seems almost exclusively to mean simply more leadership of a type similar to poor leadership (*e.g.* Kellerman 2004; Tunbrå 2004), which is often treated as synonymous with weak leadership (Burns 1978).

So is there anything called too much leadership? Should management consultants occasionally recommend that organisations adopt a little less leadership? Looking at some of the most powerful leaders in history, such as Josef Stalin and Genghis Khan, it is obvious that less would sometimes have been better.

It is simply not reasonable to refer to all leadership that leads to misery as poor leadership, as also pointed out by Alvesson and Spicer (2011). When credulous souls follow their leader into destruction, the problem is not only that their leader has lunatic ideas – many of us have. Lunatic ideas only become a problem when the lunatic succeeds in luring or leading others to follow, as such lunatic ideas soon wither away if not sustained and linked to effective leadership. The more lunatic the idea, the stronger the leadership needed to enforce it. Really good ideas do not require any leadership at all.

The scanty basis of leadership discourse

The previous sections addressed our analytical approach, and we will return to the problematic idea of leadership as a solution in the last chapter of this book. The focus in chapters 2–9 is on empirical examples. The sheer volume of the leadership literature makes it difficult to say anything definite about its empirical basis. We are nonetheless under the impression that as far as the leadership literature is based on empirical studies, despite being comprehensive in terms of the number of publications or the years spent by researchers carrying out field studies, the empirical basis is both narrow and inadequate. If one wants to learn more about leadership, another study of the same kind will not provide the answers one is seeking. Blake and Mouton's (1964) classic study of leadership styles was based on observations of the American oil industry. Sune Carlson (1951/1991) based his conclusions about the fragmentation of managerial work on studies of company directors in Sweden. Henry Mintzberg (1973) studied managers working in various professional environments, such as hospitals, consulting firms, and industrial enterprises.

The same Mintzberg (1973) also claimed that most material published on the subject as of early 1970 was not based on any empirical evidence whatsoever. Today, there is a large and growing number of empirical studies (which of course still could constitute a minority of the material published, as was the case more than four decades ago, according to Minzberg). The problem with these empirical studies of leadership is that they largely tend to follow in the footsteps of Blake and Mouton, Carlson, and Mintzberg: that is, the studies address the particular problems within, and peculiarities of, contemporary bureaucracies.

For certain, modern life is very much structured by bureaucracies such as businesses, public organisations, and voluntary associations, and it is in this disarray of empirical bases that current leadership researchers find their inspiration. The crucial question is whether this disarray might not be a little too specific and uniform to allow for new and unexpected conclusions. As the reader will notice, it is simply impossible to avoid mentioning leaders of contemporary bureaucracies in a book like this. After all, the bureaucracy is a dominant organisational form in our time. The point is that when considering the leaders of modern bureaucracies, we should be aware that they are special cases within a range of variants: they do not necessarily represent the average manager or leader.

We believe that the present theoretical framework would gain from leadership studies extending somewhat further, outside the normal framework. Our starting point is not any specific flaws in the concept or theory of leadership. It is a gigantic field with kilometres of shelves stacked with publications that, despite what we said about unanimity, is replete with conflicting ideas and theories, albeit within a relatively narrow framework. The chapters in this book are all driven by empiricism, *i.e.* the studies we carry out determine what flaws will be addressed and discussed.

But what is leadership?

A clear definition of leadership is difficult to find, and we do not want to torment the reader with a long-winded attempt at trying to formulate such a definition. Nevertheless, some sort of positioning as regards the concept is needed.

A common assumption is that leadership refers to the behaviour of leaders and the effects of this behaviour, which implies that one must first decide who is a leader in order to find out what leadership is. Members of the respectable Peter F. Drucker Foundation (Hesselbein, Goldsmith & Beckhard 1996, p. xii) have a very simple definition: 'The only definition of a leader is someone who has followers'. The problem with this definition is that it is too broad to be useful. At the same time, it might exclude activities that could probably also be classified as leadership, at least if leaders are defined too restrictively.

Others define leadership as a practice or process and stress that it involves not only the leaders but also the followers. Alvesson and Spicer (2011) argued, for example, that leadership is a process of influencing, adding that it 'involves some degree of voluntary compliance by those who are influenced' (p. 4). This is also a broad definition, although somewhat more specific.

In his well-known textbook, Yukl (2012) communicated quite reasonable views and knowledge of leadership. However, even Yukl gave up on trying to define leadership, instead citing a dozen different experiments. He concluded that leadership is far too multifaceted a concept to be captured by any one definition. We could not have said it any better.

Accordingly, it seems challenging to formulate a reasonable and useful definition. Some even believe that we know too little about leadership to train leaders in the first place (Barker 1997). We do not intend to address this gap; instead, our aim is slightly more modest though no less ambitious: we want to find out more about leadership as a multifaceted phenomenon.

Who are the leaders?

Much of what is said about leadership and leaders is circular in nature. When attributing importance to leaders, leadership becomes important. When a political party loses an election, we often blame it on poor or weak leadership. The party leader is forced to resign and once a new leader is elected, the future suddenly looks a lot brighter. The same applies to business leaders. When a business leader is superannuated and replaced, there will be considerable expectations – even though the new one is often simply a copy of the old one. Once one has experienced several such leader iterations, one might begin to question the importance of the leadership idea and wonder whether we know what we are talking about. We use the term 'leadership' fairly accurately, but do we actually understand what it means?

Textbooks on leadership have long maintained that leadership does not necessarily involve certain personality characteristics or traits other than in very general terms. For example, clever and sociable leaders are thought to cope better than others (Greenberg 2011). We would have been disappointed had that not been the case.

The less complex literature emphasises the importance of charisma and an entrepreneurial personality, which is not always wrong either. There is simply a lot that we do not know. However, assuming that many different types of personalities and characteristics are good and useful, although in different ways, at different times, and in different contexts, makes it very difficult to say anything general about what to look for in a potential leader.

It is not difficult to find things about leadership that we ought to know more about. However, when it comes to how leaders *should* act, it seems as though we know enough and have plenty of ideas. Some variations of this can be found in the following list of the characteristics of good leaders:

> Good leaders seek wisdom
> Good leaders create guiding values
> Good leaders have an inspiring vision
> Good leaders set meaningful goals
> Good leaders identify opportunities
> Good leaders thrive when the going gets tough
> Good leaders build positive relationships
> Good leaders seek self-awareness
> Good leaders make good use of their time
> Good leaders practice what they preach
> (foretagande.se 2017)

One can only agree. Obviously, we would like to think that the leaders we follow and perhaps admire possess certain attributes, being better and more noble than the rest of us. The reader, on the other hand, might be of the opinion that the list is simplistic and non-representative of leadership. We agree. Not all leadership authors are hopelessly unrealistic, but the list is still a good, if extreme, example as it was the second hit of 1,460,000 using the Google search engine.

The impression one gets when searching for popular literature and other material about leadership is that the market is dominated by information about what makes a good leader and how to become one.

One particular genre focuses on poor leaders and leadership, not criticising the idea of leadership in general, but rather offering an instructive contrast to good leadership. This fixation with good versus poor leaders is futile; some form of realism is clearly needed.

Leadership and change

It is not our intention to belittle the importance of leaders – or perhaps it is, but only to a certain degree. We do not find leaders unimportant, although we hope to demonstrate that their importance is not always what it appears to be.

High on the list of types of leadership and in demand for quite a long time now is leadership that in various ways drives or enhances change. Making changes appears much more sophisticated than simply making a business run smoothly. No manager with any self-esteem will want to be seen without a transformation project in the pipeline. One does not need to be particularly old or ultra-conservative to wonder what all this change is about.

One hospital director we studied had managed, as a result of clever and skilful work, to stay in the same job for more than ten years – a long time, considering that county councils in Sweden find it easy to replace their managers. Throughout his ten years in power, this hospital director made everyone aware of his transformation projects. His many talks about change, together with all the related meetings, conferences, training courses, and seminars, may well have led to some changes. However, the hospital in question is confusingly similar to other hospitals of similar size and character. Everyone has changed and so did this hospital – sort of. This hospital is in no way any better or worse than other hospitals. There is the same pressure for efficiency and the same problems with adopting new technologies and therapies as well as focusing on the individual patient and allocating resources.

Change is a curious word. It would be interesting to know who the actual heroes were that made the hospital function despite the lack of real attention from its change leader. If this change simply meant adapting to the constant, ongoing flow of new pharmaceuticals, new medical devices, and new budget constraints, does not the objective and the rhetoric of change seem a bit ironic?

What do we know about leadership?

Many of us know a great deal about leadership based on our own experiences, books we have read, conversations we have taken part in, etc. This knowledge usually includes everything from pure nonsense to really interesting thoughts and contributions. In the field of leadership research, the good leadership theories ought to outcompete the not-so-good theories, *i.e.* the theory that we teach, and as often practice, should be the best of all theories. However, many really strange ideas and ill-founded theories have been remarkably persistent. One example is that of the flat organisational structure that incorporates an implicit but self-contradictory leadership theory. It seems widely accepted among advocates of flat organisations and autonomous groups and among left-wing leadership critics that if we had fewer leaders – or fewer managers – there would be less control, more open and democratic organisations, and the realm of freedom would come knocking on our door. In Scandinavia, Jan Carlzon's (1985) book about how he created a flat organisational structure at Scandinavian Airlines (SAS) has enjoyed widespread popularity. Two of us, however, in an earlier study concluded that SAS had probably become more controlled from the top over time, not least because of the 'flat' reform (Ohlsson & Rombach 1998). It was probably a good thing for SAS at the time, but the fact remains that less leadership is not created by fewer people having more to say.

As we have now mentioned left-wing leadership politics, it is only right that we should also say something about right-wing leadership politics. Neither has any advantage over the other in terms of knowledge. Particularly ill-conceived are right-wing policies on compensation for leaders. Is the search for the best leaders really enhanced by financial incentives? Organisations need more than being led, and if one person is to get paid more than others, then maybe the pay packet ought to reflect the costs of training that leader or contributions made to the business. 'The market!' someone shouts on the right. Of course, truly market-conforming management remuneration would likely drive down managerial salaries considerably, as there are many more who feel called to such jobs than are actually needed. As regards larger organisations, true market dynamics might even result in people not being paid to lead or even wanting to pay for the pleasure of leading (for more about the market and salaries, see Fransson 2007).

Going through all the research on leadership is of course impossible, but there are some who have made a valiant attempt. Peter Sun and Marc Anderson (2011) are among those who tried some time ago, concluding that most research covered the same ground. 'New' concepts presented in leadership journals are often derived from the typical problems faced by organisations in practice, meaning that there is not much to be surprised about.

Another person who also tried, but earlier, is Mats Alvesson (1996). He believed that leadership studies should be less driven by the strict theoretical frameworks found in industry, instead being more open to alternative interpretations and analyses. We gladly agree with this, and especially with the related argument that any analysis of leadership ought to reflect the particular situations in which it is exercised. Therein lies, as we see it, the problem. Theoretical frameworks may be overly strict and blind to the opportunities offered, though equally serious is that the realities studied almost exclusively concern how today's leaders of businesses and public authorities could and should behave.

We want to highlight two research directions that we deem more promising than others. The first is based on detailed studies of what leaders and managers *actually* do. Rather than speculating about what they do or reporting on what one believes they do, the actual work of leaders should be observed and studied in detail (Carlson and Mintzberg and their surprisingly few followers). The second research direction looks at relationships between managers and employees, *i.e.* leaders and followers. When considering leadership as relationships, it is impossible to ignore the fact that the employees, *i.e.* the followers, contribute to the creation of leadership. Studies and analyses in this research direction shed light on things that have often been obscured in past leadership studies.

And what about those who follow?

Leadership is not all about the leader, because leadership is largely constituted by followers. Recent decades have seen a fair amount of research into 'employeeship' (*e.g.* Tengblad *et al.* 2007; Sveningsson & Alvesson 2010; Velten, Tengblad & Heggen 2017). From these studies we learn a great deal about the relationship between employees and leaders, and about how leaders can support enhanced employeeship. These studies contribute primarily to a better understanding of leadership from a management perspective.

Studies making a serious effort to find out how people follow are generally not referred to as leadership research. In his now well-known experiment, Stanley Milgram (1974/2009) wanted to see how far ordinary, decent students were prepared to go in tormenting fellow students with electric shocks just because they were told to do so by a person of authority. As we know, the result was frightening: many students obediently tormented their victims without any intimidation or persuasion whatsoever. There were those who refused to obey the temporary authority of the person leading the experiment, but Milgram's (1974/2009) final conclusion is still very unpleasant:

> A substantial proportion of people do what they are told to do, irrespective of the content of the act and without limitations of conscience, so long as they perceive that the command comes from a legitimate authority. (p. 189)

The last century will go down in history as one with many examples of strong and horrifying leaders. What if we instead said that the last century was one with a multitude of extremely docile followers? After all, when Theodor Adorno and his colleagues (1950) studied the fascist man, it was not called leadership research. Studies like those carried out by Robert Blake and Jane Mouton (1964) of the middle management in American companies are, however, seen as leadership research. These studies tell you how great '9:9 leadership' is – or democratic leadership, as Blake and Mouton called it, possibly from a slightly different perspective from that of Lewin *et al.* (1939).

In the last chapter of this book we will return to discussing leaders and followers based on the empirical examples presented in this book.

A continuing saga

Where is the leadership exercised that makes up the bulk of the cases treated in this book? What are the circumstances of the leaders that we studied?

We will begin with a chapter about leadership on vast expanses of snow and ice. The now legendary and well-documented polar expeditions of the early 1900s offer much in the way of charismatic leaders, dramatic adventure, heroism, and the most frightful stupidity.

The next chapter is about ambulances, rescue services, and the police in a major crisis. It is another story of charismatic leadership, dramatic adventure, heroism ...

Not all the chapters in this book are about adventure and drama. To slow down the pace a little, Chapter 4 is about monastic life. Here, where the everyday life is about meditation, self-discipline, and love (*agape*, of course, not *eros*), leadership is challenged with the task of resisting change, a truly delicate task.

The eternal question is: Who are good leaders? Are they people with formal authority, or do *éminences grises* perhaps represent true leadership? Chapter 5 is about the consultants and experts who assist by offering up their knowledge and advice – or maybe their leadership.

Much of what is written about leaders feels imaginary. Accordingly, in Chapter 6, we take the plunge and analyse how M leads James Bond, Agent 007, not because the case is imaginary but because it comes very close to actual leadership in an extreme context.

Another aspect of the fictional is life on the Internet. Many people spend just as much of their life in the virtual world as in the real world, and there is a marked likelihood of the two worlds colliding. In Chapter 7, a leader in Gladiatus sends us a virtual report on leadership from ancient times and his kitchen table.

We then present a study of leadership during crises. A colonel in war-torn Bosnia, a manager who becomes a victim of employee sabotage, and a flotilla commander who suffers a fatal accident that leads to the decommissioning of the flotilla are only a few examples of circumstances when it is not so pleasant to be a leader. So what does one do in a crisis? This is the question we ask in Chapter 8.

It is tough to lead, and not only when there is a crisis. Despite a number of undeniable benefits, many people are reluctant to accept offers of leadership. Or perhaps they merely pretend to be reluctant and are in fact secretly happy to be asked? If being a leader is so desirable, then why do not more people want to become leaders? Chapter 9 is about involuntary leadership.

These eight chapters are followed by a final chapter in which we attempt to look deeper into the concept of leadership as a problem. We will also reflect on the consequences of our findings and potential continuations, including a wish list of what else we would have liked to include in this book. Children as leaders is a clear gap in the literature. Children are untainted by the discourse of leadership but still lead one another and occasionally adults. Management by fear is an area with apparently weak empirical backing. There seems to be a multitude of empirical gaps.

Yet the main problem is surely what we can do with the concept of leadership. How can the discourse of leadership be developed further? We are not alone in analysing and speculating about this, and want to be involved and make a contribution. However, we hope that our readers are ultimately the ones who will contribute the most. If we compare the relationship between us and the readers to that between leaders and followers, then the goal is not for the readers to think like us – heaven forbid – but to be inspired and draw their own conclusions.

CHAPTER 2

Cold leadership

Björn Rombach and Östen Ohlsson

This is a study of an extremely cold form of leadership. Cold leadership sounds interesting, but can it possibly be that good? Everything that dictator x did was characterised by an ice-cold callousness: 'The men turned white with fear when he spoke and the women got migraine when he gazed at them with his icy and steely grey eyes'. Or perhaps there is something good about cold leadership? You can undoubtedly be cold in many different ways.

Maybe a leader should be cool instead? 'And when Gregor, the group's cool leader, thought that something was good, no one would say anything else. However, what begins as the night of all nights soon turns into a struggle between life and death when they realise that death himself is on the guest list. Panic spreads quickly when one after another falls victim to a masked killer'. This is how the film *The Pool* (2001), directed by Boris von Sychowski, was described in the online movie magazine *Vujer* (vujer.com 2007-09-25). Hardly a film worth watching. However, it is worth noting the cool leader that no one dares to disagree with.

There is otherwise nothing special about 'cool leaders'. It is the name of a South African air-conditioning company (www.coolleaders.co.za). And 'COOL' is the name of a leadership programme for US students, standing for Campus Outreach Opportunity Leagues (http://evergreen. loyola.edu and www.news.cornell.edu), as well as a characteristic of those who used the Motorola v70 (www.w5internet.com). The word has multiple uses and definitions.

Problematising leadership is of course possible. It has often been done and for a long time. The following quotation from *Moby Dick* will cheer you up:

... so for the most part the Commodore on the quarter-deck gets his atmosphere at second hand from the sailors on the forecastle. He thinks he breathes it first; but not so. In much the same way do the commonalty lead their leaders in many other things, at the same time that the leaders little suspect it. (Melville 1851, chapter 1)

Let us go back to square one. The leader is the one the rest of us think we are following. Let us not assume anything else right now. It would be more daring to go from cool to cold leadership. However, a cold leader is not necessarily 'cool', nor is he or she necessarily cool as in 'chilly'. Neither of which is a desirable characteristic. As a characteristic of a leader, being cool is primarily attributed to male leaders (skolverket.se).

Leaders can be cold in different ways. They can keep a cool head or have nerves of steel, which are roughly the same thing. Keeping a cool head is probably more to everyone's benefit. Nerves of steel are only occasionally needed. The rest of the body, however, ought not to be cold. Those with nerves of steel must not let it affect their heart, as a cold heart is seldom a kind heart.

Nerves of steel, on the other hand, make you cold. Perhaps not towards others, but in actual situations. You tend to be cold towards those you do not like. You might even make a frosty remark about someone. This is where it gets a little bit complicated. Making a frosty remark does not necessarily mean that you are cool, calm, and collected. Rather the opposite: you are more likely to be hot-blooded. Naturally, a cold gaze is often connected with a frosty remark, but the blood is more likely to run cold in the person on whom the gaze falls than in the person gazing.

Some leaders regret their actions and get cold feet. Though this is not the trait of a strong leader, it does point towards some insight. Cold hands are meant to be a sign of a warm heart, but we are not sure if hands and feet can be lumped into the same category simply because they are attached to the rest of the body via limbs. A leader should have a firm handshake and, at times, be able to point with the whole hand. It is possible to conclude that the hand is lukewarm – a temperature that is not very becoming for a leader. There is something too passive and uncharismatic about it.

The preferred temperatures of other body parts of a leader are unknown. We note, however, that being hot-blooded is fine. On 25 April 2008, the Swedish radio programme *Dagens Eko* ('Today's echo') covered a 'hot-blooded candidate aiming for the White House' (www. sr.se, Sveriges Radio 2008-05-13). The person in question was the 2008

Republican presidential nominee John McCain. People said he was beginning to boil inside. Perhaps it was his hot blood that kept him heated.

The fact that cooling is a relative characteristic does not make the matter less complicated. What we consider hot or cold depends on what temperature we have experienced most recently and what we are used to. The average Swede would not consider the climate in southern England to be cold. However, Fanny, the heroine of Nancy Mitford's *Love in a Cold Climate* (1949/2010), has a friend, Polly, who has just returned from India to southern England with her parents, Lord and Lady Montdore – hence, the book's title.

The definitions of cold and warm, however, are not entirely clear-cut. The range from ice-cold and red-hot includes many nuances. We might shudder at the thought of a cold leader but the opposite characteristic might not be much better. We would all prefer our leaders to lead with warmth, not with heat. A cool head coupled to a warm heart is perhaps the perfect scenario. But what are we to make of cool leaders?

When thinking of where to look for examples of cold leadership, searching for opinions about cold leaders in the literature is as good a place as any to start. There is, for example, an extensive literature about psychopathic leaders (*e.g.* Babiak & Hare 2006), who are bound to be ice cold. The leadership literature that psychologises about leaders and their characteristics often loses itself in speculations about cold leaders compensating for an unemotional and callous upbringing by seeking success and confirmation of their capacity as leaders later in life. A loveless upbringing should therefore create a cold leader – kind of. It is very tempting to immerse oneself in the profusion of books and articles on this subject. However, let us keep away from the psychopaths and keep it short on the subject of leadership theories and instead focusing on leaders with cold experiences. How do cold leaders lead, or rather, how does one lead in a cold climate?

It can be difficult to identify whether a leader is cold or not. The body temperature is not a very accurate measure. Instead, one ought to look for cold leaders in a really cold climate. Perhaps the manager of a cold-storage facility would be good. The problem is that in his break, he would go to the staffroom, take out a Thermos flask, and drink the hot chocolate that his wife made for him. Suddenly the situation is unbearably warm, not only because of the hot chocolate but also because of the warm kindness that his somewhat old-fashioned wife showed him. Well, the example of the cold-storage supervisor is after all from the 1950s. These days, the manager would be expected to make his own hot chocolate, turning down the warmth a little and becoming more politically correct.

Truly cold examples will have to be sought at other latitudes. Let us look at the leadership of the great and famous polar expeditions. What could be more natural? As few leaders have the same heroic status as the leaders of expeditions to the North and South Poles, four classic polar expeditions are analysed in this chapter.

The leaders of the icy expanses possessed varying characteristics of coldness. One of them might even have been hot-blooded. Perhaps he had a cold heart, though hardly nerves of steel, along with an overheated brain. Others kept a cool head. The combination of a leader with odd ideas like Andrée and men who needed a leader seems to be the reason why two of the expeditions failed. The question is what these men, who met their fate on the icy polar expanses, were searching for. A leader is one answer; adventure and heroic status is another.

Amundsen, Cook, Scott, and Andrée are 'heroes' that we used to read about in *Pojkarnas Julbok* ('Boys' Christmas book'). Would these travellers to cold regions withstand a close examination? To be called a hero, a leader must be both kind and clever. Is it reasonable to assume that this refers to a kind heart and a cool head? But some of these leaders had cold hearts, while others had overheated heads that needed cooling off.

A thought on selection

When writing about the early polar explorers, one should ideally mention all of them. However, we do not intend to do so. There were not that many of them, but still, there were more of them than can fit into this chapter. A selection must therefore be made, a selection that we can already say will consist of men only. The battle for the North and South Poles 'through the most inhospitable areas on Earth, the brave Polar scientists advanced ... until they gained final victory' (*Allers Family Journal* 69th, p. 3), was fought entirely by men.

In modern times, Helen Thayer has demonstrated that it is perfectly acceptable for a middle-aged woman to pull her own sleigh to the North Pole (Thayer 1993/1994). Liv Arneson showed that women can ski to the South Pole while Ann Bancroft showed that a woman can reach both the South and North Poles (Duncan 2002, p. 41). Another role model is Monica Kristensen (1987/1988), who successfully led expeditions until she lost her halo in connection with a fatal accident during the

Aurora Expedition in 1993–1994 (see also Duncan 2002, pp. 197–199). Additional women have played important roles in other expeditions. Well worth reading is Sheila Nickerson's portrayal of the Inuit woman Tookoolito who saved the completely wrecked Polaris expedition (1871–1873) of Charles Francis Hall, who was himself murdered (Nickerson 2002). In her book, Nickerson also tells of other women who played much more important roles than ascribed at the time. Also astonishing are the experiences of Jerri Nielsen as depicted in *Icebound* (Nielsen & Vollers 2001).

It is difficult to ignore the adventurers and scientists who tried to reach the South Pole around the turn of the 19th century. Antarctica was the last continent to be explored, insofar as it was a continent at all, though a lot seemed to indicate that it was. A Belgian named Adrien de Gerlache was the leader of one expedition that set off in 1897 (see south-pole.com), whose participants included the successful explorer Roald Amundsen (1872–1928). The great achievement of Amundsen was to spend the winter in Antarctica in 1898–1899 on board his ship. Scurvy and a lack of vitamin D plagued their existence. Not everyone survived this ordeal, but one participant by the name of Cook persuaded the others to eat what the local environment had to offer. Penguin might not be gourmet but is better than tinned food. The motions of the sea-ice were measured, giving indications that corresponded well with the assumption of an expanse of mainland. Vast amounts of ice constantly glide out to sea, creating giant icebergs. Such thick ice masses must form over very large land areas and then slide laterally, breaking off into the ocean. It was thought that, if interpreted correctly, the drift of such ice could indicate the presence of a vast landmass. Another expedition, led by Carsten Borchgrevink, spent the following winter on mainland Antarctica, enduring many of the same hardships as Amundsen had (Andersson 1945).

More renowned is the expedition of Sir Ernest Shackleton to the latitude of 88° 23' south, reached on 9 January 1909 (Shackleton 1909, p. 203). The expedition then had to turn around without reaching the South Pole: starvation and cold prevented the expedition from reaching its ultimate goal and returning alive. Shackleton could have exemplified someone with cold feet and even a cool head, but his third expedition in 1914–1916 was so disastrous that he does not deserve a place among the more clear-headed leaders (Andersson 1945). However, Edward Shackleton's (1960) book about Fridtjof Nansen is a useful reference.

If you want to find someone who has kept a cool head, it is probably best to look elsewhere and not among adventurers with contempt for death as their most prominent trait. Instead, the old *Pojkarnas Julbok* (Boys' Christmas book) tells of someone else who more than hundred years earlier managed to get farther south than anyone else of his time: Captain James Cook (born 1728). Moreover, he kept his men in good health and spirits over years of hardship and misery, ensuring that no one suffered from scurvy (Hector 1894). Cook's apparently easily won success perhaps explains why he is the only one in our selection (as far as we know) whose achievement has *not* been made into a feature film or drama, though his story has been fictionalised in literature (Nilsson 1957, p. 70).

Among those in our selection who possibly had a cold heart is Captain Robert Falcon Scott. The combination of an overheated brain and a considerable insensitivity to his and others' plights seems to be extreme in his case, although Shackleton, Amundsen, and others were perhaps equally obsessed. Amundsen, on the other hand, can be eliminated from our selection. He was indeed successful but we have already found our successful hero in James Cook. Amundsen reached the South Pole on 14 December 1911. Scott followed a month later, though he and his men did not survive their return trip. Amundsen's success and Scott's failure can possibly be explained by their equipment and the routes taken, but perhaps it is also a matter of mentality and attitude. 'Scott wanted to be a hero, Amundsen just wanted to get to the South Pole. Scott with his sense of the dramatic played to the gallery while Amundsen focused on the task at hand and not his audience' – wrote Roland Huntford (2003, p. 436) in his book about Scott and Amundsen. Though the characterisation might seem a bit unfair (see, *e.g.* Holt 1975), it supports the inclusion of Scott in our selection.

Among the Swedish North Pole researchers, Salomon August Andrée must not be overlooked. However, Andrée never got to explore anything and is mostly known for having in 1897 flown in a hydrogen balloon from Danes Island in the direction of the North Pole. Unfortunately, the balloon crashed on the way and Andrée died alongside his crew. Not until 33 years later was their final camp on the island of Vitön discovered by two Norwegian scientists. Apart from the corpses of Nils Strindberg, Knut Fraenkel, and Andrée himself, a lot of equipment and a number of diaries and notebooks were also found. The findings led to renewed interest in the expedition and to the great success of the book *Med Örnen mot polen* ('With the Eagle towards the pole') (Andrée *et al.* 1930), 'based on ... notes found on the island of Vitön', and of a major commemorative exhibition at the Liljevalchs Art Gallery in Stockholm in 1931 (see catalogue). Much has been written about Andrée, but it comes as no surprise that someone who as a student was 'bold, proud and a little arrogantly defiant' (Grenna Local Folklore Society 1931, p. 49) would eventually lead to his brain overheating at some point in his career.

As to the benefits of polar research, the following is found in the afterword of a youth book from 1929: 'One often hears the following question being asked: What is the point of all of this? Surely, the gains and losses of polar expeditions are not in proportion to each other? That depends, of course, on how one calculates. Homebodies and the ignorant would probably say that they are not – but they are wrong! You might as well ask: What is the point of any cultural work?' (Ahlman 1929, p. 547).

Then there is the difficult choice between the Finn-Swede Adolf Erik Nordenskiöld and Fridtjof Nansen, both of whom were researchers. Nordenskiöld sought clues to how the Earth was formed in the Ovifa meteorites (1870) and discovered the non-existence of Greenland's hypothesised inland forest in 1883 (see, *e.g.* Hedin 1926; Bergquist 1981). In addition, he was the first man to have navigated the Northeast Passage, a sea route north of Europe and Asia, connecting the Atlantic and Pacific oceans, aboard his ship Vega.

When Fridtjof Nansen attempted to cruise towards the North Pole, his ship got stuck in the pack ice (starting in 1893). Needless to say, this attempt failed as did his and Hjalmar Johansen's attempted dogsled trip from the ship to the North Pole. However, he confirmed the theory of ice drifting across the North Pole. The fact that Nansen was later awarded the Nobel Peace Prize distinguishes him sufficiently from Andrée to earn him the second place in our list of North Pole leaders. Nansen ought not to be seen as a patriot and madman with a death wish but as 'someone who would go to great lengths' (Wetterfors 1932, p. 9). However, according to Edward Shackleton (1960, p. 166), depicting the entire lifework of Fridtjof Nansen 'could not be done within the framework of a book', let alone a chapter.

Another aspect of the selection process is what sources one should trust or refer to. There is an incredible amount of written material in Swedish (Swedish Polar Research Secretariat 1993, 1994), but we chose to consider only what has been written about polar scientists as leaders. The selection made for this book is limited, as is obvious from the reference list. Our intention is simply to become better informed, so this will do for now.

A cold heart

'The real story of one of the greatest explorers who ever lived' is the description on the back cover of a big book about Captain Robert Scott (1868–1912) by Ranulph Fiennes (2003). Captain Scott reached the latitude of 82° 17' south in December 1902, placing him closer to the South Pole than anyone before him. His method of travelling by sledge across Antarctica had never before been attempted and contributed greatly to the mapping of the continent – for which he was greatly rewarded on returning home. Besides being lauded and bestowed with various honours, he was also awarded the Vega Medal by the Swedish Society for Anthropology and Geography in 1905.

We suspect that Scott would have been a footnote (Grafton 1997/1999; Solstad 2006) to the history of exploration had he not returned to the Antarctic in 1911 with a large expedition to compete against Amundsen in a race to the South Pole. With Scott's status as a hero, some compared his achievements to those of Nansen and even Albert Armitage, who discovered the Antarctic plateau – a far more remarkable geographic achievement (Huntford 2003).

In November 1911, Scott set off with four faithful companions. When the group arrived at the geographic South Pole, they found that Amundsen had already been there a month earlier. On their way back, both Scott and his companions perished. First, Edward Evans fell and injured himself, dying soon after in a confused state of mind. Lawrence Oates developed frostbitten toes and, in a terrible state, essentially committed suicide when he left the tent and disappeared into a snowstorm. Captain Scott and his companions Edward Wilson and Henry Bowers died together on or around 29 March 1912. In November 1912, a rescue expedition was sent out and found the three men in their tent, only about 20 km from a supply depot that could have been their salvation. In a final letter to the general public, Scott defended the purpose of his expedition, asking that the families of the expedition members be cared for.

The fate of Captain Scott and his companions is so well known that it is difficult to decide what relevant sources to include in the reference list. We read about Scott and his men in *Rekordmagasin* ('Records magazine') and in books for boys long before we realised the point of footnotes. However, we were too young to see the film *Scott of the Antarctic* (1949). Worshipping girls and boys were moved to tears by their hero Scott's laconic notes in his diary about Oates getting frostbitten toes and how it slowed down everyone. Finally, Oates decided to leave the tent, never to be seen again, perhaps hoping that it would help the others reach the supply depot before it was too late. They never did, however, and there are many explanations as to why the expedition failed:

They used horses instead of dogs but the horses could not cope with the harsh environment and had to be put down, so the men ended up pulling the sleighs themselves. Their provisions were insufficiently varied.

The expedition set off too late: Scott left 12 days later than Amundsen and missed valuable time in the middle of the Antarctic summer.

Scott and his men were so discouraged by the fact that Amundsen had reached the South Pole before them that they could not muster enough strength to return to safety.

Scott purposely delayed their return for the privilege of dying as a hero rather than having to face the world as a loser (Huntford 2003).

Scott himself blamed the failure on bad luck. His letter to the general public begins thus: 'The causes of the disaster are not due to faulty organisation but to misfortune in all risks which had to be undertaken' (Huntford 2003, p. 526).

As expected, the news of Amundsen's winning the race to the South Pole stirred up a certain degree of chauvinist frenzy in Norway. The British, however, were less enthusiastic: after all, Amundsen had chosen an easier route to the South Pole than had Scott, which surely must be seen as cheating. Nansen went on to defend Amundsen in English newspapers and in letters to Scott's wife, Kathleen. Nansen and Kathleen had been romantically involved when the Captain himself was away, though this came to an abrupt end when Nansen took sides with Amundsen (Huntford 2003, p. 528).

When it eventually became known in 1913 that Scott had not only lost the competition against Amundsen but had also lost his life out on the icy expanse, he became the subject of extensive adulation, both at home and elsewhere. His widow played a big part in that process as did the literary talent that Scott had displayed in the notes and letters he wrote towards the end of his life. Myths and legends about the value of Scott's sacrifice for a noble or possibly nonexistent cause came to be used in the propaganda of the First World War, which broke out the following year. Roland Huntford quotes *the Times*: 'the real value of this Antarctic expedition was spiritual, and therefore in the truest sense national' (2003, p. 543). It is uncertain whether the same adulation would have occurred had Scott and his men returned unscathed: 'As it was, things could not have turned out better. ... Kathleen and the country preferred a dead lion to a live donkey' (Huntford 2003, p. 541).

However, the question that concerns us is how Scott behaved as a leader. Our chapter title suggests that he had a cold heart. The letters and notes that he wrote during the arduous journey back seem to suggest that, apart from being a skilled writer, he also displayed concern and compassion for his unfortunate fellows. Or perhaps his writing represents the attempt of an egocentric to create his own heroic halo. If so, he succeeded beyond all expectations. Scott's personal attributes have been subject to much controversy. Roland Huntford (2003, p. 160) describes Scott as irresolute and sluggish, and even Scott's great admirer Ranulph Fiennes (2003, p. 17) admits that Scott, despite being trained in self-discipline, frequently struggled with tendencies towards depression, moodiness, and indifference (see also Diski 1997/2004, pp. 127–129). Most in favour of Scott are Gordon Fogg and David Smith (1990): driven by nationalism, they make the following reference to Huntford (2003): 'Much has been written about Scott and, after more than half a century during which he was looked on as the quintessential English hero, it was inevitable that some would itch to besmirch the image' (Fogg & Smith 1990, p. 54).

Looking at Scott from a contemporary perspective, he seems rigid and authoritarian. If there is any truth to the notion that leadership is a characteristic, or perhaps behaviour, depending on those who are led rather than those who lead, our two main sources, Roland Huntford and Ranulph Fiennes – despite disagreeing on many other things – agree completely on one thing: the four men following Scott were unswervingly loyal to the very end. It is difficult to find out much more about these four men; they stand in the background.

... with an overheated brain

'Reaching the geographic North Pole is not actually of that much interest from a scientific perspective' (Imbert 1987/1998, p. 65). The word 'actually' might as well be removed here – it is of no interest. When Winnie the Pooh asks Christopher Robin what the North Pole is, he replies 'it is something that you discover' (Milne 1926/2003, p. 102). Reaching this northern latitude in a large hydrogen balloon would in no way contribute to science. The attempt of Salomon August Andrée (1854–1897) to reach the North Pole in a hydrogen balloon was merely an adventure, though this did not stop it from being an undertaking of great magnitude and difficulty in terms of preparation and implementation. Even today, the story is still being retold, (*e.g.* by Havemose 2008).

Salomon August Andrée is sometimes said to have been a pioneer for his expedition to fly to the North Pole (*e.g.* Rönnbäck 1944; Laktionov 1960, pp. 143–148). Participating in the project from the start were Nils Gustaf Ekholm (born 1848, associate professor of meteorology) and Nils Strindberg (born 1872, B.Sc. in physics). Ekholm was given the task of choosing the right balloon, but was ultimately told not to order the one with the densest fabric but one that turned out to be rather permeable (see, *e.g.* Kjellström 1995, p. 51ff.). Issues regarding the density of the balloon and the estimated flight time eventually led Ekholm to leave the project. Among the many interested, Knut Fraenkel (born 1870, civil engineer) was chosen to replace Ekholm. None of the three men had any prior experience or knowledge of the polar region.

Ekholm's departure from the project is interesting and rarely commented on (except by Sundman 1968 and Kjellström 1995). Being ignored rather than being hailed as a hero can almost be seen as a punishment for refusing to sacrifice oneself for the cause. The safety issue was dismissed by Andrée: 'Sitting at the edge of an unfamiliar continent, thinking of every safety aspect possible and then demanding a five-fold safety margin is one sure way of ruining an entire project' (Havemose 2008, p. 186). This is the attitude expected from an adventurer, not a responsible leader.

On 11 June 1897, the balloon named the Eagle lifted off from Spitsbergen in Norway, heading towards its final destination 4 000 km away. However, the Eagle was leaking gas, which was not unusual for hydrogen balloons at the time. If this was not what forced it down, it was probably ice accumulation on the balloon. In addition, the balloon became extremely difficult to control after two or three of its ropes detached and fell off during lift-off and much of the ballast had to thrown overboard early into the flight over Danes Island. The Eagle managed to travel only around 500 km and not even in the desired direction. Better balloon construction would probably have resulted in a longer flight and more in the right direction. However, the possibility of a sledge ride ought to have been foreseen and the necessary equipment organised.

Everything indicates that Andrée, the leader preparing for the flight, was over-optimistic and ignorant of Arctic conditions and appropriate technology (see, *e.g.* Lundström 1997). Andrée was stubborn and found it difficult to absorb information. For example, the balloon was delivered directly from the manufacturer in Paris to Svalbard in Norway. When it was discovered that it leaked more gas than was initially anticipated, Andrée did not let this affect his plans. There are credible examples of

Andrée appearing to be interested in practical details, displaying awareness of the cold and being proactive (Nilsson 1997, pp. 62–63), but when
it came to the actual balloon and its flight, Andrée was neither willing or
able to see the bigger picture (*cf.* Havemose 2008, p. 200ff.). Much was
well prepared and thought through (see, *e.g.* Abersson 1906), but the
project failed nonetheless.

After the balloon crashed, the expedition set off on an arduous trek
for which they were not very well equipped, materially or mentally. The
reason why they eventually perished is unclear to this day. Various causes
of death have been considered (see, *e.g.* Hempleman-Adams 2001/2002,
p. 303ff.). The most common suggested cause of death is trichinosis food
poisoning from eating semi-raw polar bear meat, carbon monoxide poisoning from the Primus stove, or freezing to death. All this seems highly
unlikely. Other explorers have consumed polar bear meat for longer periods without becoming sick, and the symptoms identified did not match
those of food poisoning. The stove fuel had not run out and the stove
had been turned off; the men had sleeping bags and other equipment
for protection against the cold. We tend to agree with the notion that
the men eventually died from the cold because they no longer had the
will or strength to keep going (*cf.* Kjellström 1999) – they were simply
too exhausted. Botulism may even have been to blame (Hempleman-
Adams 2001/2002, p. 308). The exact cause of death, however, is not
that important.

Much positive has been written about Andrée as a leader: 'The
personal qualities of Andrée as a leader are reflected in the mature way
in which he cared for his younger companions and his indomitable will
to remain positive, even in the most difficult situations' (Minnesalbum
1930, p. 49). Carl Gustaf Nilsson, a carpenter involved in the preparations at Spitsbergen, wrote the following in his diary: 'His [*i.e.* Andrée's]
handshake was masculine and heartfelt while his speech and demeanour
were reassuring and commanded respect. To follow such a man to the
end of the world, if needs be, would seem a pleasure to me' (Nilson 1997,
p. 22). There are many more examples of how many 'found it an honour
to work for Andrée's North Pole Expedition' (p. 43). A strong will is a
trait that is often highlighted. For example, Gunnar Abersson wrote:
'When searching one's memory for attributes with which to describe
Andrée as a person, it is his strong and firm determination that emerges
the most' (1906, p. 65).

Andrée has also been described as a victim of the nationalist frenzy
that the media created around the project and of growing pressure from

his sponsors (Sundman 1968). If we delve further into the negative comments made about Andrée, he is even seen as a cynic who deliberately marched towards death together with the two men whom he had persuaded to come along. However, Per Rydén (2003) argues energetically against this being the case. He seems to think that Andrée's unawareness of the Arctic wind conditions (one example of his inability to listen to others and bow to evidence) was the reason for his failure. Rydén claims that though 'a distrust of others coupled with an overconfidence in his own ability' applies to Andrée, it might equally be 'a prerequisite for the traditional explorer' (p. 149) – which seems completely unfounded. Moreover, if Andrée was overconfident in his own ability to make decisions before and during the balloon journey, why was he not equally overconfident during the return journey?

A cool head

Captain James Cook (1728–1779) led three major expeditions to explore large parts of the Southern Hemisphere. Apart from New Zealand and Australia, he also reached the Antarctic Circle on two occasions. On 30 January 1774, during his second voyage, James Cook got as far south as he would ever get: 70° 10' (Andersson 1945).

Exploration of the South Pole region began fairly recently. It is just over a hundred years ago that Roald Amundsen was the first to set foot on the geographical site of the South Pole and planted the Norwegian flag there. It is just over two hundred years ago that people began thinking of the South Pole as situated in a separate continent.

In the 18th century and probably before, most geographers believed there to be a land mass in the Southern Hemisphere that corresponded to and balanced the large continents of the Northern Hemisphere. Numerous expeditions were sent out to find the large continent in the south – *Terra Australis*. Surely, such a large continent would be full of natural resources and arable land. South America had been discovered, of course, but there had to be much more out there. Many expeditions were sent out by the great powers of Europe, the results of which were difficult to interpret and, at times, completely ludicrous. Tales of seven-headed monsters did not make the discoveries any more believable.

Captain James Cook, commissioned to find out the truth of these claims, was both methodical and persistent. On 27 January 1775, Cook wrote the following in his logbook: 'It is true that most of this southernmost continent (if there is such) must lie within the Arctic Circle where the sea is so full of ice that any land would be inaccessible. The risk one must take when exploring the coastline of these unknown and icy waters is so immense that I can be bold enough to say that no one will ever venture further than what I did' (Cook 1768–1780/1982, p. 183). He sailed as far as he could before the ice put a stop to his voyage: cold conditions and other problems meant that he soon had to return north to find rest in the South Pacific.

On his third voyage, Captain James Cook was beaten to death by natives in connection with a brawl (Danielsson & Burenhult 1991, p. 298). There is extensive debate on how Cook met his end and how this should be interpreted (Hacking 1999/2010). Having previously been hailed as gods by the Hawaiians, Cook and his men ran into conflicts and problems with them on their last visit. The Hawaiian women paddled in great numbers out to Cook's two sister ships to help themselves to the sailors. The women were presented with gifts in the form of iron nails pulled out of the hull of the ship. Various thefts occurred, and when a crucial lifeboat was stolen from Cook's own ship, he, with a group of his men, tried to get it back. This led to a scuffle on the beach. Cook fired his pistol and killed one of the Hawaiians, as a result of which he and four of his men were killed. One eyewitness, David Samwell, surgeon on the Discovery, described Cook's actions as measured and wise (1786), but more recent interpretations suggest that Cook had displayed a great lack of judgement, perhaps due to the onset of Alzheimer's disease (Obeyesekere 1992a). Obeyesekere (1992b) further concluded that because the clearly hungry Englishmen kept asking such odd questions about cannibalism, they must themselves have been cannibals. The Englishmen, for their part, came to the same conclusion about the Hawaiians based on their interviews with 'the natives'. As far as we know, Cook's divine status continued after his death and there are some unpleasant details about what happened to his remains. Although the death of Cook should be treated with respect, we would like to return to his achievements in life.

Captain Cook had risen through the ranks in part because of being the best navigator in the Royal Navy. His many biographers describe Cook as an extremely receptive man. He taught himself geodetics on a voyage to the north of North America, and on his first expedition to the Southern Hemisphere, an astronomer on board his ship casually taught Cook the complicated technique of observing the moon. Cook was of humble origins and the conservative British Navy thought long and hard before making him an officer, despite his outstanding ability. A genuine tribute to his noble character can be found in a classic book for boys written by David Hector (1894) that describes Cook as a kind and loving son. Written material about James Cook is otherwise very sparse. One important thing to remember about Cook's expeditions is that his performance and results were exceptional, surpassing everything that anyone could have asked for or expected: his list of discoveries is long.

Another important factor was Cook's unique ability as a commander. It is not that he was unusually kind to his men: flogging was common in the Navy and Cook followed tradition. Doing anything else was probably not an option, although that is nothing but a meagre excuse. For example, he had two men flogged for refusing to eat fresh beef (Aughton 2001, p. 52). He might have done the same to those who refused to eat sauerkraut, though Cook himself described the matter somewhat differently: according to Cook, the crew eventually ate the cabbage, albeit after much deliberation, once they saw that the officers were happy to eat it. The sauerkraut played an important role.

In those days, the most common cause of nonviolent death on long sea voyages was scurvy. The ships that Cook commanded were all equipped to endure several months at sea. As was customary, there were huge supplies of salted, dried, and smoked food. The traditional onboard diet was deficient in vitamins, so it was not unusual for people to perish on long voyages. Cook solved this problem by provisioning his ships with large amounts of sauerkraut, and on his remarkably long voyages, Cook managed to keep mortality rates very low. When approaching Portsmouth after his second expedition, Cook wrote the following cheerful comment in his logbook: 'I have been away from England for three years and eighteen days. During this time and despite climate changes, I have only lost four men and only one due to illness' (Cook 1768–1780/1982, p. 196; Moorehead 1966/1967). On his first expedition, the mortality rate was a lot higher. No one died of scurvy, but when the ship had to land at Batavia on her return voyage for some repairs, many of his men met their death. During the three months that the ship was anchored in Batavia, many of the crew contracted malaria and later dysentery (Aughton 2001); many died, though it was hardly Cook's fault.

The mortality rate of the Swedish East India Company was much worse than Cook's, especially on voyages from Gothenburg to China and back. On a total of 134 expeditions launched every other year for 74 years, at least 2000 men perished (popularhistoria.se) – and these expeditions were not traversing any uncharted waters. James Cook clearly saw it as an advantage if his crew survived, and he had the skills and initiative to ensure that they did. He also made some amazing discoveries in the Southern Hemisphere. His extensive circumnavigations revealed, however, that the *Terra Australis* that everyone had been dreaming of did not exist. 'But maybe his greatest achievement can be found in a completely different area – hygiene. Cook's stringent demands for cleanliness onboard his ships, together with his successful battle against scurvy, signified a new era in circumnavigational technology' (Andersson 1945, p. 33).

Depictions of James Cook portray him not as adventurous or daring but rather as careful and calculating. He was clearly equipped with a brilliant intellect and relentless energy. He seemed to exercise his leadership with an obvious and, at times, perhaps brutal authority. There was some dissatisfaction with his leadership, especially among the scientists who accompanied Cook on his voyages. They often wanted to go ashore to collect plants and complained that it was a waste of time to journey to Antarctica, where no plants were to be found. Cook was not always sympathetic to their wishes and probably would have preferred to set sail without them (Andersson 1945). A list of Cook's virtues would not likely include compliance and diplomacy.

A warm heart

Fridtjof Nansen (1861–1930) was 'an outstanding scientist and specialist in zoology, oceanography, astronomy, and mathematics' (Andrist 1962/1963, p. 64). It seems likely that it was research itself and the search for empirical evidence that motivated him to embark on polar science expeditions, although he too got carried away by the adventurous spirit prevailing at the time. Nansen's own descriptions in two volumes, *Fram öfver polarhavet i & ii* ('Across the Arctic Ocean', i & ii) (1897a, 1897b), are markedly pompous and, as such, completely in tune with his times.

Nansen knew that parts of a steamer, Jeannette, which had run aground in the ice north of the Bering Strait in 1881, had been carried 2900 nautical miles from where it had foundered (Imbert 1987/1998, p. 61). The ice had moved the wreckage all that way at a very good pace. It was also known that the Inuit regularly found wood from Siberia that had drifted across the North Pole. This and similar information indicated that ice drifted across the Pole.

His project involved committing a purpose-built ship called Fram to the ice and letting the ice carry the ship and its crew of 13 men towards the Pole. This would enable Nansen to prove his theory of a constant ice drift from Siberia across the polar regions while allowing him to reach the North Pole. It is often said that the theory was perceived as unlikely and the project as too bold, making it difficult to fund (see popular works such as Andrist 1962/1963, p. 65 and Imbert 1987/1998, p. 61).

However, Nansen eventually amassed the funding and 'the ship was launched from Ekevik's shipyard in Larvik on 26 October 1892' (Byström & Sörensen 1940, p. 71). The journey began at Midsummer in 1893. The ship was very well built, its equipment well thought out, and there were sufficient food provisions to last for five years. In the autumn, as planned, the ship became stuck in the frozen ice. Life onboard was very comfortable, although somewhat monotonous. Food seems to have been an important aspect of life, which led to both double chins and round bellies (Kjellström 1995, p. 96). However, there was hardly any alcohol onboard (see, *e.g.* Brögger & Rolfsen 1896, p. 337-338).

The adventurous aspect of the project was not a success, as the ice moved more slowly than estimated and partly in the wrong direction. Fram came closer to the North Pole than any other ship before it, but not even in the second winter did it make it all the way. Nansen and Hjalmar Johanssen then tried to reach the North Pole on a dog sledge. It is never a good thing when the leader leaves his ship, though he did not do so because of the cold conditions or danger, challenges that would surely have made him stay. Nansen was simply bored. It is not unusual for a leader to embark on new activity after a long time of no action whatsoever. Nor is it unusual for a leader to seek new activities that would have been unnecessary had he had the patience to wait a bit longer.

After many preparations, the sledge expedition got under way 'to a resounding salute' (Nansen 1897b, p. 29) on 14 March 1895. However, it went slower than expected and the two men had to spend the next winter on Frans Josef Land. Interestingly, what they both really missed was the possibility of reading. One frequently cited event was when Nansen threw himself into the icy waters to capture the two kayaks that were drifting away with all their equipment (*e.g.* Nansen Høyer 1958, p. 91). In June 1896, Fridtjof Nansen and Hjalmar Johanssen came across Frederick Jackson who was exploring Frans Josef Land. Jackson brought the two men back to his camp and eventually back to Norway.

Once Nansen had left Fram, it was Otto Sverdrup who became the expedition's leader and commander and took over the task of keeping a logbook. His mission was 'to find the shortest and safest route to open waters and back home' (Nansen 1897b, p. 448). In the middle of August

1896, the ship and its crew were safely back in Norway. Some time later, the ship of Frederick Jackson sailed into Tromsø where Fram already lay at anchor.

Nansen's voyage to the North Pole with his ship Fram was not a particularly important scientific achievement. It was a significant polar achievement, though it accomplished nothing that had not been done before: ships had already got stuck in and drifted with the sea ice. However, Nansen's specially constructed ship Fram coped much better with the ice than had any other ship before it. The best known of the ships that did not survive the ice is perhaps the Jeannette, of the eponymous expedition (1879–1881, see above) led by George Washington De Long (see, *e.g.* Kjellström 1995, p. 20ff.). The logbook record of Nansen's expedition reveals a lot about everyday life on the ship and the very long periods of simply waiting. Spread over such a long period of time, little that was adventurous was actually going on.

Fridtjof Nansen was well prepared for his voyage. He drew on the experience of others and on earlier expeditions. Fram was an exceptionally well-designed ship, and there were plenty of provisions and equipment as well as dogs. Many crew members already had 'a lot of Arctic experience' (Edberg 1961, p. 60). This suggests that Nansen, as a leader, was well organised. On a radio talk, Roald Amundsen described the planning skills of Nansen as 'a complete transformation of polar expeditions' (Byström & Sörensen 1940, p. 151). A leader who is capable of successfully manning, equipping, and planning a project sounds almost too good to be true, and this preparation should have led to a successful expedition. However, one must not forget that Nansen and the Fram were not actually that successful, though it is difficult to explain this lack of success by referring to his good character and sound traits. In this case, a good crew, the right equipment, and a brilliant plan were simply not enough.

It has also been said that Nansen was 'much beloved, generous and happy at play' – probably a very true description. However, that Nansen was 'a champion' (Edberg 1961, book cover) or 'a genius scientist' (the radio broadcast referred to above and cited by Byström & Sörensen 1940, p. 151) is far from true. After all, this would imply that he had won or discovered something. Nansen could be described as someone with an interest in competing, as is often the case with sportsmen (Sannes 1942).

The Nobel Prize that Nansen received in 1922 (nobelpeaceprice. org) was for his notable diplomatic activities, in particular, the Nansen Passports issued to stateless persons, and had nothing to do with polar exploration or science. However, it does confirm that Nansen, on the whole, was a nice guy.

The downside of too much leadership

OK – so we are back where we started. The data is spread across the cold (!) floor and something should be said for our collective knowledge to move forward. One is struck by the thought that something must be seriously wrong with the heroes of our childhood books, who all insisted on getting to the Poles. And those who followed must also have had a screw loose. But was the same screw loose on those who followed as those who led? Loose screws may also be what the two old academics see when they look in this direction.

Two things usually happen when researchers start working. First of all, we like to compare statements and documents over time, setting today's benchmarks against those of the past. This can be useful, since it gives us perspectives differing from those of our own time. For example, it allows us to put nationalism aside when examining these polar scientists and, as a result, better describe the lack of scientific contributions they made on their adventures. It also makes it nearly impossible to understand the strong urge to follow these leaders on their ill-conceived polar expeditions.

Another thing that researchers like to do is to bring statements and documents closer to home. For example, we transform polar explorers into researchers, or hold the manager responsible for the work environment. Polar adventures would be much easier to understand if we let them be what they are – adventures. When looking for literature on polar researchers, we came across *Ice: Tools and Technique* by Duane Raleigh (1995). The book is about ice climbing. In the spring, the snow melts during the day; at night, it refreezes into sheets of ice and into icicles several decimetres long. The book is about climbing similar ice sheets and icicles but on a massive scale. We are talking about icicles of 30 metres or more.

When it comes to this type of ice climbing, I think we all agree that, in itself, it is not a research task, although a lot of research probably goes into actually doing it. The act is obviously very difficult, being an ultimate test of skills and requiring specialised equipment and preparation. Nevertheless, despite the best preparation, the ice could detach at any time, smashing to the ground with its climbers. Ice climbers usually work in pairs, one leading and the other following. Comparing Andrée's expedition to a climbing expedition casts it in a completely different light than if we compare it to a group of researchers studying the financial management of the City of Gothenburg.

These adventures appear less adventurous when seen from our own perspective. Take the South Pole, for example. Is it really such an amazing place to discover when others (Skinnarmo & Tell 1999) have already been there? Is it so difficult to plan what equipment to bring when Donald Duck has already pointed out the importance of warm clothes at the South Pole (Disney 1959)? These days, it is even possible to buy complete 'adventures' to exotic Antarctica. You may even be offered a discount on 'explorer packages' (hurtigruten.funnit.no).

We started by considering the amount of leadership needed. The examples presented here confirm our suspicion that there can in fact be too much leadership. The leaderships of Andrée and Scott seem to have consisted of an unfortunate combinations of foolishness. Scott and Andrée were one type of fool, while the faithful men who followed them to the very end were another type. One type of fool must make contact with the other for strong leadership to emerge. If Strindberg had not come across the engineer Andrée, he might have become a civil servant and married a nice girl.

However, one assumes that adventure and heroism was sought. Polar research was one of many paths available – after all, there was lots to discover in Africa too. The army and navy also had dangerous pursuits to offer. Ice climbing too, for that matter. And it was never the intention of this leadership to study budgets; rather, the focus was on spectacular adventure. The question is whether anyone was persuaded to participate against their better judgement: Here we are on the ice – I thought we were meeting the Budget Director?

If bringing this matter closer to home is wrong, what is less wrong when it actually happened? It is very possible and completely independent of time and place for a leader to be given great responsibility. We can, of course, try to understand, but we do not have to accept. We have every right to argue that it would have been preferable if the leader had known better. This is probably not what Urban Wråkberg (2004) meant, but what has once been discovered cannot be rediscovered. The undiscovered is gradually eliminated, forcing adventurers higher and higher up the wall of ice. Should we take responsibility for those secrets that still remain?

Many researchers argue that leadership is a relationship rather than a trait or characteristic of an individual (see, *e.g.* Hällsten & Tengblad 2006). We would like to point out that such a relationship might not necessarily be positive, but could often be one of self-righteous people with fixed ideas meeting people in search of a vocation. But the question is if this really is what we have seen.

Martin Wood (2005) maintains that leadership research should concentrate on leadership as a process and not on the characteristics or behaviour of the leaders themselves. Nor is it about the behaviour of the followers. Rather, it is about the process in which both parties are involved. We conclude that leadership is something that never ends, at least not as long as the parties involved are still alive. Given that approach, the leadership of Scott across the icy expanses might just as well have been reinterpreted and developed while the toes and noses were becoming frostbitten. Let the truth be told: 'The opera ain't over 'til the fat lady sings' (popularised by Daniel Cook).

In praise of the cool leadership

So, back to the question of leadership temperature. Our hypotheses about leaders with a cold heart have not been confirmed. Both Scott and Andrée appear heartless, but this is hardly what made them leaders. It is more a matter of lack of coldness a bit higher up than that. Here, the qualitative or normative significance of temperature is apparent. Nothing that we have seen so far speaks against good leadership being facilitated by a warm heart or a cool head. If this is what we are searching for, then we need look no further than Cook and Nansen.

The question is where, in all the leadership literature that is not about temperature, do we find anything about leaders with a warm heart and a cool head? Starting with a cool head, we find this in a place that we have not visited for a long time, either theoretically or normatively. We can see the advantages of a cold righteous bureaucratic leadership over a hot market- and media-oriented entrepreneurial leadership. We are old enough to know that the situation was no better in the past, but not everything has gone from strength to strength. 'Progress' often runs off in one direction where it all turns into shambles, as a result of which it then backtracks and runs off in a completely different direction.

We feel that we are currently at such a crossroads. We can either rush off on a tangent and embrace everything that is new, convenient, 'healthy', appealing, and easily available. There is nothing wrong with that. After all, that is the direction that most of us choose, and it normally gets us where we want to go.

Or we can change direction. Let us take the public sector and its traditional bureaucratic leadership as an example. We could embrace a slightly colder leadership and apply a conception of fairness, ethics, stability, predictability, and justice. Good leadership can get employees to embark on inspirational journeys to new continents and make new discoveries. It also makes sure that they return safely. After all, those who survive get to see more. How about it?

The publisher would never allow us to take up the space needed to defend bureaucracy against all those who currently believe or who, over the years, might have believed that other ways are better. Despite there not being that many of us, we are not alone in arguing in favour of bureaucratic forms of leadership. We do not mean 'post-bureaucratic leadership' of the kind that Warren Bennis (1970) and others have been expecting for many years, but 'old-school bureaucratic leadership' as it stands with its ethos and everything else included. However, this is not an integral part of traditional bureaucracy.

Readers looking for additional proponents need look no further than Alexander Styhre's *Byråkrati* ('Bureaucracy') (2009). His book briefly deals with not only those who criticise but also those who defend the institution. Obviously, Max Weber (1922/1998) cannot be counted among the most eager advocates of bureaucracy. As he found the problematic role of bureaucracy in relation to modern rationality, many see him as the inventor of bureaucracy.

Paul du Gay has written several articles about the advantages of bureaucracy that are well worth reading (2000, 2005/2009). Charles Goodsell (2004) and Stewart Clegg *et al.* (2011) can be added to your reading list although du Gay made little impression. Let us not delve deeper or stir ourselves up; we have said what we wanted to say.

CHAPTER 3

Disobedient leadership at the accident site

Eric Carlström

This is a story about organisations in which orders are the norm, obedience is taken for granted, and formalities reign supreme. It is about the ideal image of leadership and control which assumes that everyone will keep to the schedule and that everything will work out as expected, even if it does not. Let's illustrate this with an actual event.

One sunny day in mid September, two passenger cars collided head-on along a rural road in Western Sweden. An elderly woman turned left at a crossroads, directly in front of an oncoming car travelling about 90 km per hour. The collision had serious consequences. The elderly woman was trapped in her car, and she and the driver of the oncoming car suffered life-threatening injuries. Once in hospital, they both had to undergo emergency surgery for internal bleeding – with successful outcomes. They both made full recoveries from the ordeal. Fortunately, this accident had a happy ending. However, it was nonetheless marked by confusion among the emergency staff attending.

The approach usually taken in traffic accidents follows *the Swedish Prehospital sjukvårdsledning,* in English 'prehospital medical management and communication model ("PS Concept"),' (Rüter *et al.* 2007). The staff dealing with the accident had all been trained to follow this model.

Flowcharts and management concepts, such as the PS Concept, are common in the work of accident and emergency services. Such concepts are based on the assumption that problems can be anticipated and solutions predicted (Weick 2002). The structure of these and similar concepts requires that certain basic elements be identified and acted on before further elements are added. They are based on strong rational ideals and a belief in the possibility of standardising the work. Standards are supposed to create order and reduce confusion and unorganised behaviour in stressful situations (Weick 2001; Kendra & Wachtendorf 2003).

The most common types of charts used when applying such concepts to accident response are *organisational charts* and *flowcharts*.

An organisational chart or organogram provides a detailed geographic schematic of where and how the participants are placed relative to one another at the accident site. This is a standard model illustrating the physical layout of the activities taking place at the site of an accident. An accident or emergency site is often separated into 'cold' and 'hot' zones, each of which requires different skills and equipment, depending on the particular task. In the case of a shooting, the monopoly on violence exercised by the police officers means that they are best placed to act in the hot zone. Fire and rescue services and paramedics have to wait in

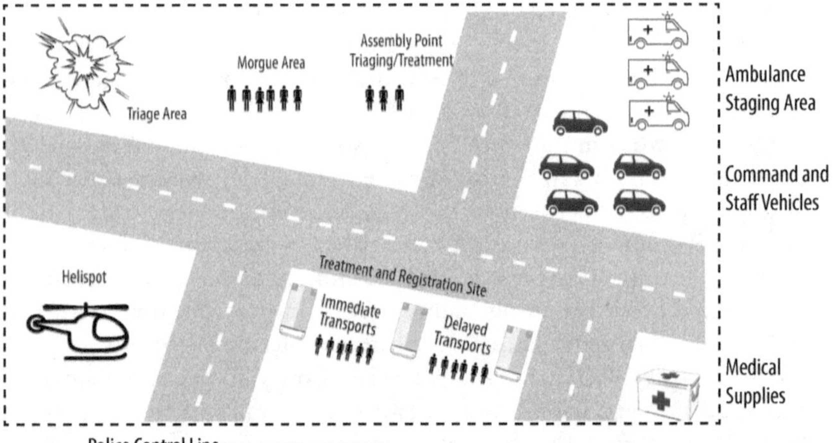

Figure 3.1 Example of the standardisation of an accident site in the form of an organisational chart (Auf der Heide 1989).

the cold zone until the site has been 'secured'. In the case of an incident involving chemicals, the paramedics of the fire and rescue services are the only ones allowed to work at the actual site of the incident. The other two responding organisations, police and ambulance services, have to wait until the area has been decontaminated and any victims removed from the site.

In the cold zone, units are set up to deal with various problems. A major incident will have various assembly points for the uninjured, shocked, or deceased as well as places where medical care is given to the injured. There will also be incident command points, assembly areas, medical evacuation sites, as well as suitable locations for airborne transportation. In addition, there will be roadblocks, pedestrian barriers, and a media briefing centre. (Figure 3.1)

The second type of chart mentioned above, the *flowchart*, gives a detailed description of the flow of activities taking place at an accident site. A flowchart illustrates the order in which communication occurs, for example, who of the rescue staff communicates with whom. The chart also regulates the conduct of vertical communications between the rescue service management and staff on site, controlling relationships between staff members by restricting their communications to certain predetermined levels. This means, for example, that communication with colleagues is allowed while communication with anyone else is prohibited. The purpose of this is to bring order to the accident site and to minimise time-wasting activities. (Figure 3.2)

Standardised charts and models are often derived from military models (Morgan 2006; Weick 1995). The two above examples illustrate how to behave (Lewis 2006) based on the perception that control and therefore leadership, in the form of a standardised action programme, will

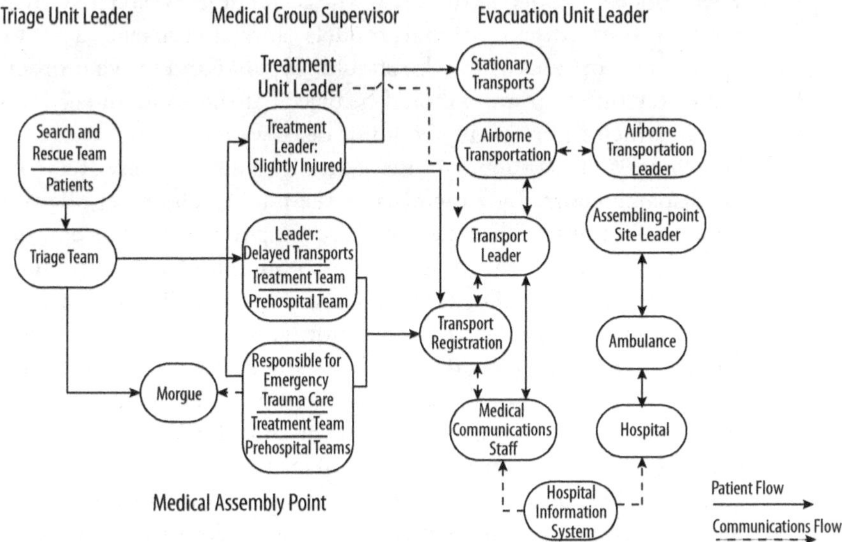

Figure 3.2 *Example of a flowchart for the care of the injured at a major accident site (Auf der Heide 1989).*

have the expected and desired effects (Anthony & Govindarajan 1995).

This brings to mind the concepts of formal and informal leadership, in that a leader may either act in line with a standardised schedule, *i.e.* formally, or deviate from such a schedule and act informally. The difference between a formal and informal leader is that the formal leader is appointed and paid to carry out the task of being a leader. Consequently, formal leaders are defined as managers and informal leaders as 'leaders for the time being' (Carlström 2009). It would be more useful if the concepts of formal and informal leaders instead focused on how the leader is acting, regardless of whether he or she is appointed 'by the book' or has simply temporarily taken on the leadership role. By this definition, a formally acting leader is someone who does what he or she has been told to do, while an informally acting leader can be unconventional and act outside the norms.

We will return to the site of the road accident in Western Sweden; in addition, later in this chapter, we will look at what happened in the initial phase of a well-documented landslide. We will also consider how emergency services (*i.e.* ambulance, fire and rescue services, and police) operate in line with governance models, how these models deviate from the need for governance, what makes a leader, and how a leader handles certain situations.

The PS Concept applied at the site of the accident in Western Sweden incorporated both organisational models and flowcharts. The PS Concept consists of rules as to who should say what and in what order, how and where different units should be placed at the accident site, and the order in which the accident should be dealt with.

When there is an accident or emergency, it is usually reported to a regional dispatch centre by a member of the public. The most relevant emergency service unit is then alerted. According to the PS Concept, the first ambulance to reach the accident site communicates a preliminary 'windscreen report' by radio, targeting the other rapidly approaching units. The windscreen report contains information about the situation at the accident site and gives details about any access roads, obstacles, risks, as well as the extent of the actual accident. It also signals that there are now people in place to take control of the situation.

According to the PS Concept, the ambulance arriving first at the site of an accident should carry one registered nurse trained in prehospital care and one paramedic (ambulance staffing according to the Swedish standard). The paramedic leads the medical work while interacting with the incident commander and the police. The registered nurse finds out how many people are injured, makes an assessment, and performs triage. The registered nurse then reports to the paramedic who, if required, requests additional resources, finds out which hospitals can receive patients, contacts these hospitals, and determines in what order the rescue work is to be carried out. When more ambulances arrive, it is still the crew of the first ambulance that leads the work at the accident site (Rüter *et al.* 2007).

A minute or so after the accident had occurred along a country lane in Western Sweden, it was reported to the national dispatch centre by a passer-by. The call was received by an emergency operator. The alert message was 'traffic accident trapped', and the fire and rescue services, police, and two ambulances were alerted. Later on, an air ambulance was also called to the site.

The ambulances and air ambulance were assigned Incident Communications Channel 1 by the dispatch centre while on route to the accident site. The ambulance arriving from the south had not programmed in Channel 1; the ambulance crew notified the operator at the dispatch centre about this, suggesting that they would instead use Channel A of the fire and rescue services.

A few minutes later, the ambulance from the south arrived at the site of the accident. Upon arrival, the ambulance crew gave the dispatch centre an accurate 'windscreen report', which the other rapidly approaching ambulance and the air ambulance were unable to hear.

The windscreen report provided by the first ambulance arriving at the site of an accident is routinely recorded in writing by the dispatch centre and relayed in text form to all other units on their way to the incident. This routine is intended to prevent misunderstandings or insufficient information due to poor radio audibility. However, there was not enough time to relay the text in this case. In a subsequent interview, the emergency operator said:

> We usually write down the information received by the first ambulance arriving at the site, which we then pass on to others that are on their way, but we response desk operators do not always have time to do this. (Operator, dispatch centre)

Consequently, the reports received by the dispatch centre were never passed on.

The ambulance from the south was first to arrive at the site and was therefore responsible for taking command. The ambulance staff indicated this by putting on yellow incident-command vests. They were expected to take command of arriving units as well as report on and allocate tasks until the last patient was removed from the site. The paramedic spoke to the fire officer in charge of the three fire engines and 10 firefighters on site. The fire officer explained that there were two people in one car and a sole woman trapped in the other.

The registered nurse and the paramedic in the ambulance from the south immediately began providing medical care to the two most seriously injured motorists. Neither of them had time to comply with the management guidelines of the PS Concept. Instead, they chose to care for the most seriously injured patients. Shortly afterwards, the second ambulance arrived from north of the accident site.

The later-arriving ambulance crew did not know that another ambulance was already on site. The radio had been quiet during the journey and no 'windscreen reports' had been received via Channel 1. Moreover, the dispatch centre omitted to announce the arrival of a second ambulance. To complicate the matter further, the ambulance from the south was hidden by the fire brigade.

As a result, the crew of the second ambulance began acting like a 'first-ambulance crew', *i.e.* deciding on who should do what and putting on the same yellow incident-command vests as worn by the crew of the first ambulance. They thought it was their responsibility to take command of the incident site.

When the newly arrived paramedic went to talk with the incident commander, he was surprised to hear that another ambulance crew was already busy providing the injured with emergency medical care. At the same time, the air ambulance landed in a nearby field. The rapidly increasing number of people at the site called for additional management and organisation.

Regardless of the guidelines of the PS Concept, the newly arrived ambulance crew took the initiative to lead and allocate the work. Despite the PS Concept principle that the 'first on the site leads', the paramedic of the second ambulance from the north took charge of the emergency medical care. Staff were allocated tasks, hospitals contacted, additional transportation requested, data obtained with the assistance of the police, and work with the Rescue Extrication Unit coordinated.

Once the situation had stabilised somewhat, the paramedics from the south and north ambulances met for the first time, whereupon the following dialogue took place between them:

Were you already here? I did not see you arrive.
We have been here for a while. Didn't you hear our windscreen report?
No, we haven't heard anything.
Didn't the dispatch centre report our arrival?
No, not that either.
(Paramedics, ambulances 1 and 2)

The paramedic of the first ambulance from the south chose not to lead, but instead cared for the most seriously injured motorists; he commented on his actions as follows:

It would be very strange to just stay by the incident command point when there are people lying injured nearby. It is not right that I should turn my back on people when they need my help. If you are on your own at the site then, naturally, you do what you can for the injured. The concept that we should remain at the incident command point in such circumstances is unreasonable. (Paramedic, first ambulance on the site)

The virtue of obedience

In emergency services, orders given by the top to the bottom are expected to be carried out (Berlin & Carlström 2009). These organisations have a simple hierarchical chain of command that involves a clear and simple division of responsibilities, right down to the 'bottom floor'. The idea is that everyone should know the rules and who it is that makes decisions. They are also characterised by a strong target orientation, *i.e.* all tasks must be carried out quickly and efficiently. To aid this process, there are schedules, rules, and general plans of action.

This form of organisational structure is seldom found in slightly slower-paced operations such as municipal and government administrations providing public services at a normal pace.

Emergency services, however, act in urgent situations where there is a threat to life and property and insufficient time for negotiations. They do not engage in employee empowerment, nor do they circulate matters for comment and review. If these services must respond to an accident or any other threat, they take it for granted that there will be resources with which to address the trouble without delay. That is why there are emergency services, to deal with accidents, violence, fires, and natural disasters promptly.

Obedience is therefore a virtue in emergency services. Operations are governed by rules and schedules that are based on an ideal of how rescue work should be implemented. These rules and schedules are mandatory models that must be followed. They act as operational laws and directives from government agencies and supreme authorities and are expected to be obeyed. They fulfil an important function. In a reverse-case scenario, *i.e.* if there were no rules and schedules to follow and everyone acted on their own initiative, there would be considerable chaos. The absence of a disaster recovery plan would cost lives and property. This is evident from the Caribbean where the islands are regularly subjected to hurricanes. Before 1960, there were no national agencies in the Caribbean to deal with natural disasters; since then, both national and sub-national agencies have been formed. Before these agencies were formed, all major incidents were dealt with on an ad hoc basis. Every time disaster struck, the police and military would supervise the improvised and badly organised relief work. This tragic sequence of events would then be forgotten and no preparations made before the next disaster struck, when the ad hoc response was repeated once again. This lack of disaster preparedness cost many lives and a large amount of resources (Poncelet 1997).

Another proof of the need for order and clarity at the site of an incident is illustrated by the concept of *second disaster*. The concept refers to a situation in which self-imposed and unorganised rescue staff impede more than facilitate the rescue work at the site of an incident. This is particularly obvious in international disaster situations. The relief work provided by visiting aid agencies is often perceived as inadequate and even misguided due to their inability to follow a common disaster recovery plan. Language barriers and cultural differences are often the reason for this (Noji & Toole 1997). One such example is the 2010 earthquake disaster in Haiti, when certain aid agencies operated in their own self-interest rather than in the interest of others. The medical journal *The Lancet* (2010) described how aid agencies compete to show the media how proactive and professional they are rather than conforming to local procedures and practices.

However, obedience can also make it difficult to make directional changes. If rules and regulations are given priority and are not negotiable, whatever the situation, not even local leaders will have enough influence to induce an organisation to change direction. Accordingly, members of the organisation will continue to act according to predetermined schedules and well-practised routines. This is exemplified by

Karl Weick's (1993) description of the death of 13 firefighters in connection with a forest fire. What was initially considered a forest fire under control soon developed into an inferno that threatened the safety of the firefighters. When the flames were coming closer, the local fire chiefs gave an unexpected order, far outside the normal action plan. One of them shouted: 'Drop your tools!' (Weick 1993, p. 635).

The idea was that the firefighters would drop their heavy equipment and quickly flee the fire. However, the firefighters had not been trained to flee, let alone drop their equipment. No such thing was mentioned in the formal action plans according to which they had been told to act. They were all well-equipped *firefighters* who fought fires with bravery and skill. Rather than following the order given by the Fire Chief, the firefighters made a slow retreat, still carrying their heavy equipment, until the flames caught up with them. The firefighters proved difficult to direct in a situation that deviated from the norm.

Blind obedience to one's leader implies that gaining recognition is more important than achieving. Rules and regulations continue steering even if they sometimes steer off course. High levels of blind obedience may end in failure in which the actual purpose of the activity is lost.

Leaders can also, as in the case of the forest fire, issue an instruction that contravenes the rule with the aim of letting ends justify means. Subordinates too can act contrary to issued orders or to the established plan of action and still carry out their duties, examples of which are presented in this chapter. Such autonomous behaviour requires the ability to act alone and sometimes manifest disobedience, especially when the governing action plan is inadequate.

One such situation was a major train accident that occurred in Norway, as described by Christina Lindblad (Lindblad & Sjöström 2005). The ambulance staff dealing with the incident deviated from the rules. They went around to the people trapped in various sections of the train, letting them swallow doses of painkillers that, in other circumstances, were meant to be injected. The paramedic in charge had the ability to improvise, even though it meant deviating from the usual routines.

Another example is the 'Gothenburg Fire' of 1998 when a party venue caught fire, killing 63 youth and injuring 213. On that occasion, *smart tags* were used, *i.e.* folding paper tags hung around the necks of the injured indicating their level of priority. Those assigned a lower level of priority and expected to wait for transport were themselves able to see the level of priority assigned, in this case, a green tag with a picture of a turtle, which meant that they had to wait at the site. This led many of the youths to re-mark their tags, folding the paper to get a higher level of priority and faster medical care. As it was, the front of the tag was coloured red and had a picture of an ambulance. This same behaviour spread among the injured youth. Once the medical staff realised what was happening, the marking of paper tags stopped. The action plan had not had the desired result. Consequently, those in charge began acting disobediently: they deviated from established routines and stopped using the 'smart tags' (Suserud 2001).

One routine that was partially abandoned in conjunction with the Gothenburg Fire was the documentation requirement. Only a quarter of the staff produced any form of report on the incident, while most did not report at all. The incident site was dark, grimy, and full of injured people. Difficult ethical considerations were involved in prioritising the patients. This required an ability to make quick and drastic decisions. One ambulance paramedic or nurse could be surrounded by 20–30 injured young people. Standard routines were bypassed and assessments made based on an ability to disregard one's training (Suserud 2001).

Matthew Cooke (1999) highlights the problem of standard routines taking control of the course of action and calls for the possibility of allowing assessments to be adapted to the situation at hand. This can be summed up as 'doing much for many', which requires the ability to change strategy in a critical situation. Cooke believes that it might be necessary for a leader to be 'disobedient' in a precarious situation. Controversial decisions must be made when 'desperate times call for desperate measures'.

Another relevant example is that of an earthquake in Turkey. Sitki Corbacioglu and Naim Kapucu (2006) described how local rescue services, for the first time, decided not to wait for permission from the Prime Ministry Crisis Management Centre to obtain the equipment needed. The incident took place in connection with one of the largest earthquakes in Turkey, in Marmara in 1999. When the leaders of the rescue operation arrived at one of the logistic material depots, they found the door locked because the working day was over. They decided to break down the door to get the much-needed equipment, violating the strict rules governing rescue operations in a disaster. 'Obedient' rescue leaders would have waited for a central order, which in turn would have led to long delays because of the breakdown in communication. To put it another way, those trapped under tons of rubble would have had to wait for a decision from the central authorities before the emergency services could get access to the equipment needed to get them out. When the

Marmara earthquake struck in 1999, the disobedient local rescue leaders ignored this protocol for the first time.

When an incident happens that deviates from the norm, *i.e.* an incident that requires a different form of behaviour from what hierarchies, action plans, and other models of conformity mandate, this creates a threshold of confusion, making it difficult to choose a different path.

Karl Weick (1990) illustrated this by reconstructing the sequence of events that led to the fatal plane crash in Tenerife in 1977 when two aircraft collided on the runway. The accident claimed 583 lives. In the cockpit of the Dutch KLM aircraft were three crew members: 1) the captain, 2) his first officer (under the captain's command), and 3) an aircraft engineer under the command of the other two pilots. The KLM aircraft stood farthest away on the runway, waiting for clearance from the air traffic controller. On the same runway a Pan Am aircraft was taxiing through the fog towards the KLM aircraft. The captain on board the KLM aircraft was highly experienced and qualified: not only was he a commercial pilot, but he was also the Director of KLM's Flight Training Department. He had himself issued the much younger co-pilot his pilot's licence. There they were, side by side, the captain, his first officer, and the aircraft engineer: three levels of command with the captain at the top of the hierarchy.

Then, the captain made a fatal mistake. He gave the order to prepare for take-off despite not having the all-clear signal from the flight controller. The captain acted as if he were in a flight simulator, in that he himself gave the all-clear signal for take-off. The first officer was at a disadvantage. He wanted to show that he was competent, assuming the role of an 'obedient' and compliant first officer to his older and much more experienced captain. The aircraft engineer, however, realised that they were on their way towards another aircraft in the middle of the runway. The Air Accident Investigation Commission could hear him say on an audio recording: 'Is he not clear then, that Pan Am?' (Weick 1990, p. 580).

His gentle protest indicated that he did not want to get involved, and he instead focused on monitoring the power supply and systems. He followed his own flowchart of rules for aeronautical engineers and turned a blind eye to the bigger picture, *i.e.* a safe and secure take-off. A broader and less controlled focus would have helped the aircraft engineer prevent the accident from happening.

Karl Weick (1990) referred to the relationships in the cockpit of the KLM aircraft as a 'top-heavy hierarchy'. A top-heavy hierarchy, according to Weick (1990), contributes to deadlocks and narrow-minded behaviour. The 'obedience' or compliance and respect that the first officer and the aircraft engineer showed the current order of hierarchy had disastrous consequences.

Dominance and submission are therefore not always favourable. The risk is that those who are submissive may refrain from reflecting and protesting when a situation is likely to 'fail'. In such circumstances, the organisation lacks the necessary protection against flawed decisions.

Leading under time pressure entails certain problems. In emergency services, there is seldom scope to make the leadership see sense by reporting on and discussing possible deviations from protocol at management meetings or by making proposals. In an environment in which decisions need to be made quickly, there is little room for discussion. Employees cannot always spend time going through normal decision-making channels when a house is burning to the ground, injured are bleeding to death, or a passenger plane is taking off. On the other hand, when the regulated actions of an action plan expose an operation to risks, it is usually the responsibility of the local leadership to correct the mistake.

The administration of painkillers after the train crash in Norway and the discontinued use of smart tags after the fire in Gothenburg are examples of behaviours outside the norm. The leaders were consciously 'disobedient' in these cases. However, bearing in mind the circumstances at the time, it is difficult to criticise these behaviours as they probably reduced the suffering of many people and saved more lives than if the behaviours had been traditionally obedient. The obedience that the first officer and aircraft engineer manifested in the case of the KLM aircraft in Tenerife had the completely opposite effect, and led to disaster. The words of the captain continued to apply until the last few seconds before the disaster happened. This can be a problem, particularly in organisations in which obedience is expected. As illustrated by the example of the forest fire, the overriding plan of action had greater influence than did the local leader.

In the above examples, instructions on how to carry the equipment, rules on the order of hierarchy and the administration of pharmaceuticals, the tagging of injured in a mass casualty situation, and the permission needed to access rescue equipment either jeopardised or could have jeopardised the entire emergency operations.

Why is there then this expectation of obedience? One explanation is the lack of time in 'extreme situations'. There is simply no room for time-consuming negotiations. Another reason might be that the top leadership has access to more comprehensive information. Yet another reason might be that the leadership has the tools and expertise needed to comprehend the complete picture. A person dealing with only a limited portion of a sequence of events might see a given top–down decision as overly restrictive, short-sighted, or even incorrect. Even so, the decision might be well thought through, justifiable, and beneficial to the overall situation.

Does this mean that an established action plan is always the best option? Of course not. The difficulty of understanding a complex situation can result in somewhat mixed messages and updates reaching the leadership. The circumstances and progress of events combined with an inability to get an overview of the situation can lead to mistakes. This is very much the case when emergency services are involved. The progress of events is often random and chaotic, everything is done under time pressure, and the information passed from to bottom to top often ends up being delayed.

Obedience in Småröd

One dark evening, 20 December 2006, a section of the International E-road number six (E6) subsided in Western Sweden near Småröd close to Skredsvik, just south of Munkedal. Around 500 metres of a motorway and one kilometre of the Bohusbanan railroad collapsed. Some ten cars were caught up in the subsidence, creating a vast accident site. It was extremely difficult and hazardous to reach the vehicles on foot. The 500-metre-wide pit was full of clay and had steep, loose edges that were gradually crashing into the centre of the pit. The rescue operations were organised from Munkedal, north of the accident site, and from Uddevalla, south of the landslide (County Administrative Board 2007).

At the dispatch centre, the emergency operators handling the incident were seated at different desks. Some of the emergency operators dealt with incoming 112 calls (the European emergency telephone number), while others listened to the calls at the same time as organising emergency services. The first person reporting the incident in Munkedal was a lorry driver who, when calling the dispatch centre, was hanging upside down in his lorry in the middle of the crumbling pit. The emergency operator taking his call described it as follows:

> A man called in. I replied: 'National dispatch centre here, how can
> I help you?' The man said calmly, 'Hello, my name is xx, the E6 is
> collapsing in Håby'. 'Sorry?', I replied. 'The E6 is collapsing here in
> Håby', continued the man. Then his lorry probably fell into the pit.
> All I could hear was the man screaming: 'The E6 is collaaaaaaaps-
> ing!' Then I thought the lorry must have overturned. It was com-
> pletely silent. (Operator, dispatch centre)

None of the other emergency operators registered this first and dramatic
call. The emergency operator sensed immediately that something out
of the ordinary and major had occurred. She wanted to get everyone's
attention. According to normal procedure, the operators can activate an
electronic alarm in the event of an incident, and the others will be quickly informed via their computers and headsets. In this case, the operator
decided to do something unusual, contrary to the established routines:

> I stood up and shouted: 'Is anyone else getting calls about the E6
> collapsing?' Then, more calls started to come in about Småröd.
> There is a big difference between Håby and Småröd. It was in the
> afternoon on a December day at ten past seven and it was dark, cold,
> and damp. I contacted the incident command centre in Uddevalla
> and told them that they would probably have to come from two
> directions. I did this over the radio. I said it over the radio so that
> everyone could hear. The ambulance service switched over to the fire
> communication channel. (Operator, dispatch centre)

The behaviour of the emergency operator got the others' attention,
which was her initial intention. The other operators were now also
focusing on the incident in Munkedal. The emergency operator deviated
from the routine in two further respects. She used the 'open channel' so
that all the units could hear her radio transmissions, in addition to which
she asked the ambulance service to switch over to the fire communication channel. In the established routine, the ambulance service does not
normally use the fire communication channel. However, that is what
happened in conjunction with the landslide in Munkedal. As a result,
everyone involved was simultaneously updated as more and more information was received by the dispatch centre. Every call was important,
resulting in vital information being forwarded to the emergency staff on
site and to those who were on their way to the site. An example of this is
the next call received from one of the incident victims:

> In the middle of it all, we received a call from a mother. She and her
> baby were trapped in their car that had been caught up in the land-
> slide. She did not know where she was. She described how her car
> had suddenly turned upside down. We kept 'juggling her' between
> us, talking to her while at the same time sending out alerts and
> keeping everyone involved up to date on the situation. When the
> ambulance helicopter was getting closer, she said, 'I can hear some-
> thing now'. I then called the helicopter crew, asking them to look
> out for her. She had a blue car. I had her in one ear at the same time
> as maintaining radio contact with the helicopter. After a while, she
> said 'I hear voices, I hear voices'. We had juggled her between us all
> this time. She went from one operator to another, whenever anyone
> had a moment to spare. (Operator, dispatch centre)

The dispatch centre alerted the emergency services in two different
locations – another example of action inconsistent with the established
routines and plan of action. Normally, only the emergency services in
the municipality where the incident has occurred are called out. The
operator used 'common sense' before taking any action. She gave the
following explanation: 'When the entire E6 is blocked then you have to
come from two directions' (Operator, dispatch centre).

Emergency services in two different municipalities were called to the
site, one from the north and the other from the south. They both set up
incident command points. First on the site were the fire and rescue services and ambulance service from the north. When the road collapsed,
the section leading to the nearest hospital had also gone. A paramedic
on-board one of the ambulances from the north described the situation
as follows.

> It was dark, dirty, and impossible to see anything. All we could see
> was the edge of the landslide and the darkness beyond. We had no
> idea what was happening on the other side or how far the landslide
> stretched. It took a while to take it all in and, at the beginning, it
> was not clear who should take the initiative and do something. We
> hesitated to go into the pit as it was very dangerous. It was some
> time before we had an update on what was being done on the other
> side of the pit. (Paramedic, north edge of the landslide)

The first on the site was the ambulance service followed closely by the
fire and rescue services, air ambulance helicopters, and the on-call para-

medics from the south side of the incident. The first paramedic on the site told how the task of leading was not passed upwards in the hierarchy when other more qualified staff arrived, which is what should have occurred, according to the established routines:

> I am not very good at the different relations in a situation like this, but neither the on-call paramedic nor the air ambulance doctor wanted to take the lead. Most people would usually want to lead a rescue operation like this as it is seen as a valuable merit. This time, however, they said, 'You handle this, we'll keep in the background'. I worked without a break for seven hours and I am not even a full-time nurse. I think they were just as unsure as I was about what to do. Nothing was the way we had been taught. (Paramedic, south edge of the landslide)

Close to an hour after the accident, the incident commanders on either side of the landslide managed to make contact with each other. Because of the darkness and the distance from one edge of the landslide to the other, it was impossible to get an overview of the entire area from north to south. The two incident commanders therefore decided to continue working as they had begun with two locally led rescue operations. The extent of the incident site and the number of cars buried in the landslide emerged slowly and painstakingly. Throughout the rescue operation, the two incident commanders continued to lead the work from two separate directions. The accident report reads as follows:

> Three firefighters continued through the site towards the lorry. Behind the lorry, on the embankment of the landslide, they found a passenger car. No one was inside or near the car. It later transpired that the driver of the car and his two sons had abandoned the car and managed to find their way out of the area in a southward direction. The left door of the overturned lorry was open. The driver of the lorry was lying halfway through the door. His legs were trapped between the steering wheel and driver seat. To be able to dislodge the lorry driver, hydraulic rescue tools had to be brought on site. The work of dislodging the lorry driver was carried out near the high landslide embankment, which was threatening to collapse at any time. Once the nurses and paramedics came close enough to give the driver pain relief, he was dislodged and brought on a stretcher to the assembly point south of the area. At the same time as assessing

the situation of the lorry, a woman was heard calling for help close by. It was a woman with a ten-month-old baby. The woman and child were found outside a car positioned slightly higher up in the pit where it was hidden from view behind a mound of earth. The woman had repeatedly called 112 to report the difficult situation in which she and her baby found themselves, whereupon the dispatch centre had talked to her, giving her advice and trying to keep her calm. One of the firefighters helped the woman and her baby out of the landslide area. (Swedish Accident Investigation Authority 2009, p. 55)

Two geotechnicians on the south side of the incident site assessed the area to be at risk of further landslides. Consequently, the incident commander decided to move the incident command point a further 200 metres to the south, which made it even more difficult to survey the area. Nor was there any possibility of putting up floodlights around the area to help assess the extent of rescue services required (Swedish Accident Investigation Authority 2009).

The use of two incident command sites was later criticised by the Swedish Accident Investigation Authority when evaluating the rescue efforts. This approach was found not to comply with the intentions of the Prevention of Accidents Act (2003:778), which stipulates that an incident should be overseen by only one incident commander. The *organisational chart* the Authority referred to shows a cohesive leadership regardless of the size and extent of the incident site. The legal responsibilities in terms of the rescue efforts and any subsequent responsibilities create a need for a single incident commander. However, the legislation does not stipulate where the incident command point should be located. It could be located at a distance from or close to the incident site. What matters the most is that there is an incident command point on site.

However, the absence of a visual overview rendered it more difficult for the incident command centre than for the incident commander on site to follow the sequence of events (Berlin & Carlström 2009). It was the particular circumstances of the incident that led to deviation from *the organisational chart*. Once the two incident commanders had made contact with each other and obtained an overview of the situation, they appointed a coordination officer responsible for relaying information and coordinating the rescue operations on the north and south sides of the incident site – an improvisation that deviated from 'how things ought to be done' (Swedish Accident Investigation Authority 2009).

Good and bad obedience

Landslides are not that uncommon in Sweden. The area described in the above case was located close to Skredsvik (in English, 'The bay of landslides'). The name Skredsvik, and consequently the phenomenon of landslides, can be traced back almost 700 years in the area. Road accidents are an everyday occurrence in Sweden, as in the rest of the world. However, the weather and visibility conditions can be quite difficult in Sweden, especially during the winter. The rescue services from Munkedal were unable to get an overview of the extent of the incident and it took some time before the details of the incident emerged, allowing for the establishment of an appropriate rescue strategy.

According to legislation, all incident sites should have one incident command and one incident command point or centre (Swedish Accident Investigation Authority 2009). The advantage of having one incident command is obvious: it prevents confusion, redundant instructions, overlapping responsibilities, and an unclear reporting process. An incident command is necessary for transparent accountability. Every rescue operation should incorporate an incident command responsible for making careful assessments and decisions. This creates scope for regulating and establishing practices. Berlin and Carlström (2008) described how a competition for prestige sometimes develops between staff from the rescue and ambulance services and the police, resulting in serious delays in rescue work. The commanders of the three groups are sometimes unable to agree on a mutual incident command point and therefore end up at various distances from the incident site, while remaining in visual contact with one another. After a bit of squabbling, one of the commanders comes out the winner, while the others 'creep to the cross', agreeing to a mutual incident command point.

There is usually only *one* incident commander at the site of an accident, though on some occasions, this may be fraught with problems. The work of the incident commander leading the rescue work is facilitated by a good visual overview of the site. However, incident sites can be vast and difficult to survey, such as a train derailment involving many carriages along several hundred metres of track or a forest fire threatening the safety of many communities and spreading rapidly across large areas. Other extreme examples of unfathomable events are the bombings in Madrid in 2004 and the terrorist attacks in Oslo in 2011, which occurred in different locations at the same time. In the case of the Madrid bombings, a major government investigation identified the necessity of routines and incident commanders being flexible and adaptable to unforeseen events and circumstances (Eriksson 2004).

The approach taken in Munkedal was characterised by flexibility and creativity. The difficult situation was handled to the best of everyone's ability despite the extremely complicated and serious circumstances. The setting up of two incident command points, one to the north and the other to the south of the incident, was a necessary consequence of the specific character of the event. Emergency units from both sides were alerted; it was only about one hour later that the two incident commanders made contact and could start working together. The appointment of a coordination officer was not part of the plan either but a joint creative solution devised by the two incident commanders.

That the operator at the dispatch centre alerted the emergency services in two different municipalities was also a course of action outside the norm. Requesting the assistance of emergency services from another municipality incurs costs that are regulated between the municipalities. The municipality requesting the assistance normally ends up paying for the assistance requested. Consequently, it is a procedure that requires a qualified assessment and an authorised request. The operator at the dispatch centre took matters into her own hands and therefore saved time, property, and likely lives. Because the area around the landslide was cordoned off promptly, more vehicles were prevented from plummeting into the rubble and there were no further delays in initiating the rescue work.

The road accident bears some resemblance to the above situation but also differs in key ways. The rescue operation for the landslide in Munkedal deviated from the usual organisational chart as did the rescue operation for the road accident in Western Sweden. When the second ambulance arrived at the road accident site, the crew did not see the other ambulance parked behind a fire engine. According to regulations on the positioning of vehicles at incident sites, smaller vehicles and the site itself are to be protected by larger vehicles such as fire engines. The positioning of the vehicles was therefore correct and in keeping with the organisational chart but nonetheless counterproductive, seeing as the crew of the second ambulance thought they were first on the site. Ideally, an incident command point should have been established from which the paramedic, fire chief, and chief police officer could lead the rescue operation. This did not happen in the road accident case as the paramedic decided to leave the incident command point and instead give medical help to the passengers of the oncoming car. The ideal model conflicted with what the paramedic saw as reasonable behaviour. To remain at the incident command point, waiting for the next rescue unit to arrive, was perceived as lower priority when there were patients in urgent need of medical care.

Communication is thought to have been the main problem in this case. However, a number of respondents claimed that it is not uncommon for such situations to be chaotic. There are no established routines for coordinating communications when the rescue work involves multiple units. Certain routines, such as the relay of information by the dispatch centre, had failed to function amidst the hectic rescue activities. The use of incident communication channels was also difficult to manage.

The appropriate conclusion from these cases is not that we should surround ourselves with constantly disobedient leaders who act on their own initiative regardless of established routines or procedures. Nor should we surround ourselves with naively obedient leaders who, considering the situation, are unable to make an optimal decision out of respect for organisational charts, legislation, or senior officers. What is required is a sensitive and reflective leadership that can interpret a situation and act accordingly (Dreyfus & Dreyfus 1986). The models shown in Figures 3.1 and 3.2 include guidelines that need to be questioned in the case of critical situations. The question is whether or not the models facilitate the rescue work in conjunction with particular incidents. The same question can be illustrated as the difference between a map and a sketch.

Map or sketch?

The incidents above deviated from the ideal organisational chart and flowchart. However, according to subsequent interviews, this is not unusual. As mentioned earlier, organisational plans and flowcharts are based on legislation as well as on routines established by the operations leadership. One important question is whether these models are seen as *maps* or *sketches*.

This alludes to the concept that maps are images that shape our perception of reality. We trust that a map will lead us to the target. In contrast to a map, a sketch is a guide that can be adjusted as and when required. Leaders who can follow their intuition, read a situation, and deviate from the simplified official model treat action plans as if they were drawings. Leaders who stay true to the rules and act as the policymakers expect, *i.e.* according to the motto 'rather precisely wrong than almost correct', treat action plans as though they were maps.

Plans seen as sketches allow for manipulation of what is depicted. If the sketch is unreasonable or inaccurate, the matter is simply dealt with in another way. Efforts are changed according to the needs and the situation. However, if plans are seen as maps, the situation immediately becomes more difficult. If the topographic conditions do not match the map, which, after all, constitutes 'the truth', then trees must be felled, rivers rerouted, and hills levelled. In the case of an accident, the map logicians believe, regardless of the situation, that there should be only one incident command point and that the incident commander should focus on leading even if the need to take care of the injured may seem more important at the time.

The sketch perspective can be a help when handling complex situations during emergencies, even though the map perspective still dominates in emergency services. The reason to prefer the sketch perspective is that crisis management often differs from standard management in public organisations. Such management has moved from top–down hierarchies to laissez-faire and further to transformational–transactional leadership in order to encourage staff to self-regulate. Various types of team organisations have emerged as well. They have moved from multi- to trans-professional, from differentiated to complementary, and from sequential to synchronous (Rickards & Moger 2000; Hall & Weaver 2001; Berlin & Carlström 2008; Carlström 2012). However, leaders in emergency services still seem to prefer top–down hierarchies. They often have a collective self-image of always being in the first rank, acting decisively, and having a high level of competence (Berlin & Carlström 2009 2015). One upshot of this is that they can find it difficult to stand aside and leave room for others. Previous studies have referred to this behaviour as 'impression management' (Boin *et al.* 2005), *i.e.* trying to display superior skill and courage in order to impress colleagues during the work at the emergency site. Such behaviour is nowadays difficult to find in other types of public organisations, such as hospitals and universities. It is known to lead to a situation in which different action options are not examined, risk assessments are not carried out, and difficulties arise in interacting across boundaries (Weick 1996). On the other hand, leadership at an accident site is more unpredictable than in other types of public organisations. The leadership at a hospital or university does not depend on what member of the staff happens to arrive first at the office. If this method of appointing the one in charge were routine, the situation would probably be quite confusing at these institutions as well. In some organisations, staff would intentionally arrive late at work, to avoid being leader for the day, while in other workplaces, there would probably be a competitive early-morning race to be the one in charge. Furthermore, when staff arrived at work, there would also be some confusing moments before they identified the manager. Such confusion is comparable to the situation during the Western Sweden traffic accident mentioned above. The discussion between the two paramedics form the south and north ambulances illustrates this: 'Are you already here, I did not see you arrive?' 'No, we haven't heard anything'. Another effect of shifting leadership would be changing agendas, changing ideas of what to do, and different directions in management from day to day. This could be one reason why emergency services follow established routines, are perceived as conservative, and are map-logicians. Another difference between emergency management and management in other public organisations is the effects of failure. Emergency work at an accident site is critical, fast developing, and often involves life-or-death decisions. A wrong decision can have devastating effects just a few moments after the order is given. In contrast, typical public management is often characterised by changing assignments, dissolving targets, and fuzzy ideas, but still works fairly well. Consequently, public-sector managers often have lots of time to correct poor decisions.

The rules in public organisations are not always followed in the way that the stakeholders suppose. When a routine of management control is implemented, the staff can avoid acting according to the new regulation. The consequences of obstructing the system, however, are not always especially painful. In some cases, management will not even notice that the routine has not been followed. It is different when we come to emergency management. In the case of the road accident in Western Sweden, the routine of keeping the radio updated had failed in the south ambulance: Channel 1 was not programmed and, as a result, the radio was quiet during the journey and no 'windscreen reports' were received.

Routines are a help to a certain extent but they can be a hindrance when circumstances change. The real challenge when organising rescue services is to decide when to act 'by the book' and when to make exceptions because of shifting circumstances. One way to handle such a dilemma is to use a drawing perspective, *i.e.* let the models and rules be the organisational skeleton but simultaneously be aware of the potential need to act outside the established framework. Such an approach is not easy to embed in emergency services. There are still remnants of a 'stiff-upper-lip approach' in the crisis community (Boin *et al.* 2005). Whether the accident site is on the road, in the woods, on a mountain, in the summer or winter, when the weather is pleasant or there is a raging storm, the routines are carved in stone in the form of advanced established models.

An ability to act organically is of great value, as the empirical examples in this chapter illustrate. Efforts will, when necessary, be made and adapted to the conditions at the site of the incident. A good example is the operator at the dispatch centre who, against all the rules, decided to stand up and call out to her colleagues at the other emergency response desks. The same applies to the two senior commanders on the south side of the landslide in Munkedal who preferred to stay in the background. The situation could not have been handled any better despite the work being led by temporary staff.

So why is there a tendency to regard action plans as maps? The underlying mechanism is our need to view the world as something we take for granted and that is predefined, comprehensible, secure, and stable. This need is constant but increases significantly at the site of an accident. The absence of stable reference points facilitating the comprehensibility of the situation implies that a threat of subjectivism and relativism is around the corner. This tendency to make a complex sequence of events more comprehensible can be seen in causal metaphors such as 'the Trojan horse', 'the shot in Sarajevo', or 'the Titanic and the iceberg'. This way of thinking has strongly influenced how we like to organise and comprehend various contexts. Sten Andersson (2004) has referred to this as our need to classify, find causes, and identify action or remedy in an easily comprehensible and appealing manner.

These concepts of models and rationality are represented in emergency services (Balaban 1990). Comprehensive action plans not only specify what is expected to lead to B, that is A, but also give long-term projections, that is, what B will lead to. The model is a means of bringing order into chaos, of sharpening minds when the onset of paralysis threatens, and of sorting out a problem that initially may seem unsolvable. However, plans may deviate from reasonable assumptions about the behaviour of individuals (Tsoukas & Knudsen 2003). Experience suggests that symmetries are broken and trusted linear activities challenged (Kiel 1994). Astrid Scholtens (2008) criticised the dogma of supreme command and operational leadership, instead recommending collaboration and individual decision-making in order to achieve effective preparation (Berlin & Carlström 2015). Such a course would call for wise leaders with the ability to act outside the ordinary 'map', if required. The formal appointment of a leader does not always mean that behaviour has to be guided by formality. This puts focus on the style of leadership rather than on the leadership itself.

Conclusions that may influence our view of leadership are therefore as follows: Successful leadership requires the ability to consider other options and alternatives beyond what is already defined and specified. In keeping with that definition, a leader is a person who not only acts in a formal and correct way but also has the ability to make a wise choice between formal and more informal logics of action. Such a leader can even be disobedient if and when favourable to the situation.

CHAPTER 4

Preservative leadership

Anna Cregård

They stand in two lines, facing each other. They wear the same clothes – grey robes with a black wimple and a white crown with five red dots. It is in the middle of the day and time for one of the day's ceremonies. One line of women begs the other line of women for forgiveness for any 'words or deeds, signs or gestures' that may have caused them offence. The other line of women replies that they forgive 'wholeheartedly'. Then the women switch roles and the same words are repeated. The same ceremony has been performed daily for hundreds of years. For the nuns at Vadstena Abbey, it is an essential routine.

As organisations, abbeys provide perspective on what 'long-lived' means, many having been founded in the Middle Ages. How can it be that some organisations remain seemingly unchanged for such a long time? Are they especially good at adapting to changes in their environment, following every fluctuation in society and thereby always being perceived as right? Are their products and services so strong, important, and coveted that they make the organisation imperishable? Or maybe it is the organisation itself that has been successfully promoted?

In this chapter I discuss one way of looking at long-lasting organisations: as organisations that give their members stability, a core of never-changing missions and routines, as well as a coherent view of life. I call the leadership of such organisations preservative leadership, and Vadstena Abbey constitutes the case. Preservative leadership is a concept focusing on something quite different from what is usually treated in the leadership literature: change management. However, to create organisations that do not fall apart under the challenges of being different, leadership cannot promote change solely, but must also secure stability in the core of the organisation. Preservative leadership does that. Since such organisations are created to accomplish something very important in the eyes of organisation members, they must change only in order to preserve what really counts.

The case

In Sweden, there are around 200 nuns and 30 abbeys/convents. The tasks and activities of the abbeys vary, and while some are active in their local communities (*e.g.* running preschools, refugee centres, and nursing homes), others practice a more contemplative way of life, prioritising prayer. Most abbeys are Catholic but there are also those that follow the Lutheran faith or principles of ecumenism. This chapter focuses on the Catholic nuns at St. Birgitta's Abbey in Vadstena. The Abbey complies with the monastic Order of St. Birgitta from c. 1370.

The Order of St. Birgitta has four branches: the medieval branch (incorporating five independent abbeys in Europe including the Abbey of St. Birgitta Pax Mariae); the Spanish branch (incorporating four independent abbeys in Spain and four in Mexico); the Swedish branch (with a mother house in Rome and about 50 communities across the world); and the Birgittine Monks (established in Oregon in 1976). In addition, there are missionary Birgittine Nuns in Mexico and Venezuela, who are not yet recognised by the Roman Catholic Church. Common to the Birgittines is that they are based on the Order of St. Augustine from 300 AD. This means, among other things, that the nuns should pursue godly fellowship while committing themselves to the vows of poverty (community of property), celibacy (chastity with a pure and undivided heart), and obedience. The rules also stipulate when and how the nuns (and monks) may leave the enclosure of the abbey, say their prayers, and carry out their work (*e.g.* in silence).

I stayed with the Birgittine nuns in Vadstena Abbey for two days, during which time I was given access to at least some of their daily routines. The nuns follow a strict schedule of prayers and work, and refrain from participating in the common prayers at canonical hours only for extraordinary reasons. First, I conducted a group interview of all the nuns in good health and at home, meaning that 10 out of 12 were able to participate. The group interview involved general what, why, how, and when questions about life as a nun. I then conducted a separate interview with the Abbess, Mother Karin, during which we mostly talked about the meaning of being appointed leader of the Abbey and how such leadership was exercised. A third interview was conducted with the Advisory Sister, in which leadership, among other matters, was discussed from an empowerment perspective (*e.g.* when the Advisory Sister is requested to assist in the everyday running of the abbey by the Abbess or the rules of the Order). Later on, a colleague and I also participated in a seminar concerning convent leadership, in which three convents were represented. This seminar was held at Vadstena Abbey with 12 nuns together with one vicar general from the diocese. My colleague and I acted as discussion leaders, and for approximately three hours we considered issues such as recruitment, leadership and organisational development, core values, administrative tasks versus professional and spiritual tasks, delegation and coordination, and workload.

Other empirical materials used include *The Revelations of St. Birgitta of Sweden*, an account of St. Birgitta's view of monastic life, life in general, and her communion with God. I also consulted material found on the website of the Order of St. Birgitta, including three of their DVDs about St. Birgitta, monastic life, and what it means to be a nun.

I have taken an ethnographic approach to collecting and analysing the data. It is worth emphasising, however, that I tried to get an unbiased view and understanding of the monastic life of the nuns. This means that behaviours and ceremonies that may seem irrational to anyone outside the Abbey enclosure are depicted based on their function for the initiated. Although my approach is essentially based on a desire to understand, it does not preclude analysing the organisation and leadership of the Abbey from a more critical perspective. It is of course impossible to really understand someone or something after only a few encounters. For example, I asked Mother Karin if she would read my empirical description. She read it and made many pertinent comments (which, together with other e-mails from Mother Karin are obviously included in my data). However, the one comment that stood out the most was that Mother Karin did not think that my text truly reflected how happy she and her fellow sisters were to be part of the monastic community at the Abbey. This is a very significant comment as it illustrates how fervent the nuns are about their lives and how strongly they identify with their organisation and its activities. Now, let us turn to what the nuns do and how they live their lives.

Activities of the nuns

The Abbey of St. Birgitta Pax Mariae is part of the Catholic Order of the Most Holy Saviour and housed 12 nuns from six countries when I first met them in 2011. By the end of 2015 only eight remained, the attrition being due to old age. They live together in Vadstena Abbey, a popular destination for people looking for a few days of peace and quiet while staying at the Abbey guesthouse.

The guesthouse is not a main priority for the nuns but is an important part of their livelihood. Other sources of income are retirement pensions and gifts. The nuns prioritise prayer, as God has called them to the Abbey for the purpose of praying. The nuns at the Abbey thus lead a contemplative existence. The Abbey website (quoted from birgittaskloster. se) has this to say about prayer:

> It means first and foremost the praise of God. It means giving that thanks which all creation wants to give God who has loved us so much. It means prayer for those in active service, it is our way of backing them up. It can also mean prayer for many, many others who ask us to pray for them when they are in some sort of crisis. It means prayer for all those who never pray at all, for those who have forgotten that God has given them their life.

The prioritisation of prayer means that common prayers are said and hymns sung at certain times – or canonical hours – in the daily routine of the nuns. Prioritising prayer also means that delayed prayers are not allowed, so all other work stops at the times of prayer. It is also evident from the website (birgittaskloster.se) that preference is given to simple chores and tasks, as these have less of an effect on the concentration of the nuns in constant communion with God.

The canonical hours at the Abbey are as follows: 7.15 a.m. (called *lauds* and *tierce*), 11.15 a.m. (*none*), 4.25 p.m. (*vespers*), followed by a holy mass and a final canonical hour at 7.30 p.m. (*compline* and *matins*). The time between the canonical hours is devoted to work mostly in silence in the Abbey and the guesthouse, but there is also time for cooking, reading, teaching, etc. Following lunch, the nuns have an hour of free time, for example, for resting and walking (within the monastic enclosure). Another 40 minutes are set aside in the afternoon for handicrafts and conversation. The nuns dine in silence or while listening to a reading. After the monastic night-time liturgy or matins, the Abbey falls completely silent. The day begins again with meditation at 6.15 a.m.

Recruitment, community, and rules

The aspiring nun has approximately eight years in which to try out what life as a nun in the abbey is like. But the nun herself is tested too: Does she have the right motivation to embark on life as a nun? Is she called by God and, if so, to this particular abbey? Is she strong enough mentally to cope with living in this community for the rest of her life? One of the nuns explained that it is quite common these days for a psychologist to be asked to examine the mental health and motives of those with a desire to become nuns.

'Who can become a novice and then a nun?' I asked. 'Most aspiring nuns are screened out immediately', replied Mother Karin. One of the other nuns said that it is not unusual for women to call the abbey because they are tired of their husbands or children and just want to come to the abbey for some peace and quiet. These women are immediately told that they were not meant for a monastic life, though they are welcome to a retreat at the guesthouse. Others seem called by God, though, as it turns out, not to Vadstena Abbey. The 12 nuns living at the Abbey at the time of my first visit all sought out the Abbey and proved that they belonged there. 'How do you know that this abbey is the right one for you?', I asked. 'The path is different for everyone', the nuns explained: 'It is very individual'; 'Common to everyone is that they had a calling from God'; 'They felt drawn to the abbey – God brought them here – they felt that they belonged here'. One of the nuns put it like this: 'It is about listening and believing that God means what he says, and that he is helping me along the way'.

One of the nuns said that it was not difficult to become a nun. All that is required is a bit of common sense, humour, and willingness to accept – as well as strength and determination to cope with living in a community. The community aspect is important. The nuns share everything except their nightly rest: they each have their own sparsely furnished room, which is small and not ornate in any way. 'What is so typical of an abbey', said another nun, 'is, in fact, the community and the values we share'. The nuns did not chose monastic life because they believed it would offer them the most out of life; they did not really choose at all, but rather were called. One nun likened it to being picked up by the hair and dropped into the Abbey.

The nuns come from different parts of the world. They vary in age but are all women. Mother Karin explained:

St. Birgitta envisaged *one* communal abbey consisting of two convents or communities – one for women and one for men – physically separated from each other by the abbey church. St. Birgitta thought in terms of cooperation, *i.e.* men and women complementing and not competing with each other, each with a specific duty.

The nuns have different experiences from their previous lives and different skills and educations too. They told me of the advantages of not being equally skilled in the same things, as there are so many tasks to do. They also said that their work is valued equally – not as in the rest of society where different jobs confer different social status and value. The nuns explained that all people have talents of their own, all of which are gifts from God. Everyone is equal and of equal value in the eyes of God, so it would be wrong to value one another's skills differently.

Entry into the abbey means living together with the other nuns, which is part of their godly duties. The nuns must live together in companionship without having chosen one another. They must love one another, which has nothing to do with what the nuns call 'superficial emotions'. This love goes far deeper and has to do with willingness and duty. One of the nuns explained:

> The companionship found within these walls is much different from that found on the outside. It is here all the time, avoiding it – even a little bit now and then – is not an option.

Nor can it be questioned because the nuns believe that it is God's will for them to share a monastic life. However, the nuns were keen to point out that it is this companionship that allows them to 'support one another' in carrying out their calling. These ties go very deep and are linked by one common denominator: God. 'God is the basis of life', said the nuns. Without belief in God, their monastic life, prayers, and hard work would be meaningless.

The clothing strengthens the sense of community. The nuns wear a grey robe, a wimple, and a crown with five dots on it. The nuns' clothing constitutes an important symbol and was ordained in detail by St. Birgitta. The same type of clothing was described in the original rules of the Order (comprising the rules of the Order of St. Augustine from late 4th century AD, supplemented by St. Birgitta in 1370, and reinterpreted and approved in 1987). For example, the fourth chapter of the original rules of the Order stipulates the following:

> The wearing apparel of the sisters shall consist of two petticoats
> of white homespun, one for everyday use and one as a change of
> clothes, a robe of grey homespun with a hooded cowl, the sleeves of
> which should not be longer than to the base of the middle finger.
> And any tail that hangs down over the hand shall, similarly to other
> sleeves, be attached to the arm in a simple and straightforward way
> when the nuns are working. (cited in Lundén, 1957–59, translated
> from Swedish)

The grey robe is a sign of poverty, as only rich people could afford to dye their clothes at the time of St. Birgitta (see www.birgittaskloster.se). The crown symbolises Jesus' crown of thorns and the five red points His wounds during the crucifixion, on His feet, hands, and the side of His body. The wimple covering the hair is the way women used to cover their hair before everyone but their own husband in St. Birgitta's time. The nuns wear their wimples as a sign of having committed their lives to God. The robes are sewn by the nun who is the best at sewing and are the only clothes that the nuns wear, even when venturing outside the abbey. All the nuns wear identical clothes; the only thing that distinguishes the Abbess from the others is that she wears a necklace from which a cross hangs. 'Well', wrote Mother Karin in a letter, 'postulants wear lay clothes until they become novices, when they get to wear the same robe as everyone else but with a white veil. Once the first time-bound commitment is made, the white veil is replaced with a black veil, and when the final commitment is made, the black veil is supplemented with a crown and ring.'

St. Birgitta had to work hard to obtain permission to found her abbey. In a DVD film from Vadstena Abbey, one of the nuns tells of the opposition to Birgitta (she went to Rome and had to wait from 1349 to 1370 for permission from the Pope). While her hard work eventually led to approval from the Pope to establish the abbey, time had run out for Birgitta to become its first Abbess, a role instead taken on by her daughter Katarina (Vadstena klosters minnesbok, 1918/1984). However, the rules of the Order of St. Birgitta and her written notes on righteous living essentially govern the way in which the nuns live and work.

The nuns all take perpetual vows. This means that the nuns, subsequent to an introduction period (consisting of a postulant and a novitiate period, and then a period of a temporary vow), promise to live, work, and die within their enclosure. In other words, after taking their perpetual vows, they will never perform any duties or work outside the abbey walls. The principal canons are based on obedience, chastity, and poverty (according to The Revelations of Saint Birgitta of Sweden 1377/1957–59, the nuns should lead a humble life in chastity and poverty). 'These are difficult values to live by', said one of the nuns, 'especially in this day and age'. That is why it is so important to have an introduction period.

Vadstena Abbey dates to the Middle Ages, and the nuns pursue an old-fashioned way of life. 'Traditions give structure to our lives ... It is like wearing a corset', said one of the nuns. These rules and patterns of behaviour originate from long before the abbey was established. The nuns said that they found a book written in Old Swedish about the practical aspects of monastic life under the rules of the Order of St. Birgitta, which has since been interpreted and translated into modern Swedish. When reading the book, the nuns discovered that much of their way of life was already recorded and that, in fact, very little had changed. The book dates from the late 1400s (Vadstena Abbey was an important publisher of religious books in the Middle Ages; see, *e.g.* www.medeltidshand-skrifter.se). I asked the nuns what behaviours and rules are mentioned in the book, to which they replied that it covers everything, though some things are deemed more important than others, for example, the order and manner in which the nuns should enter the abbey church, how and when they should kneel, what clothes they should wear, what hymns they should sing, how they should behave towards one another, and the general daily structure of their lives. Some things are learned through the study of texts, others by imitating the ways of the older nuns.

Showing respect for the older and more experienced nuns is important. One nun described how she noticed that one of the younger nuns, when in church, stood with her feet angled at 45 degrees, not parallel like all the others, and how this gradually changed over time, without anyone ever mentioning it, as the nun noticed the example of her senior colleagues.

Anyone breaking the rules can be expected to be reprimanded. It is evident from the older rules of the Order that a serious violation of the rules could be punished with not being allowed to attend mass. 'This [rule] is no longer applied', explained Mother Karin. She continued in a letter: 'It is always possible to reprimand someone by using facial expressions, words.' During the focus group interview, the nuns also mentioned that if a nun breaks the rules, she might get a written warning in the presence of two nuns. 'But', said one of the nuns, 'only when we are at our wits' end'. Only in an extreme case would a nun who has taken her final vows be asked to immediately leave the abbey. Mother Karin said that she knows of only one such case in which a nun was forced to leave her monastic community – in the 18th century. Such action requires 'compelling and outwardly apparent reasons for which the nun is held accountable based on legal evidence', explained Mother Karin. The Canon Law of the Catholic Church (*Codex Iuris Canonici*) deals with this, among other issues (vatican.va 01.09.2011; see also CIC 694–703 §). 'It is, however, rare for any rules or informal agreements to be broken', said one of the nuns, 'everyone has joined the community of their own free will. They want to be as good nuns as possible, so it is important for them to carefully follow rules, traditions, and practices, as intended by St. Birgitta'. A good nun is diligent and loving and follows the words of God with a pure heart. The nuns pointed out that God sees every action and thought. He knows each person's feelings, motives, and genuine will, but he is also forgiving as long as one does one's very best.

The Abbey and the world around it

Although the walls surrounding the Abbey constitute a boundary between it and the outside world, this does not mean that the nuns have no contact with that world. They are allowed to visit their families for one week every four years. Friends and family are also welcome to visit the nuns in the Abbey and, for example, write letters and e-mails to them. One of the nuns told how her sister, a hairdresser, sometimes comes for a visit and to give all the nuns haircuts. Other relatives help out too, for example, by replacing or mending broken things in and around the Abbey. However, friends and family are not meant to take up too much of a nun's time, as this might interfere with her work and concentration on communion with God.

Despite getting some help now and then, the nuns essentially do all of the work themselves. For example, when I visited the Abbey, a water pipe that began leaking in one of the guest rooms was immediately attended to by one of the nuns. Since the nuns are meant to live in poverty, they have few financial resources for getting help from the outside world.

The nuns' contact with the outside world is not only via friends and family. They read newspapers, watch a summary of daily news on TV, and sometimes listen to news broadcasts on radio. They also read books. 'Though not crime fiction of course', one of the nuns pointed out, 'but literature that strengthens our faith and knowledge of society'. News and other information about society outside the walls give the nuns input for their prayers.

Others who contact the nuns are, for example, children and young people studying Catholicism and convents, journalists wanting to write about the nuns or get comments about religious matters, or people with spiritual questions. Mother Karin usually handles matters of a spiritual nature but sometimes the other nuns help out too.

The leadership function

The Order of St. Birgitta states that the Abbess should provide the nuns with everything they need. In essence, the Abbess decides upon everything material as well as on other matters.

Mother Karin has held the position of Abbess since 1989. It is a burdensome responsibility, according to Mother Karin, who would love for someone else to take over. However, since 1989, the other nuns have repeatedly chosen her. An Abbess is chosen by means of democratic elections once every six years. Three priests act as election officials, whereupon the Bishop determines and announces the election results. To be elected Abbess, there must be a two-thirds majority; a run-off election is held if no one receives such a large proportion of the votes. A run-off election requires an absolute majority for appointment, and if no one is elected yet again, then a third and final vote will be held and the nun receiving the most votes will be appointed Abbess. Following this, the Abbess-elect will be asked the following question: 'Do you want to become the Abbess of this abbey?' To which the nun may reply 'No'. 'However', says Mother Karin, 'it is important to remember that you have been elected and that God will show you grace ... [which] means that God will help when needed.' Mother Karin described this as God standing by her when she lacked knowledge or expertise, because it was impossible to know everything from the start. Mother Karin also referred to St. Birgitta, who worked hard to establish an order and implement what she believed in, though she was unable to enforce much of what she fought for. Doing one's best is what matters, and one should not expect things to be perfect every time. Mother Karin said that she behaved 'like an idiot' at the beginning, continuing to describe in a letter how she tried to understand and get involved in everything, which led to an enormous and unhealthy workload. These days, she is better at delegating and putting her trust in the Prioress (ranking next to the

Abbess in the formal hierarchy), who complements her leadership and compensates for her shortcomings. 'But sometimes nothing happens or something has been forgotten', said Mother Karin, 'and then I just take over from them. I say "I'm going to do it myself!" and then, that is exactly what I do'.

A Prioress is elected to her position in much the same way as is an Abbess. The primary duty of the Prioress is to assist and support the Abbess. A third elected position is that of the advisory sister, whose duty is to also provide support. The Abbess is elected for a period of six years, while the Prioress and advisory sister are elected for three-year periods.

If the Abbess is not re-elected or declines to be nominated for re-election, she does not leave the abbey, as is often the case in other abbeys, though she might be away for a short period of time. Once a new Abbess is elected, it is important for the former Abbess to make it clear that she is no longer the leader of the abbey and start shifting her responsibilities to the new Abbess.

In addition to the election of leaders, the supervisory process includes certain control functions. Every three years, an inspector from the Catholic Church arrives to check the activities of the Abbey and, in particular, determine whether the Abbess is fulfilling her duties as the leader of the monastic community. This is seen as precaution but may also provide a forum for complaints.

Abbey leadership comprises three main components, *i.e.* administrative, professional, and spiritual leadership. Administrative leadership involves making sure that there is a functional work distribution. In addition, the Abbess must secure the financial future of the abbey, which is sometimes difficult, according to Mother Karin. It is then the responsibility of the Abbess to think of other ways in which to bring in more revenue, for example, by making and selling candles or hand cream. Mother Karin pointed out that it is her duty to deal with strategic and financial issues or they might not afford to keep the Abbey.

Professional leadership relates to certain aspects of monastic life, such as advancement in knowledge of religion, monastic rules, and traditions. There are several ways in which the nuns can improve themselves and undertake further studies, such as education for nuns-to-be, special seminars, and listening to readings during meals. They can also have religious conversations.

Spiritual leadership is about motivating the nuns to continue living and working together in a good and loving way, and touches upon the innermost lives of the nuns. It is about striving to get closer to God. An

Abbess must always be available to give the other nuns spiritual support and guidance. She can never demand that the nuns open up and speak to her, though the nuns can demand that their Abbess should listen to them. The position of Abbess usually means that the other nuns see her as a spiritual role model and, therefore, as someone whose advice and guidance they may seek in spiritual matters. Mother Karin believes that the duty of earning the trust of the others is bestowed upon her by the grace of God. In other words, God gives the strength and support needed in order to grow with one's duty, from both the practical and spiritual perspectives. The other nuns know that God will help the Abbess, should she need it. They should also try to be helpful to the best of their ability – this is an important responsibility of the other nuns. This is part of monastic life, as is showing leniency if something does not go according to plan.

The obligation of confidentiality is another important aspect of leadership and monastic life. An Abbess can never relay anything that a nun has revealed in confidence. This does not constitute the seal of confession but is simply a matter of showing discretion, and is a deeply rooted, strongly held principle. The Abbess is in a vulnerable position. For example, she might hear a lot about what is happening in the diocese or about the various sides of an argument among the nuns. 'It is difficult to deal with an argument or problem when you cannot disclose what you have been told – you end up sitting on the fence', said Mother Karin.

Spiritual leadership takes up varying amounts of time, as some nuns need more guidance than do others. As a guiding principle, Mother Karin tries to talk with each of the nuns at least once a month, but she said: 'At the moment, one of our nuns is having a bit of a crisis, which means that I simply do not have as much time for the others'. Spiritual conversations of various kinds are an important aspect of abbey life, and are interwoven in the daily schedule.

An Abbess is both a formal and informal leader of the nuns, though 'everyone is a leader at some point, in whatever duty or situation that may be', explained Mother Karin. For example, someone might be very good at technology and IT while another is good at organising celebratory occasions, a third is good at cooking, and a fourth is a role model when it comes to prayers, and so on.

The nuns – including Mother Karin – have each been appointed a confessor. Mother Karin is also friends with other Abbesses, and the one she confides in the most is, she believes, a completely different person from herself who leads in a completely different way. She also regularly speaks with the former auxiliary bishop. When receiving troublesome information about the internal affairs of the church, it is not unusual for Mother Karin not to relay this to the other nuns. The nuns must be able to ignore such things – after all, it is Mother Karin's job to consider how much of such matters the others need to know. Mother Karin is usually the one talking to the media, in conversations that she finds difficult as they often involve misunderstandings. One of the nuns once spoke with the press, responding nicely to the questions put to her; her answers were then distorted and the nun ended up sounding silly. 'It is not easy – you can be too trusting sometimes and not think about what you are responding to', Mother Karin commented. She has asked the nuns to be a little more cautious when it comes to responding to and dealing with the media. Mother Karin reiterated that it is not the responsibility of the Abbess to decide whether or not someone should agree to an interview; this is decided by the chapter.

Relations, hierarchy, and conflicts

Diligence and mutual help form important parts of monastic life. Everyone is expected to do as much as and the best they can, including those who would be deemed pensioners outside the Abbey's walls. Although everyone differs and should remain so, these same differences can sometimes lead to friction. The nuns describe how they must constantly reassess themselves and their way of life, as everyone has a different opinion on how things ought to be done:

> How can I change my ways? It can bring out an unexpected side of yourself. And it can be fun. You can liken it to fragments of rock from a number of different rock blasting sites. Twelve fragments are thrown into a concrete mixer and, after a while, are turned into cobblestones.

There is a hierarchy of authority in the abbey, which Mother Karin and the nuns often refer to as an 'upside-down hierarchy'. Admittedly, the Abbess is at the top of the formal hierarchy, followed by the Prioress and then the Advisory Sister (followed by the other nuns according to their number of years in the monastic life). However, the pyramid is not governed by power, but by love and care. In other words, the nuns are meant to 'bear and support one another' in their everyday life and duties.

Although the Abbess has the authority to decide on certain matters such as the distribution of work, providing care and support is of prime importance. This is a significant responsibility that increases with age and rank. However, the Abbess noted that the responsibility of caring is so fundamental that the organisation of the Abbey could be likened to an upside-down hierarchy with her at the bottom, bearing everything on her shoulders: 'Everyone bears as much as they possibly can', she said.

Caring entails being able to ask for, receive, and offer forgiveness. When people are so close to one another every day, there will always be conflicts and arguments, whether small or large, explained the nuns. Such conflicts and arguments must be resolved. 'How do you do this?', I asked.

> You have to dig deep into your heart and spirit, scrutinise yourself, and ask the other for forgiveness. And then forgive each other.

Resolving of conflicts and forgiving form part of the daily vesper service mentioned at the beginning of this chapter. The words said when asking for and giving forgiveness must be heartfelt and sincere. The nuns say the words even when it is difficult, and everyone knows in her own heart whether the words are heartfelt and sincere. Scrutinising oneself is an important start to this process, which entails a constant connection with God, who knows how one feels and what one thinks. One nun described how she was responsible for ordering heating oil for the Abbey. She told how God had given her many reminders that she, because she was busy doing other things, had simply waved off with the excuse, 'Yes, later'. The following Friday evening, she realised that she ought to have ordered the oil a long time before. She prayed to God that the last drop of oil would last the weekend, as it was in the middle of winter. The nun continued:

> God said, 'You should have thought of that before', and the little oil that was left did not last the weekend. On Saturday morning, it was both dark and cold in the Abbey. I felt ashamed and asked the other nuns for forgiveness for what I had omitted to do. They all replied, 'We forgive you wholeheartedly', and on Saturday evening, we sat grilling by one of the fireplaces.

'This story is not just about asking for and giving forgiveness', explained the nuns, 'but also about taking joint responsibility and supporting one another with celebration, not coldness.' According to the nuns, there is nothing written about how to handle conflicts, other than in connection with the vesper service. Most important, however, is to scrutinise one's own behaviour and do one's best. Such scrutiny of one's own actions and behaviour is done in the evening.

Spiritual leadership in the Abbey: Karin and Birgitta

Leadership at Vadstena Abbey is both extensive and comprehensive. I am not referring just to the relationship between the formally appointed leader and her followers, as leadership has many significant contributors. Leadership not only influences the work of the organisation members and what can be seen on the outside; it also influences what is on the inside of the members, such as their attitudes, values, and other deeper-seated beliefs. Consequently, leadership at the Abbey can be described as spiritual leadership (for a review, see Reave 2005; Fry 2005).

Fry (2005) talked about spiritual leadership in terms of altruistic love, inner life, self-transformation, and fellowship. He argued that leadership affects the basic needs of people, whereas spiritual leadership focuses on the inner devotion and fundamental values of the individual and on relationships of trust. This contributes to optimised organisational performance and human well-being, according to Fry. Spiritual leaders do not build their leadership on values such as self-interest or prestige (as is expected of other leaders, according to literature on spiritual leadership) but on 'ultimate ethical values like integrity, independence and justice' (Fairholm 1996, p. 12).

Spiritual leadership is said to consist of three components (Fairholm 1996; see also Fry & Cohen 2009). First, spiritual leadership does not compromise on its fundamental ideas and values, instead challenging those who believe otherwise. Values are important as they connect the individuals living under such leadership (the members of a spiritual organisation are assumed to have the same values), in addition to having arisen from a common belief. Second, spiritual leadership emphasises stewardship, not ownership, as this creates equality, *i.e.* the leadership role is borrowed for a while so as to achieve what is best for the community, which in itself constitutes power as it allows everyone to contribute to the leadership to the best of their ability. Everyone is responsible for doing the best they can in their fields. The third important component is community and fellowship, which determine collective behaviour and generate a sense of belonging. The emphasis on leadership as relational is prominent in discussions of spiritual leadership.

Leadership at Vadstena Abbey closely fits the description of spiritual leadership presented by Fairholm (1996; see Table 4.1).

Table 4.1 Spiritual leadership at the Abbey

Spiritual leadership components (Fairholm 1996)	Practices in the Abbey connected to the components
Not compromising on fundamental ideas	Fundamental ideas are ever present and learned; only strong believers are admitted; and everyday life is fully adapted to the fundamental ideas of poverty, chastity, and obedience, prioritising prayer and leading a contemplative life in the service of God.
Stewardship rather than ownership	The Abbess, Prioress, and Advisory Sister are elected; the present leadership functions follow the basis of St. Birgitta; and everyone is seen as a leader in some respect.
Community and fellowship	The nuns spend all their time together; the walls create a boundary excluding life outside them; the long introduction period and the specialised clothes contribute to a sense of exclusiveness; and all nuns have heeded a special calling from God to precisely this life in close community with Him and one another.

For example, the nuns' fundamental values are strong and distinctive. Aside from values that may be deemed typical of nuns (*i.e.* poverty, chastity, and obedience), other Catholic values are also prominent in their written materials and customs. The Bible is of course an important text, as are the rules of the Order and other texts written by or about St. Birgitta. The everyday lives of the nuns are permeated with values, and they talk and read about how to live and behave in order to be good nuns. Fry's terms (see above), such as altruistic love, fellowship, and devotion, closely describe the leadership of the Abbey. The essence of spiritual leadership is that people's spiritual realm (*i.e.* one's basic values and outlook on life and humanity) is linked to the outside world of work and social relations. At the Abbey, these values, together with a faith in God, are linked to a particular outside world – not just any outside world but one adapted to the spiritual, inner world of the nuns. The nuns first of all serve God, and other more profane tasks are not allowed to take over either their time or thoughts.

Mother Karin is the elected leader of the Abbey, and the concept of spiritual leadership describes her leadership well. She can be seen as a trustee of St. Birgitta's values and beliefs, which profoundly influence the lives of the nuns. Accordingly, St. Birgitta is a clear leading figure and a benchmark for Mother Karin and the other nuns (*e.g.* when it comes to deciding who does what around the Abbey). A spiritual leader has the important task of motivating his or her followers and ensuring that their spiritual realms are connected with the community or organisation to which they belong. At the Abbey, St. Birgitta is a prominent figure who motivates her followers to engage in persistent and godly work and who, in her writings, graphically describes the inner and outer lifeworlds as connected by a moral life. In this respect, St. Birgitta is a spiritual leader, regardless of when she lived.

The third concept, fellowship, is a matter of course at the Abbey. According to the rules, the nuns should spend all their time together, apart from their night's rest, and share everything. The long introduction period of approximately eight years, during which the aspiring nun is taught how to think like the other Birgittine nuns (and that ends with the nun receiving her robe, crown, and ring), lays the foundation for a sense of belonging, unity, and community. The aspiring nun seeks out the community because she feels drawn to it. The extent of the community at the Abbey contributes to creating a 'total institution' (Goffman 1983).

The word spirituality has positive connotations, suggesting someone who is spontaneous and emotionally alert at the same time as being witty and entertaining, someone who cares for others and is free thinking. However, spiritual leadership does not just bolster these attributes; it can also support a community fully identifying, beyond question or doubt, with uncompromising values, stewardship, and fellowship if the leadership goes deep enough (Cregård, 2017).

Change, manage, and preserve

The stewardship of Mother Karin means that she must understand the values, life philosophies, and patterns of behaviour that St. Birgitta stands for. She must motivate her fellow sisters to continue advancing in their lives as nuns, in their contemplative duties at Vadstena Abbey. Her management task is important. It entails preserving the heritage of St. Birgitta in terms of the community's goals and mission, the distribution of work duties and schedules, as well as the implementation and results of production. However, in the role of manager and leader, Mother Karin is not expected to change or develop the organisation; rather, the opposite is the case, as the organisation and its core operations should change as little as possible. In the 600–700 years that the Order of St. Birgitta has existed, much in the organisation has remained unchanged – except that Vadstena Abbey has not always been home to the nuns. In 1595, the nuns of the Order were deported from Vadstena to Poland and did not return until 1935 (see svenskakyrkan.se).

An extensive leadership literature describes and propagates a development-oriented notion of leadership. For example, the book by Gary Yukl (1981/2004), which is a standard work in the management training literature, begins by pointing out that a leader's most important task is to take the lead in making changes. Many courses are designed to teach managers and leaders to be more open to change, and to teach them to teach their own staff to be more open to change. The following are examples of introductions to such courses:

> Every day, a leader with a good idea fails at change management. Most fail because they can't get beyond vision. Successful leaders need to take a holistic approach to organisational change: working top–down to influence stakeholders and mobilize support, and bottom–up to keep projects and people moving forward. (http://www. ecornell.com/certificates/leadership-and-strategic-management/ change-leadership 2015-10-02)

> The pace of change is only going to get faster. How do you remain an effective leader no matter what crises or surprises come your way? It's not easy, but it can be done. (http://www.inc.com/minda-zetlin/how-the-smartest-leaders-cope-with-constant-change.html 2015-10-02)

> Change used to be episodic. It was deliberated, planned, and executed. But in today's turbulent environment, change is a constant. You could argue in fact that change is your real job. And when it's part of your daily routine, you need more than one approach for leading it. (http://executiveeducation.wharton.upenn.edu/for-individuals/all-programs/leading-organizational-change 2015-10-02)

Typical of the above quotations and similar promotional texts is that they give the impression that the need for change is inevitable and cannot be resisted. As a representative of an organisation, one has no other choice than to change oneself in order to keep up with the changes of the surrounding world. Another aspect emphasised is that all organisations are affected by the changing world around them, irrespective of their production, size, or dependence on their surroundings (or the type of change). These are 'constant' too. Researchers have been keen on reproducing this. For example, Todnem By (2005, p. 370) stated in a frequently cited article regarding what the change management literature has come to agree upon:

> Firstly, it is agreed that the pace of change has never been greater than in the current business environment ... Secondly, there is a consensus that change, being triggered by internal or external factors, comes in all shapes, forms and sizes ... and, therefore, affects all organisations in all industries.

The rhetoric of change and the need to manage it in an organisational manner and with the help of leaders appears to be based on threat: constant and uncontrollable changes affect us all, indiscriminately and recklessly. However, the effects of the pressure for change *can* be managed, given the right leadership, courage, and preparedness. Those who can handle change as well as the need for change will reap the rewards. Such is the rhetoric of change.

Furthermore, the rhetoric of change signals that organisational change itself can be seen as something good. Organisational change indicates that the organisation is forward thinking, flexible, and development oriented. Change is expected to be synonymous with development and improvement. An organisation should preferably be so open to change that it is the first to make a change. This requires a leader or manager who can take the lead in the process of change, create opportunities for change, and knowing how to deal with potential resistance. Furthermore, such a leader must have a feeling for what change is needed, which essentially means that he or she must be well placed in the surrounding environment to be able to assess how it will react to organisational changes.

At the Abbey, in contrast, change is not seen as the ultimate solution. The rhetoric of change seems not to have gained a foothold. Mother Karin has no duty either to assess or respond to the surrounding environment as it appears outside the Abbey walls, other than to answer direct questions if she or the chapter find it suitable. However, if Mother Karin's predecessor had taken that stance, then Vadstena Abbey would not have been re-established back in 1935. Mother Karin's mission is to safeguard the traditions of bygone days as illustrated in the Order's texts and practices. It goes without saying that some change must take place, for example, in interactions between the Abbey and the outside world. However, Mother Karin's leadership concentrates on maintaining and managing what already exists. She endeavours to create strategies to avoid any potential changes in what is perceived as the core organisation. Hence, her leadership can be described as a preservative leadership. In the next section, I will explore what I mean by that.

Preservative leadership

The literature on spiritual leadership is silent about organisational change. Rather, spiritual leadership is said to be more about facilitating individual change and, in particular, the connection between one's inner and outer selves. The spiritual leader has the important duty of preserving the essential values of the organisation. That is not to say that spiritual leadership is the same as keeping things as they have always been. In this chapter, I have deliberately considered various aspects of preservative leadership, as it appears to be both a central and an interesting part of life at the Abbey. Mother Karin does the same as the leaders of many other organisations, in that she distributes work tasks, mediates conflicts, listens to the problems and concerns of others, manages daily financial matters, and handles other administrative work. She does other things as well, such as taking responsibility for the spiritual and material needs of the other nuns (as stipulated by the rules of the Order), making sure that they study and learn from important texts and supporting them in their constant rapprochement with God. Based on my observations from Vadstena Abbey, the main responsibilities of its leader are *managing the core organisation, controlling time and space*, and *making sacrifices* for the benefit of others. That is what Mother Karin does – although not on her own. Preservative leadership is relational, as is any other kind of leadership: St. Birgitta, her fellow nuns, God, and of course Jesus are important partners of Mother Karin in exercising her leadership. Table 4.2 summarises some aspects of what I call preservative leadership.

Mother Karin manages the concepts and organisation of the Birgittines. She borrows and enacts the leadership from St. Birgitta for a period of time, and then passes it on to someone else. When her time as Abbess ends, she will return to being a nun without a formal leadership role (unless she is elected as Prioress or advisory sister). This process prob-

Table 4.2 Aspects and practices of preservative leadership

Preservative aspect	Practiced in the Abbey
Manage core organisation	– bringing life to values: bringing together the inside and outside worlds – following and giving meaning to artefacts, routines, and ceremonies
Control time and space	– regulation of daily schedule and prioritising prayer – the concept of the present is connected to both the past (*e.g.* the times of Jesus and St. Birgitta) and the future (*i.e.* the afterlife) – regulating Abbey space and reinforcing the boundary set by the Abbey walls – regulating holy spaces, common spaces, and individual spaces
Make sacrifices	– leaders give up their time for the good of the cause and to benefit the community – nuns give thanks on behalf of everyone else

ably in itself promotes preservation. Mother Karin is not in a position to introduce new reforms, as she knows that she will soon be replaced but still within the Abbey. The nuns also have a good idea of what rules and routines apply at the Abbey, as determined by St. Birgitta. Mother Karin guarantees this by ensuring that everyone gets to study the texts and by bringing important values to life. One important task is to bring together the spiritual inner world with the outer world (though still within the walls) and to ensure that certain values are transformed into prayer, contemplation and other activities. The other nuns also contribute to preserving important values and transforming them into practice. They must accept the values and make them their own, if they have not already. When talking about the Abbey, one of the nuns quoted above cited an example of how these values are intertwined with their everyday lives, when she forgot to order heating oil for the house. Her example illustrates not only how the spiritual inner world is linked to the everyday lives of the nuns but also how the other nuns are involved in the leadership. Like Mother Karin, they too bring important values to life, making sure that they are preserved. This type of preservative leadership is enhanced by the fact that the organisation complies with certain highly institutionalised rituals, ceremonies, and schedules. Artefacts linked to institutionalised activities, such as the cross, the chancel (next to the altarpiece), and symbols (including the clothing of the nuns), reinforce the sense of belonging to another time, which, in turn, reinforces Mother Karin's efforts to manage the organisational concepts of St. Birgitta.

Another important aspect of preservative leadership, apart from managing, is the regulation of space and time. Time is carefully measured and divided into various carefully specified categories. The same categories applied in the time of St. Birgitta, except for slight alterations: from reading informative letters on paper to watching the news on television, and from refilling oil lamps to changing lightbulbs. However, the most important category, prayer, has not changed much at all, except for the delicate modernisation of certain parts of the prayers and some changes in pronunciations and endings. The regulation of time is always present as is the regulation of space. The nuns' own rooms are regulated in terms of size and furnishings, and their spatial sphere of life is defined by the Abbey walls. As they do not expect to be disturbed by the world outside the walls, how Mother Karin handles contact with that world, when necessary, is important. She does not always tell the nuns about events outside the Abbey, only those that she feels they ought to know about. The rhetoric of change prevalent in the outside world, as well as the need for and willingness to change, must not take root in monastic life. Almost all of the nuns' time is devoted to other, more timeless matters inside the Abbey walls.

A third concept that I would like to mention in connection with the preservative leadership of the Abbey is 'sacrifice'. I have already touched on this. Both St. Birgitta and Mother Karin have sacrificed themselves to be leaders, a fact that neither of them tries to conceal. Instead, their sacrifice is put on display: Mother Karin shows it by wearing a necklace from which a cross hangs, while St. Birgitta showed it in her writing.

The Order of St. Birgitta tells of the diligent work of St. Birgitta and how she encountered setbacks and sceptics but was given strength by the grace of God to stand up for what she believed was morally right. St. Birgitta gained many followers (and many opponents) and was relatively well known throughout Sweden and Rome during the Middle Ages. Despite her connections with the Swedish royal family and nobility as well as the Pope, her power was hard-won. Yet it was still difficult for St. Birgitta to establish the new order, first, because she was a woman and, second, because not everyone saw the need for another order. The Pope was concerned with other more important things. St. Birgitta sacrificed her time and a life that could have been so much easier for something that she strongly believed in. According to Keith Grint (2010), it is important to be seen to make sacrifices if you are to be considered a leader. The concept of sacrifice is obvious in the world of the nuns, and not just the sacrifices of St. Birgitta: Jesus died on the cross and the nuns themselves have devoted their entire lives to praising God and praying for other people, so the leader of the Abbey is also expected to make sacrifices. Her sacrifice is connected to others' sacrifices, reinforcing the sense of connection to the past and the future. Mother Karin sacrifices herself by taking on the role of the nuns' leader. She does not do this because she wants to, but rather because her fellow sisters – and God himself – want her to. She sacrifices her time to discharge many profane duties, time that she would otherwise spend praying, developing her spiritual self, and studying devotional writings. She does this because she knows that God will show her mercy.

The sacrifice made by the Abbey's leader not only supports the organisation's core values and emphasises the leader as a leader, it also reveals what is worth preserving. In this way, sacrifices mark a boundary around what should never be compromised, reinforcing values and the core of the organisation in the same way as do other symbols, routines, and artefacts.

Preservative leadership and other organisations

What can we learn from the case of Mother Karin and her sister nuns? From my perspective, Mother Karin's way of regarding organisational change is refreshing, both the way she emphasises the importance of not changing the core of the organisation, and her acknowledgement of change as inevitable only in order to preserve that core.

Let me summarise some of the characteristics of the Abbey's leadership that I have reported here. First, the core values (*i.e.* poverty, celibacy, and obedience together with diligence, obligation of confidentiality, and community) and mission (*i.e.* to pray) are clear and vibrant. The work performed and the lives lived in the Abbey are permeated by the Abbey's values and mission, and all matters are handled based on them. Other competing values may not outrank the core values of the organisation. The control of time and space (*e.g.* the present influence of the Middle Ages, the walls between the Abbey and the rest of society, and the nuns' restricted contacts) support these values, just as do the nuns' everyday routines, artefacts, and ceremonies. The nuns' way of fulfilling spiritual leadership in the Abbey supports the preservation of the organisation, leading to what I call preservative leadership in which change management is not considered the leader's prime task. Preservation of the core values and organisation is the prime task of the preservative leader, and change is only to be implemented when it serves the preservation of the core. Since the core values permeate all aspects of the organisation, every change must be thoroughly scrutinised before being implemented. Change is not seen as the sole salvation.

The Abbey can perhaps be seen as a slightly unusual organisation with an extreme form of leadership, or perhaps the preservative elements of the leadership are only more far-reaching than in a more secular organisation. Despite not being recognised or appreciated in much of the leadership rhetoric, a form of preservative leadership can be found in every organisation. It is a fundamental part of leadership and management skills. Even an organisation operating in a very unstable environment and facing fierce competition needs stability, core rituals and concepts that allow it to continue being that particular organisation. The members of an organisation must also be prevented from undertaking all sorts of conflicting actions and be disciplined to comply with the routines, overall goals, and collective duties of the organisation. They must be prevented from developing their own duties and jurisdictions in ways that do not fit with other organisation members' duties and jurisdictions. Presumably, one would expect the circumstances of a constantly changing organisation to be just as constant. Nor is it unusual for organisations claiming to favour development and change also to strongly favour preservation. I refer in particular to universities. Here, traditions and rituals serve as leadership conditions while managers are not only expected to safeguard what is innovative but also to promote leadership that is preservative. The leaders protect what is typically academic, and buildings, values, traditions, and artefacts (*e.g.* references) help regulate time and space at the same time as managers must be seen to make sacrifices, for example, by abstaining from research in favour of other more mundane (or profane) administrative tasks.

Much can be learned from the nuns. One lesson is that change in itself is not necessarily the same as improvement or development. Not all changes are automatically good, and some may not even be necessary. We also need leaders who can critically examine the rhetoric of change and preserve what is worth preserving in an organisation. They would probably do this by managing the core of the organisation, introducing or maintaining regulations addressing space and time, and by showing that they themselves are making sacrifices – for the sake of the organisation, colleagues, and for the good in itself (whatever that might be in that particular organisation).

At the beginning of the chapter I raised a question: How can some organisations remain seemingly unchanged for a very long time? In this chapter I investigated an organisation that started more than 600 years ago. That could be considered a long time, and other organisations have lasted just as long, including several municipalities in Sweden as well as several companies in Japan (http://www.bbc.com/news/business-16611040, 2015-10-19). It is of course impossible to answer a question this complex by examining just one long-lived organisation. One can only extract some possible partial explanations, some hypotheses, to discuss and investigate in the future. Some of the more obvious characteristics of the Abbey could serve as useful and suggestive starting points: the organisation's mission, which transcends short-term considerations; the devoted organisation members; the reduced need for external support; and, finally, the explicit performance of preservative leadership.

CHAPTER 5

Leadership and expertship

Staffan Furusten

Organisations frequently buy services from external service providers. In the last decades we have seen a number of examples of this rationalized by a need for *outsourcing*. This is one explanation to why we have seen an emergence of markets for various expert agencies. This chapter draws attention to the implications for organisations seeking external leadership expertise, often provided by what are called *management consultants*. The phenomenon in focus is that leaders tend to appoint experts who presumably are better at leadership than they are themselves. This situation is rarely discussed in the leadership literature, though there are good reasons to consider this problem. When leaders call in outside experts on leadership, ambiguities often arise concerning the exercise of leadership within the organisation. This is likely to create confusion among the organisation's employees as to how to behave towards people not employed by the organisation but presented as better at leadership than the in-house managers appointed to lead the organisation. In this chapter, this leadership dilemma is discussed in terms of the importance for managers of balancing leadership against expertship.

When someone else knows better

It is not that remarkable for leaders in organisations to surround themselves with people who have the expertise needed in different areas (Furusten & Werr 2005, 2009), but when it comes to the leadership area, it is interesting to delve a little deeper, as presumably a leader is granted the authority to lead based on the notion that he or she knows what is best for the organisation. In this light, the practice of buying the help of external leadership experts is an interesting matter.

First, they play the role of actors who know better, but they are employed by another organisation than where they perform their work. This may mean that it can be difficult for the members of an organisation to know how to relate to such 'employees' even though they are rather mundane personnel in many organisations today. *Second*, sometimes, encounters with experts are unproblematic, such as when we go to the naprapath because of a bad back or the dentist for dental treatment. We seek the help and advice of these experts because we realise that we lack pertinent knowledge to solve particular problems ourselves (Giddens 1991). Turning to experts in situations like these is both reasonable and rational, since they represent both well-functioning professional systems and organisations (Friedson 2001; Furusten & Werr 2017a).

However, there are many situations where the services of someone who knows better are clearly needed but the qualifications of their professional system are unclear. As will be discussed more in detail below, management consulting is an example of this. Because of the ambiguities surrounding the status of this professional category, how can we be sure about the status of their expertise (Furusten & Werr 2017b)? If their expert status is debatable, where does this leave the leadership in organisations that hire consultants? Has a real expert been hired, *i.e.* a person with better knowledge, or a person who represents something else? If so, what are the implications of this for leadership in organisations?

Both considerations originate from the notion of an ideal leader assuming that leadership emerges only when a leader is given the authority to lead those who need and want to be led. Reference is often made to Max Weber (1949), who defined leadership as authority being established on legal, traditional, or charismatic bases. According to Weber's terminology, leadership appears when authority emerges either from a formal hierarchical framework that clearly identifies who is the superior and subordinate or from traditions in which there is an institutionalised conception of what characteristics a leader should possess in a particular context or where someone gains authority to lead because his or her charismatic conduct convinces followers to listen and act accordingly.

All these views of leadership are challenged when leadership situations are interfered by other players than the leaders, players not employed by the organisation who represent a role that is supposed to know more about leadership than the leaders themselves but whose expert status is vague. This chapter debates this issue, focusing on the presence of management consultants in leadership situations in organisations. I suggest that such situations are not about leadership per se but about expertship, and how managers handle the presence of external leadership experts in leadership situations. I will in the following discuss this dilemma of managers based on analyses of the work of management consultants. First I discuss generally how management consultants tend to construct their services and relations between consultants and their client organisations. This is important for the understanding of the steps taken by consultants and what relations they strive to establish towards their client organisations. This analysis is based largely on previously published material (Furusten 2003, 2009, 2013), interviews with around 40 consultants and ten consultancy clients. Quotations from these interviews are used to illustrate common patterns in the material. This is followed by a discussion of how external experts are likely to be perceived in the organisations where they deliver their services. Finally, the concept expertship and its consequences for leadership is discussed as a special form of relation between leaders and experts working in the organisation while not being employed there.

External experts and their services

One way of characterising the work of a consultant is that he or she should spend as little time as possible at the workplace of his or her employer. It is the client that indirectly pays the consultants, which means that they normally work in the organisation of the client, not in the organisation where they are employed.

A common view among consultants themselves is that anyone can be called a consultant who succeeds in creating enough confidence in their own and their colleagues' abilities so that other organisations will be willing to pay for their services (Furusten 2003, 2009, 2013). This requires competence in confidence building, networking, creating trust, and maintaining relationships; it is less about excelling in formal or practical management skills. Still, consultants assume the role of experts in their client organisations. This means that when organisations hire management consultants, two types of leadership experts are performing side by side in organisations, consultants and managers. There is, however, a distinct difference between the performance and authority of these two actors: while managers find themselves in hierarchical management positions among colleagues, consultants spend their days far from their own offices, colleagues, and superiors. This means that consultants constitute a non-employed temporary workforce in the organisations where they do their work. Still, since they are not employed by and have no position in the organisational hierarchies where they work, who leads them in their actions? Can anyone who hires the services of a consultant trust that the consultant in question represents the expected, or indeed claimed, level of expertise?

Many larger consultancies, such as McKinsey & Co., recruit undergraduates directly from university and college, training them as consultants by means of graduate training schemes. These recruits are deemed particularly adaptable and therefore suitable for client firms' own training schemes (Armbrüster & Glückler 2003). These larger consultancy firms usually operate on a global scale with head offices in the USA (Furusten 2013); they often also have their roots in the USA. The consultants – sometimes in thousands – who work for a major global consultancy firm share the same benchmarks and values, and they all undergo proprietary training as new recruits (Furusten 2003). They learn how to act as representatives of the firm and how to handle the firm's models and tools in practice. Once fully trained and ready to start working as consultants, they are usually given tough assignments, expected to work intensively on certain tasks for the duration of their projects. This category of consultants is usually difficult for in-house managers in client organisations to control and direct, since the consultants are employees of large consultancy hierarchies with their own standard operating procedures for how a good consultant should perform.

The organisation of smaller consultancies (with around 20 employees), however, is based on completely different premises (Furusten 2003). Here, it is not unusual for consultants to be more or less self-reliant, so there is little scope for trainee consultants. According to one senior consultant (Furusten 2003, 2009, 2013), there is hardly any point in applying for positions in his company (employing 14) if you are under the age of forty and without extensive experience as a consultant and manager. In smaller consultancies, consultants are both sellers and service providers, and must bring in their own clients and projects. In the larger firms, however, the senior consultants are usually in charge of the sales process and of structuring the assignment, while the less experienced consultants are expected to do the groundwork. Smaller firms basically consist of senior consultants who, when needing someone to do the groundwork, usually enlist one of the client's younger assistants. Needless to say, there are varying approaches to the role such consultants play in their client organisations, and therefore also to the relations between the consultants and the client organisations.

Since it is the clients that indirectly pay the salary of the consultants, the latter have strong incentives to promote what is saleable. Accordingly, the consultant is likely to provide what is requested, while the client can only request what he/she already knows. Still, in the same way as consultants have limited capacities to invent completely new services in every new assignment, clients also have limited capacities to demand services 'out of the blue'. Although not formalised as in traditional professions (*e.g.* auditors and lawyers), there is arguably a system comprising both clients and consultants in which certain ways of doing things are institutionalised (Furusten 2003, 2013; Furusten & Werr 2012, 2017a). This system likely guides consultants in preparing a schedule of services with good chances of being demanded by what the clients are likely to understand. This system has popular managerial discourse as its basis (Furusten 1999), which means that certain general assumptions about how organisations should work and be led and about the function of consultants are shared by those who perform and demand consulting services. When asking sellers and buyers of consulting services what controls the work of a consultant, the answer is often that the professional system they possess shape what they do, although it is difficult to be very precise about what this means (Furusten 2003).

Management consultants as viewed by...

One of the interviewed consultants said that it is difficult to specify exactly what it means to be part of some sort of professional system. Professionalism in this system is not explicit, but is still available to those who have been around for a while and have learned how the system works (Furusten 2013). The consultant explained (MK1):

> It can be really frustrating, it is very difficult to sell from a subjective point of view. And when you do not have any contacts of your own – then it is beyond difficult! That is why it is so difficult for new consultants to get started. It can take a long time. We often work together on an assignment and then I can bring someone new on-board. Obviously, he or she must be good. It can be very nerve-wrecking because you do not want them to make a fool of themselves but instead show what they can do. And naturally, I want to have my fair share of the assignments too. Yes, it is difficult. That

is also why it is so difficult to recruit consultants – people who make good consultants are far and few between – most of them think it is about being technical. 'But, I am good at accounting and finance and bloody hell, I know how to do this!' Then, you bring them into the meeting and within five minutes, they are walking on the thinnest ice. For example, they might end up telling the CEO, 'but my dear, this is what you should have done!'. I can see that the client does not understand and then, there is no point in repeating yourself and saying, 'Yes but I'm the expert on this and this is what you must do'. Because the guy does not understand what you are talking about, he will not do what you tell him to do anyway. You have to calibrate this knowledge.

The above quotation is taken from an interview with a senior consultant at a small consultancy firm (12 consultants) in Sweden. He is a partner and co-founder of the firm. What the senior consultant is expressing here is the idea that consulting is more about feeling what is right in a certain situation and less about showing off your expertise in a certain area. This is a contemporary image of consulting and one that particularly applies to consulting in leadership and organisational development. In the case of administrative and technical systems, the client usually requires something more specific. In the examples of consultation referred to above, the senior consultant said that it was important not to assume the role of a 'know-it-all'. In other words, a consultant must not barge in like a prima donna and start to boss everyone around: the management consultant should not impinge on the specialist area of top management itself. Acting like a know-it-all in such circumstances can easily backfire on the consultant, who ultimately just wants to do good business. The same consultant developed this further while trying to explain the role of a management consultant (MK1):

Many people believe that consultants are experts in a certain area such as finance, marketing, research, or whatever it may be. Especially at the end of the 80s and beginning of the 90s when loads of CEOs seemed to say, 'But I am so clever at what I do, surely I can become a consultant?'. You must be technically proficient in some disciplines such as management or business management but you must also be a consultant, which is not the same thing. However, this is what many people think.

What the consultant meant is that it is impossible to clearly define the expertise on which he and his colleagues base their services, so this definition is not to be found in any book. He went on, saying that consultants with the right amount of expertise will intuitively know what to do during the consultation process. This was also mentioned by other respondents. It therefore seems difficult to trace the origin of the knowledge and skills required by consultancy firms because, as one small-scale consultant put it, 'You are constantly learning new things as you go along', to which another consultant added (MK3):

> We ask three things of anyone who wants to become a consultant. You must have specialist competence in one area where you are better than the rest, in a particular industry or sector. The next step is not only to be an expert in your field but to be able to convey your expertise in a manner that engages other people. The third and final step is to be able to sell your expertise. We get people who know A and B but not C. However, based on this, I still think we can make good consultants of them. We have our introduction programmes, etc.

The above quotations indicate that there are many definitions of management consulting (*cf.* Kubr 2005). However, Furusten (2003, 2013) nonetheless has argued that such definitions primarily concern the consultant in three roles, *i.e.* as an external resource, an intermediary, and a facilitator.

Consultants as external resources

The image of management consultants carrying out various tasks and being identified in various ways is strengthened by what is said on the matter by a selection of buyers of management consultancy services. Several definitions emerge of what a consultant is assumed to be. A frequent understanding is that consultancy happens when specialist knowledge is *outsourced* by an organisation. One buyer described a consultant as 'someone who sells specialist know-how in a specific area where we are not self-reliant. It could also refer to outsourcing of a certain activity' (K1). Another buyer described it as follows: 'Consultancy is a service that someone outside our own organisation can provide, in other words, someone that I hire and pay to do the job' (K2). Yet another buyer (K3) described a consultant as follows:

> a type of specialist, someone with specialist knowledge that you
> hire for your organisation or a service that you buy. A service that
> you acquire from outside of the company ... It could be some sort of
> expertise ... It tends to be about knowledge services.

However, the notion that a consultant is a specialist with knowledge that
does not exist in an organisation, *i.e.* a type of expert, is not universal.
Another buyer believes that consultancy is more about providing temporary expertise, defining a consultant as 'someone you hire for a short
period of time to perform duties that your own staff would normally
perform but, for one reason or another, cannot perform at that time'
(K4). His definition of a consultant is close to the notion that the pro-
curement of consultancy services may well be a question of staffing. The
organisation does not have the competence needed at a certain time, so
the needed competence is brought in from the labour market.

However, a consultant is not always seen as an external expert. One
buyer put more emphasis on the supporting function of a consultant:
'It is generally someone externally ... I mean ... help from the outside
meant to support both me and the organisation as a whole, and the
consultant must have certain expertise in the area where I need it' (K5).
A consultant does not always have to be a specialist as long as he or she
has competence relevant to the buyer. In this case, the buyer preferred
to define a consultant as someone external with whom one can discuss
one's organisation and who, in many ways, can give management guidance and advice without assuming control of problem definitions and
creating solutions. The same view was expressed by another buyer (K6)
who described a consultant as

> ... a person who can provide an organisation with advice and sup-
> port without, so to speak, taking on the role of a manager and
> instead contributing knowledge, advice, tips, planning, and structur-
> ing. The consultant should presumably also be good at finding out
> ... getting a picture of ... a person who works for someone else, I
> believe, without being responsible for any executive tasks. There is a
> kind of contract with the consultant.

The notion that a consultant is a type of adviser is shared by many;
this is also the first definition of 'consultant' found in the dictionary
(Nationalencyklopedin, ne.se).

Then there is the combined notion that a consultant is someone with competence that an organisation or a management lacks who at the same time acts as an adviser. One buyer defined a consultant as 'an adviser with the expertise that I myself do not have' (K7). Other combined notions such as a consultant being an expert and interlocutor exist too. According to another buyer, a consultant is 'a speaking partner, a resource, and an expert in areas where I myself lack the competence required' (K8).

The term 'consultant' conjures up many other notions as well. A relevant dimension of consultants mentioned by a number of buyers is that their work relates to the commercial provision of services, for example, 'a person selling his or her services to someone – to a customer' (K9). The consultant is seen as 'a person outside of our own organisation who, in return for payment, provides expertise and knowledge that we do not have ourselves' (K10).

Clearly, and not just according to the buyers quoted above, the title 'management consultant' conjures up various images and definitions; for example, a consultant is a springboard or a resource for an organisation that lacks a certain competence needed at a certain time or is someone who can provide an organisation with expert knowledge it lacks – services generally thought of as commodified expertise.

The role of a management consultant generally seen as an external resource is summarised by Furusten (2013) as:

> Management consultants are external resources for management. They are listeners and *speaking partners* and are curious, open, and sociable. They also act as catalysts and stimulators with an added ability to determine situations, identify problems, and propose solutions. They are advisers, specialists, and experts as well as mentors and supporters who guide management to make decisions, implement processes, and execute restructuring projects.

Consultants as intermediaries

However, according to providers and buyers, consultancy is not just about being available as an external resource. As expressed by one consultant (MK4):

> A consultant acts as a catalyst – when it goes well. One that gets involved and promotes the process without actually participating in the same way as an employee. A good consultant acts as a catalyst

and provider of experiences and knowledge, etc. A coordinator ...
who works single-handedly ... but who cannot take on the responsibilities of anyone within the organisation. A stimulator of processes
and a springboard for ideas, perhaps also a bit of a mentor – that
depends on the circumstances. Just to be on hand and hopefully, contribute to something positive without taking over and controlling.

In other words, a consultant is preferably someone who does not take
over but who acts as a springboard. However, this also means that the
consultant is a problem solver with something to convey, which does
not necessarily refer to expertise or at least not to any particular form of
expertise. Furthermore, a consultant is described as someone who is on
hand to assist the buyer as and when required. The consultant quoted
above (MK4) is a self-employed consultant and a specialist in the field of
quality assurance. Perhaps this explains why he sees the role of a consultant as multifaceted, depending on specific circumstances and situations.
If a consultant, similar to the one quoted above, works single-handedly
or is part of a small company, he or she should be able to take on various
roles and assignments, as it is impossible to wait for only specific types
of assignment.

Consultants working for larger companies tend to have a slightly
narrower perception of their role, for example (MK5):

A consultant is an adviser. Initially, the role of a consultant was to
be more proficient and skilled in a certain area than the organisation
or company hiring him or her. The consultant was hired because
he or she was the expert whose advice everyone adhered to. At the
beginning, a consultant was only meant to write a report ... But
when the consultancy Bohlin & Strömberg was formed in 1960, the
consultant not only had to write a report but also take responsibility
for the actual change. So, you were the expert, you were the one that
knew better ... hence, you were expected to take responsibility for
the changes needed ... Today's consultants are no more competent
than the management that hires them, except, maybe, in a particular
field ... Today's consultants constitute a way in which to obtain more
information and knowledge, a better foundation and more resources
for the implementation of changes. The consultants of today do not
work as personal advisers to the CEO ... Now, you might be part of
a team of consultants working on a certain reorganisation project,
which could have been handled internally.

This consultant believes that consultancy is mainly about giving advice and that the role of today's consultants is primarily to provide information and expert knowledge that will give management a better basis for making decisions about possible changes. This, he believes, is something that many organisations today lack the resources for. That a consultant should be an external expert who comes with a perfect solution to every problem is an outdated perception, according to the consultant. What is most noteworthy in the interview material about the intermediary role of consultants can be summed up as follows (Furusten 2003, 2013): Management consultants convey experiences, expertise, knowledge, information, new procedures, and data on leadership, management, organisation, top–down strategies, as well as holistic perspectives to their clients who are managers at the top of the hierarchy.

Consultants as facilitators

As intimated above, consultancy is also about being available as an external resource and conveying something of value, at the same time providing support. Both consultants and buyers of consultancy services seem to share the view that consultants are not technical experts on anything in particular. A senior consultant from a small consultancy firm with a background in a larger consultancy firm described consulting as follows (MK1):

> Consultancy is a profession ... it has little to do with technical competence.

> A consultant is a person who, according to the situation, has the ability to get an organisation to produce results through the implementation of processes and by using different methods or models as explanatory variables and thus get the management of that organisation to make competent decisions. A consultant must possess certain personal qualities such as the ability to listen, to be very adaptable to new situations, and to be extremely humble.

> You can only exert influence through your competence – a consultant should not take centre stage. When an assignment is nearing its end, then I go and sit in the corner of the room. The consultant is only there to help. You are of course involved to the end but you are not to take credit – it has to be the client, the owner of the organisation.

You have to be able to identify problems, identify a way forward in the current situation, but not necessarily something that is written on paper. You must be very sociable and be able to deal with different types of people in different situations. And have a sense of timing – when you can and cannot do certain things. You need to be able to multitask and be strong but not so strong that you take over.

You are the adviser ... and if you seek the advice of another profession, then you do not want eleven different types of advice, you want one piece of advice not two or more ... you must be assertive and stand tall and not say, 'You could sort of do this or that ...'.

According to the above, consultancy need not involve the provision of technical expertise. Yet the same consultant argued that consulting is a profession that requires a certain amount of competence, which he believes comprises the ability to listen and identify problems and solutions and to guide management in making decisions and producing results. Consulting requires humility, adaptivity, timing, and transparency, in that the consultant stands behind the advice given without offering a number of alternatives, which, according to the quoted consultant, is not what is expected. Other consultants seem to have the same or similar notions of what consultancy is about. Another CEO (MK6) from an average-sized consultancy firm said:

A consultant is a helper and adviser to whom one turns for help and advice on how to find new directions and solutions. We are not the experts. We do not just walk in saying, 'this is what you should do ...'. We believe that changes and developments take place when the problem owner, entrepreneur, or county council director ... finds his own solution to the problems. The solution is usually to be found within their own organisation and, in any case, there must be a desire to embrace what is new. We are ready to assist with advice on how to achieve this and how to reorganise and develop, but we will never walk into an organisation and say, 'this is what you should do'. We are very different from those who we refer to as 'expert consultants' and see ourselves more as 'process consultants' who interact with the client.

Another senior consultant, with a lot of experience in larger consultancy organisations but who, at the time of the interview, ran his own consultancy firm, explained that a consultant can never approach an organisation with ready-made solutions. According to this senior consultant, a consultant should have the following attributes (MK7):

> He or she should be curious and open-minded and, most importantly, never pass judgement or you end up bringing nothing but your own expectations instead of being interested in creating a picture of the actual situation. You enter a new environment where you are supposed to perform and it is then important to understand that environment, to take a positive approach ... I never arrive with a folder of ready-made solutions. However, there are many consultants who do exactly that – they bring their entire toolbox with system folders and everything. I believe that prevents many from seeing the situation as it is.

The characteristics of consultants acting as facilitators can accordingly be summed up as follows: Management consultants support and contribute to processes that promote the development of business concepts, quality assurance, management, leadership, and organisation.

Managers, external resources, intermediaries, and facilitators

The first two categories – external resources and intermediaries – are broad enough to contain a number of services that organisations buy from other organisations. All experts whose services are acquired on the open market and who are not part of an organisational hierarchy may in one way or another be seen as external resources. They can also be seen as conveyors of expert knowledge and information in their respective professions and areas of expertise. However, the third category is more specific to management consultancy. No one would expect a secretary who is hired temporarily from a temporary employment agency to take on the role of a facilitator. Such a person may very well be a conveyor of experience, knowledge, and expertise on administrative routines, and there is no doubt that such a person is seen as an external resource. However, the difference between a secretary and a consultant is that the former is more often hired to fill a temporary position in an organisation while the latter is expected to identify problems and find solutions that, if successful, will have long-term implications for the organisation.

Considering the presence of management consultants within organisations in this way, we also find that they have an audience, *i.e.* the employees of the organisations hiring them. Even if consultants stick to their scripts, it is how their behaviour is perceived by their audience that largely determines the significance of their presence in organisations (Furusten 1999, 2003, 2009, 2013). The consultants interviewed for this study believed that the most important characteristic of a consultant is being able to secure assignments. If the consultant succeeds in this, then the market has accepted him or her in the role as a management consultant. Still, acceptance in the role to such an extent that market relations are established and financial transactions take place is one thing, but how are consultants perceived in a local organisational context? Perhaps the role they were meant to play and are confirmed as playing by market arrangements is, in fact, not the role that organisational employees perceive the consultants as playing?

Managers and experts: two categories of leaders

It is not unusual for leaders to delegate responsibilities and authority to individuals with special competence in certain matters. This is a normal way to allocate actions and make use of different talents and expert skills in modern organisations (Giddens 1991). Seen from a leadership point of view, the problem with this logic arises when management hires people from other organisations who act in the roles of the experts discussed above, and starts giving them responsibilities and authority that interfere and compete with the responsibilities and authority of in-house managers and employees. As seen above, the consultants themselves have no desire to walk into an organisation, take control, and boss people about. They want the in-house management to retain its leadership status and authority within the organisation while they remain on the sidelines, possibly coaching the management on how to implement some of the concepts they passed on, which the in-house management can then decide whether or not to implement. They do not wish to interfere with the in-house management system. This is a transparent way of relating to the ideal image of leadership in organisations and to relations between external experts and managers, but represents just one aspect of management consultancy, *i.e.* the stylised and rationalised.

Another side of this ideal image depicts management consultants as temporary employees carrying out the assignments for which they are contracted and riding out the occasional storm alongside the other employees, and not as personnel who only step in when the workload is excessive or there is a temporary shortage of competent personnel. The work of management consultants tends to take place in a parallel universe to the everyday work in organisations. They obtain information on how the organisation works, interview employees, inform and educate about what is deemed general knowledge about organisations and managing them, and coach in-house management on how to implement changes. They also tend to come up with lively suggestions and comments on what could be done differently. Hence, the other aspect of consultancy relates to the role of management consultants in the daily life of organisations and how they are treated and perceived by their 'temporary' colleagues.

This matter is discussed below in terms of two consultant identities adopted in providing better knowledge to others: the know-it-all and the 'star'. My reasoning below will identify several nuances in how consultants are perceived, illustrating different meanings of expertship and what we can learn about leadership by discussing the implications of expertship.

Managers and employees versus the know-it-all and the 'star'

The label 'know-it-all' has negative connotations. It usually makes us think of a difficult person who comments on what everyone says and always has the last word, who constantly rates the performance of others, and who repeats what others say to make it look as if any new ideas were theirs in the first place. Anders Mathlein's cartoon character Bengt-Erik Besserwisser is a good example of a know-it-all, although somewhat exaggerated. This is how the character is described on Mathlein's website: 'The man who is always right regardless of the subject, situation, or speaking partner ... and regardless of whether or not he knows what he is talking about' (mathlein.se). Consultants do not want to be perceived as know-it-alls, but it is not automatically how they are perceived in the local organisational context. Therefore, we cannot rule out that consultants may be perceived as know-it-alls and an irritating feature of the everyday life of the organisations hiring them. We tend to think that those we refer to as know-it-alls generally behave in a smug and self-confident manner, as if the responsibility of getting it right rests on no one's shoulders but their own.

The problems faced by organisations where know-it-alls are part of the everyday work environment was highlighted in an article published in the Swedish magazine *Chef (Manager),* on 11 May 2010:

We have all come across the know-it-alls – people who just cannot stop themselves from commenting on every word you say or how you pronounce them or who corrects you immediately if you should dare to give a celebrity the wrong surname. You have the choice of not associating yourself with such a person in your private life but as a manager, you do not have that choice. You must work together with him or her, in addition to which you must also get that person to work with the others in the group ... For a manager, dealing with a know-it-all can seem relatively easy as he or she often has low self-esteem and is keen to adapt to authority. It is usually more difficult for the other employees who have to put up with their remarks and arrogant comments.

Although the relevance of the magazine article is debatable, it provides a good indication of how we generally regard someone who is a know-it-all. Here, the know-it-all is called a difficult person. In this example, the term know-it-all is used to describe someone who likes to comment on everything that anyone says. The employees of an organisation may also refer to someone as a know-it-all if he or she keeps repeating what others have already said, remarks on what others do, or makes cheerful suggestions on how things ought to be done without having any particular insight. Although the quotation refers to know-it-alls among employees, it is not uncommon to describe management consultants in the same way. Many experienced and established senior consultants are well aware of the risk of being perceived unfavourably by their clients. Particularly at risk are junior consultants who have not yet fully identified with their occupation.

As discussed above, it is hardly the intention of consultants to come across as know-it-alls; rather, the image they tend to cultivate is that of the back-stage coach. Still, if consultants are perceived as know-it-alls by their audiences, then their conduct can be viewed as disturbing the exercise of leadership in the organisation, since they were hired by the managers. The presence of a management consultant may nonetheless give rise to feelings and comments such as, 'What right does Paul/Pauline have to come here and ... ?' If the presence of a consultant leads to such feelings and comments, it will have a general effect on confidence in organisational management. If the management does not know better than to bring in know-it-alls at every possible opportunity, then why should employees feel confident in any other decisions or measures of the management?

If the know-it-all represents the negative side of the presence of external experts in organisations, then the 'star' has the exact opposite connotation. The more experienced consultants seem to believe that they actually play the role of the star, as manifested in a quotation from one senior consultant: 'I'm good at management.' Such consultants are convinced that they are among the most prominent representatives of their area of expertise and top achievers whose assignments routinely produce the desired and expected end results, at least if their clients do what they are told. It is not unusual for a failure to be rationalised as the client not having followed the advice given. If these consultants manage to maintain an image of success before, during, and after completion of their assignments and this image is shared by the employees of the client organisation, then they have succeeded in playing the role of a star rather than a know-it-all. The consultant has performed so well that management's judgement in hiring the consultant cannot be questioned: management has simply hired someone who proved to be the best and who has fulfilled – or even exceeded – the expectations.

It is common that consultants attempt to create star status for themselves by giving a detailed description on their own websites of earlier successful assignments. However, to retain their stardom, they must keep on building their image of delivering fantastic results. If they succeed in this, they are likely to have satisfied clients and a satisfied client means that their stardom status is preserved.

When the employees of an organisation perceive the consultant as a star, the leadership situation is likely to strengthen and positively reinforce the in-house leadership, *i.e.* the leadership is strengthened by expertise, although this is not always the case. It could also be the complete opposite, *i.e.* that the star status of the consultant is seen as somewhat outdated and tedious from a competence perspective. If a consultant, however, offers the best expertise available and the employees also believe this to be the case, the risk is instead that this will lead to problems for management and its relatively outdated competence. Unless management keeps up, there could be major problems to deal with once the consultant has left the organisation.

If management allows itself to be infatuated by a know-it-all consultant and does not resist both the way he or she conveys insights and the actual message conveyed, employees may lose confidence in management, especially if they feel that management has knowingly hired a know-it-all. However, if management realises that the consultant did not succeed because the employees saw the consultant more as a know-it-all than a star, management can still retain employee confidence and turn the situation around. For example, when a former government research centre was to be privatised, management brought in one consultant after another. In the end, both management and employees got so tired of the consultants recommending one thing after another that they decided to take the matter into their own hands and make the necessary changes themselves (K11). After a long period of frustration and indecision, they finally summoned the energy to do what was needed. Interestingly, the research centre actually implemented the changes previously recommended by the consultants, but as they finally did so of their own accord, they felt that they were implementing their own solutions to solve their own problems. The management in charge at the time was given a great deal of trust by the employees, who felt that it had taken their side against the consultants (Furusten 1999). Now, it was the company versus the consultants and not the consultants and management versus the employees, as had previously been the case. It is noteworthy that there had been a change of leadership not long before the consultants were asked to leave. As a result, the new management could blame previous failures on the unsuccessful efforts of the consultants and on the former management for having allowed the consultants to behave like prima donnas. This in turn strengthened the position of the new management.

Expertship and leadership

When those with expert knowledge are not employed by the organisation where they perform their duties, a shift occurs in the relationship between the expert consultants and the in-house management. It is no longer about leadership from the management's perspective but about something we may call 'expertship'. The concept of expertship relates to the handling of external experts – not taking into account the employees – who, with their specialist knowledge, authority, and responsibilities, get involved in the organisation's decision-making and development of everyday processes and procedures. It is the responsibility of management to ensure that any external recruits function in their role; accordingly, it is the fault of management if they do not. However, it is not a case of unsuccessful management but what might be called unsuccessful expertship.

One dimension of the forming of in-house expertship is the nature and degree of robustness of the expert system to be hired. Management consultancy is a vague expert system in which the relationships between client organisation managements and management consultants differ considerably from those that apply when organisations hire people with expert knowledge in fields where the prerequisites for expertise are more distinct (Furusten & Werr 2017a), for example, in systems authorising accountants or solicitors (Abbott 1988; MacDonald 1995; Freidson 2001; Brante 2014). Although attempts have been made to establish the same or similar structures for management consultants, they have not been particularly successful (Furusten & Werr 2017a). In Sweden, for example, only a few of all practising management consultants have chosen to apply for membership in the Swedish Association of Management Consultants (SAMC) and even fewer have sought certification pursuant to the international Certified Management Consultant (CMC) standards (Furusten 2003; Alexius 2017). As a group, management consultants tend to categorically oppose all forms of rules and regulations rather than endeavouring to function together as one profession governed by the same professional standards (Alexius 2007, 2017) and upholding the same ethics. As a result, the relationships between client organisations and management consultants probably vary more than in the case of other professions, such as solicitors and accountants. Robust professions like these have little professional leeway, which makes it easier for those who engage them to anticipate the service they will receive. At the same time, this situation makes it easier for know-it-alls to use their formal status in arguing that they know best. However, the opposite could also happen in that the actual specification of requirements may preclude the existence of know-it-alls. You are either formally qualified or you are not, and if you only gain recognition in the profession for having the right competence and qualifications, then it does not matter how much other people claim to know as they will never be fully included in the profession.

Another dimension of the forming of in-house expertship is that those who know better belong to a category of outsiders who step into client organisations to provide something that the organisation's employees cannot. Consequently, they are presumed to represent a category of top performers (*i.e.* stars) in their particular fields, but the line between being perceived as a know-it-all or a star is very fine indeed. In other words, even consultants with good reputations and star status on the market may be experienced by client organisation employees as self-centred and vain with an unjustified sense of their own ability, talent, enlightenment, compassion, and importance.

We conclude that expertship represents a three-way (*i.e.* manager–external expert–employee) infringement on the hierarchical leadership structure of client organisations. The first infringement occurs when management puts its trust in experts who represent a vague and elusive expert system. This can lead to dubious and difficult-to-manage situations in which certain responsibilities are passed onto representatives of such expert systems. The second infringement occurs when people not normally included in the hierarchy of the organisation are suddenly part of its everyday life. They are not part of the organisational structure, yet they work within it. They are usually hired by management but may act as intermediaries between management and employees. Someone from the outside turns up and starts interfering with the everyday work of the organisation. They do what they are contracted to do and, when finished, leave the organisation with the end result of their services and the challenge of deciding what to do with it.

The question is then what we can say about leadership on the basis of this analysis. From the management's perspective, it is a question of expertship when consultants are engaged to assist in the leadership role. The consultants' own self-image is that of experts who complement the in-house leadership structure, who remain backstage and let the client organisation representatives serve as figureheads for change processes or any other results of their guest performance. Consultants therefore do not believe that they have any effect on the prerequisites of leadership. Instead, they see themselves as people who stay at the side of management, providing assistance. In other words, they prefer to be heard but not seen – in the local context. However, once their job is finished, they like to be recognised for some of the organisational success. One studied consultant said that he saw himself as a theatre director given a cast that he has not selected but whom he must direct to perform a script that he has not chosen.

Leadership among external experts?

We have now seen that there is a connection between expertship and leadership. Accordingly, the traditional image of leadership needs to be supplemented. Leadership is not based solely on the authority created by a regulatory framework, tradition, or charisma, as claimed by Max Weber (1949). How management handles its expertship is also significant. This chapter has discussed two principal challenges facing the management of an organisation when hiring management consultants:

that an outsider with better knowledge of leadership is brought into the organisation and that a non-employee is taking responsibility for various stages of internal management procedures.

The *first* challenge stems from the fact that the external expert is expected to *know more* about leadership than the organisation's own management, at the same time as the status of management is based on the assumption that they know how best to lead their own organisation. The status quo must be maintained if both parties are to continue to function in their respective roles. In other words, the challenge concerns how one or the other party is perceived in the local context and how their image is maintained.

If the consultant portrays the management as insufficiently knowledgeable about leadership, this puts the management in an awkward position and may adversely influence the confidence that their subordinates have in them. However, it can also be beneficial and confidence-building for the management if the consultant hired turns out to be a star, adding both more and better knowledge to the organisation. The management was, after all, responsible for hiring the consultant in the first place, so if they can bask a little in the glory of the consultant, then that will bolster their leadership position. If, however, the consultant is not perceived as a star, then this will have the opposite effect on the leadership position, for the same reasons as above.

Even if the consultant behaves like a know-it-all, it is still the responsibility of the management to ensure that he or she becomes a daily feature in the organisation, which again may affect the confidence that subordinates have in their management. It is particularly awkward if the leadership know-how that the consultant brings to the organisation is deemed irrelevant and out of context. If that is the case and management wants to retain confidence and perhaps even emerge stronger from the entire experience, it is vital for management to realise that the consultant did not succeed as anticipated and to clearly demonstrate that they are still in command and know more about management in the current context than does the consultant. One remedy for this could be to recognise and clearly emphasise that there is enough expertise within the organisation and that they therefore are going to take the matter into their own hands by identifying the problems and proposing appropriate solutions.

The *second* challenge relates to *accountability in management processes*. Management is ultimately responsible for the activities of an organisation, thus it is management that should be held accountable for the results of such activities. The management of larger organisations often allocates responsibilities and partial responsibilities for different phases and areas to others in the organisation. However, consultants are not part of the organisational framework – they are outsiders. They are given assignments that they implement and deliver within the framework of their own organisation. Consultants from larger consultancy firms deliver the services requested by their superiors, who are in turn accountable for the services delivered in connection with individual assignments. The problem is then that there is too much accountability, with two organisations being accountable for one particular assignment. The client organisation is accountable for the consultant carrying out a specific task, while the consultancy firm is accountable for the assignment being completed in keeping with what has been agreed on. In addition, the management of the client organisation is accountable for the end result of the consultant's services. An added complication is that those affected by the consultant's services and expected to adapt to the consultant's proposals are also held accountable for their own performance. The same applies to the consultant carrying out the assignment. This could lead to conflict because the different requirements are incompatible in practice. When a specific process or project leads to overlapping forms of accountability, this can create confusion and uncertainty surrounding the leadership in its present context.

The issue of accountability is further complicated by the fact that consultants are seldom asked to get involved in processes that are already unclear and subject to one or more changes. In such contexts, there might be excessive formal accountability but not enough personal accountability. When that is the case, it is particularly important to differentiate between various forms of accountability and let the consultant relieve management of some of its accountability. Management can then exploit the expertise of the consultant as an argument for why certain difficult decisions must be made. Citing the expert opinion of a consultant can, for example, help management develop a strong argument in favour of cutbacks. In this way, the consultant is also held accountable for the difficult measure. Management is then relieved of accountability when the consultant leaves at the end of the assignment, taking with him or her a certain amount of accountability. As a result, management is left to focus on its accountability for other processes in the daily operations of the organisation. This is likely to work smoothly if the consultant is legitimised as a star. The outcome will be different, however, if the consultant is perceived as a know-it-all. Should that be the case, management will hardly be relieved of its accountability – rather the opposite. Unless they make the consultant into a scapegoat, they could also be held accountable for his or her conduct. However, it is still possible for management to be relieved of accountability for irrelevant ideas and zany proposals by passing them on to the consultant, who leaves at the end of the assignment along with a certain amount of accountability (or blame). So, there are several ways in which management can exercise expertship and use a consultant to be relieved of accountability.

To conclude, the management of expertship in the form of (1) too much personal accountability and (2) excessive accountability in complex situations, is significant in leadership contexts. Since most managements are busy with the everyday running of their organisations, they find it difficult to take responsibility for important developments occurring alongside the ordinary operations of the organisation. Consultants, on the other hand, can bypass these ordinary matters and take responsibility for extraordinary issues that also must be dealt with. For this to work well, however, the consultant must either have or attain star status or the management must successfully exercise expertship.

CHAPTER 6

To lead secret agents

Björn Rombach and Rolf Solli

Has anyone not seen a James Bond film? Is there anyone who has never heard of Agent 007? James Bond or 007, the fictional secret service agent created by Ian Fleming, is undoubtedly the most famous agent of his kind. James Bond has completely outcompeted other literary rivals such as George Smiley by John le Carré. James Bond is also the agent who has been given a role in this chapter of the book. For now, what Bond does or does not do stays in the background. Let us instead focus on how he is led by his superior, also known as 'M'. We know for sure that managers play a significant role as regards agents. Ask Valerie Plame Wilson who was revealed as a spy by the Busch administration, just because her husband was critical of the administration's argument for the Iraq war. What can we learn from M?

There is nothing new about secret agents. One man who became renowned for his agents was Sir Francis Walsingham (1532–1590) – the 'M' of his time, you might say (Rombach & Solli 2006a). Through organising agents all around Europe and in Britain too, for that matter, he was able to prepare for attacks from both Spain and France as well as expose plots against Queen Elizabeth I, who probably would have been dead several times over had it not been for Walsingham's contacts. The methods favoured by Walsingham were rather brutal by today's standards, usually involving torture and execution. The website of MI6 (the British Secret Intelligence Service) implies that the methods used by Walsingham to organise his agents are seen as somewhat foreshadowing those of MI6 (sis.gov.uk). It is here, within MI6, that we find James Bond and M, *i.e.* within the secret intelligence service that keeps Britain safe by keeping an eye on what is happening outside the country.

The Swedish equivalent to MI6 is presumably Säkerhetspolisen (https://en.wikipedia.org/wiki/Swedish_Security_Service - cite_note-Naming-3SÄPO, the Swedish Security Service), but it is difficult to know for sure. After all, a secret is a secret. Dennis Töllborg (1999), who provoked the Swedish Security Service for many years, estimated the number of SÄPO employees to be around 700–800. In fact, this was secret information until Töllborg got hold of it, after which it soon became general knowledge. For the sake of comparison, Töllborg also obtained information about MI5, the British intelligence agency protecting the UK's national security, which in 1997–1998 had 1860 permanent employees. At that time, 559 people were in full-time employment with the Dutch Secret Service. In fact, we would like to know the size of all the organisations in charge of foreign intelligence.

Our conclusion is that major organisations run extensive intelligence service activities. These activities are often part of government operations, although not always. To better understand the work of intelligence services, we need to apply organisational theory. To further develop the part of the organisational theory that applies to the public sector, we need to look more closely at the work of the intelligence services. There is no shortage of real secret agents, many of whom feature in various publications. If you are Swedish or want to learn, books about spies by Tore Forsberg (2006, 2009) are well worth reading, and in Norwegian, is Tore Pryser's Female Spies (2007) good reading. Or why not read a book by Boris Grigorjev (*e.g.* 2007/2009)? Yet we decided to study James Bond and M, a decision that we defend below. By now, you probably realise the direction in which we are heading: agents are secret, so you do not get close to them.

General agent theory falls within the context of national economics and is usually called 'principal–agent theory'. Generally vague economic theories are more often than not referred to as business economics. Principal–agent theory tackles the issue of how the owner (*i.e.* principal) can make the contracted executor (*i.e.* agent) work according to the intentions of the principal. In straightforward cases, this is not a problem: the principal can simply check that the agent has done what was initially agreed on and that it has been done properly. It becomes more of a problem when the principal does not know how the work should be carried out and finds it difficult to explain what he or she really wants. According to theory, the solution is found in incentives.

According to principal–agent theory, the agent will presumably meet the requirements of the principal as long as the right incentives are offered. The trick is to get the vested interests of the agent to coincide with those of the principal. It is to this end that bonuses, share-option schemes, etc., occasionally or, in fact, all too often get completely out of control. The agent is, by definition, better informed than is the principal and therefore has influence that the principal might find difficult to discern.

The question is how the principal can make the agent move in the right direction. We can dismiss the basic economic theories of incentives because they do not solve the problem. For example, Robert Drago and Gerald Garvey (1998) and Anastasia Danilov *et al.* (2013) have demonstrated that the incentives system is not very effective when it comes to leading. Even so, there is an almost religious belief in incentives as a regulator between the principal and agent. However, let us not entirely reject the idea of incentives. Perhaps elements of principal–agent theory can be combined with other theories to create something even more sensible.

This chapter looks at how a manager can induce an agent to do what he or she wants. The example or scenario that we have chosen is perhaps a little extreme. There is, however, a pedagogical point to choosing an extreme example, as it clearly illustrates the difficulties, and potentials too for that matter, of leadership. The agent who needs to be led in our example is James Bond, Agent 007, undoubtedly both an extreme and a well-known case. One thing that distinguishes the fiction from reality, however, is the reality that the world is overrun by secret agents.

Studying the leader of Bond – M

The real James Bond does not exist and never has, although Dusan Popov (a double agent who met Fleming in 1941) is often mentioned as a source of inspiration (*e.g.* Gifford 2006, p. 14). Everyone knows that Bond was created by Ian Fleming and has since been adapted by directors, EON Productions, and six actors (as of 2018) into the character we have seen on the screen. Fleming's books have certainly sold in numbers that make management authors a tad jealous, but we are fairly certain that most people have got to know Bond via the big screen.

A motion picture that is not a documentary is usually fiction, *i.e.* something imaginary and invented, although not based on an unsubstantiated whim. For us to understand what we are watching, a storyline must be comprehensible, that is, include components that we can recognise. On film, one is allowed to exaggerate to make common events more interesting. Exaggerations create transparency, not dissimilar to what we in everyday life refer to as theory. For us, theory is a device that makes something difficult easier to understand.

How something is portrayed on film does not just depict reality, but creates it as well. Real-life mafia start behaving like the mafia on film. They start imitating the way the mafia talk and shoot on screen. *The Godfather* prompted the Italian mafia to change the title of their family heads from *compadre* to *padrino* (the original film title). Movies directed by Quentin Tarantino led to the mafia carelessly discharging their guns, aimlessly spreading bullets around. James Bond and M are also certain to have influenced real secret agents and their leaders.

We will use the James Bond films in the same way as we use cases in case studies (Rombach & Solli 2006a; Rombach & Solli 2009). Others have done so but with other films. Why not read one of Lawrence Krauss' (1995/1997) or Mark Glassy's (2001) books? We have.

The study of James Bond on film turns into a drawn-out longitudinal study. The first film we examined is from 1962 and the last from 2015. Fifty-three years is an unusually long period to cover in a management study. We have concentrated on films produced by the production company EON Productions. Some of the Bond films were produced by other companies, but these are hard to come by and, as far as we are concerned, 24 films are sufficient data. The reference list shows the films we viewed in order to study M.

There is no need to give a detailed description of how we analyse films – we have done that before (*e.g.* Rombach & Solli 2006). Let us just say that we keep to what the subtitles say and what the pictures show. We have chosen not to include empirical data, as it would make the chapter far too long. However, anyone wishing to check the data will find it easily available on film.

We have also decided not to consider other people's perceptions of M and Bond. There are quite a few of them, some of which are interesting. However, seeing as they have no bearing on the following analysis, we have chosen to leave them for a future and more comprehensive study of what we can learn from Bond.

How leaders are expected to lead

We start by creating a reference framework from two ends of the spectrum, which we will then link to the rest of our study. Let us examine the idea that it is possible to differentiate between how or what a leader is expected to do (*i.e.* the large-scale, long-term, and external perspective) and what the leader actually does (*i.e.* the small-scale, short-term, and internal perspective) without rewinding the tape to the 1950s. Neither perspective is more real or correct than the other, nor can they be separated from each other. Leaders indeed focus on what can be referred to as large-scale, long-term, and external matters while also showing an interest in what is small-scale, short-term, and internal. However, we must not let our knowledge of the epilogue ruin the film.

Instead, we shall focus on the actions of the leader. If we are to bring order to our narrative of secret agents and their leaders, we must first say something about the characteristics of leadership in general. It is very tempting to start with the management classics. Henri Fayol (1841–1925), for example, is a good starting point. Many people are familiar with *Administration industrielle et générale* ('Industrial and general administration') (1916/2008). Henri Fayol created a list of 'qualities and skills that an executive of a large organisation should have':

1. Good health and fitness
2. Intelligence and intellectual flexibility
3. Moral principles
4. Good general knowledge
5. Administrative capacity
6. General insight into key functions
7. Utmost competence in the particular areas of the organisation
(Fayol 1916/2008, p. 106)

Note that the same qualities and skills apply regardless of what type of organisation the executive leads.

All executives of industrial, commercial, political, military, or religious organisations and at the same hierarchical level face the same requirements as those listed above (items 1–6). The only difference is the particular competence (item 7) required in each organisation (Fayol 1916/2008, p. 106).

'Administrative capacity' is often cited as Henri Fayol's personal view of what executives ought to be doing and what they, in fact, are doing (item 5 above).

5. Administrative capacity
Planning – the ability to develop an action plan
Organisation – the special ability to develop a successful organisation

> *Leadership* – the ability to manage people
> *Coordination* – the ability to reconcile actions and efforts
> *Control*
> (Fayol 1916/2008, p. 106)

In the literature, one often sees the translation 'commanding' instead of 'leadership', as used above, and 'monitoring' instead of 'control'. These terms are remarkably far apart. However, we shall not discuss this translation issue without first referring to the French text (*e.g.* Fayol 1966).

We then go on to the work of Luther Halsey Gulick (1892–1993). Gulick is known for the initialism POSDCORB, though perhaps he is wrongly credited, as Lyndall Urwick may have also been involved (for a historiography, see Brech *et al.* 2010, p. 86–87). POSDCORB comprises the initials of the seven main functions or responsibilities of a leader: planning, organising, staffing, directing, coordinating, reporting, and budgeting. From Fayol came 'staffing', 'reporting', and 'budgeting'; the translation 'commanding' was modernised as 'directing', while 'controlling' was more accurately described as 'reporting' (Gulick 1937/2003).

Sune Carlson's classic work *Executive Behaviour* (1951) is also worth mentioning, as is the work of Henry Mintzberg (especially 1973) and Rosemary Stewart. We shall not weigh down this presentation by rehashing what has already been repeated far too often. Nevertheless, briefly stated, Mintzberg managed to identify 10 executive roles in three different areas. However, in a postscript to Sune Carlson's *Executive Behaviour*, republished in 1991, Mintzberg admits that his scheme was not that successful (pp. 100–101).

> One begins to wonder what in the world is going on in the literature
> of management. We live in societies obsessed with management, now
> far more than in 1951. We idolize managers; we fill book stores with
> studies of them, under 'fiction' as well as 'business'; we pretend to
> train huge numbers of innocent students to become them; we have
> even created a special class for them in our airlines. Yet we cannot come
> to grip with the simple reality of what they do. (Mintzberg 1991, p. 103)

Mintzberg finally concludes (in 1991) that POSDCORB is what organisations want but do not get from their leaders. If we interpret this as 'what organisations *believe* they need from their leaders' and refrain from making organisations into subjects while instead focusing on their leadership and employees, it sounds much more reasonable. POSDCORB constitutes the expected but virtually impossible, which becomes the responsibility of the leadership (see also Carlson 1991, p. 25). 'We see it because we believe it', as Karl Weick would have said (Mintzberg 1991, p. 108). POSDCORB is what is expected of leaders, what they are responsible for, and what they themselves and those around them would say that they do. How could this possibly be falsified by case studies? Such case studies would surely only generate lists of examples of leadership resources.

Let us stop there. POSDCORB is what James Bond's superior is expected to do – but not only that. We will return to how Bond and M manage to perform their POSDCORB tasks later in this chapter.

When it comes to what leaders actually do, we can, as indicated above, go far back in time. Sune Carlson (1951) composed a list of the everyday activities of managers. The list essentially comprises four categories of activities: obtaining information, giving advice and explaining, making decisions, and giving orders (see also Carlson 1991, p. 88).

We will probably never learn what exactly managers do. In other contexts, we have relied on Colin Hales' (1986) critical review of empirical studies of what managers do, in which he wrote 'the following strands are common, if not universal' (p. 95). These days, a critical review of this kind would be more or less impossible. There is simply too much research on the subject. Table 6.1 summarises the nine variables identified by Colin Hale (1986).

Table 6.1 Hales' (1986, p. 95) variables combined with results of surveys of municipal managers in Sweden in 1995, 2000, 2005, 2010, and 2015. Values range from 0 'strongly disagree' to 100 'strongly agree'.

	Municipal manager surveys				
Hales' variables	1995	2000	2005	2010	2015
It is my duty to act as the front man of the municipality.	55	54	53	55	57
My main job is to coordinate the work of others.	73	73	72	73	70
Most of my working hours are spent supervising, filtering, and spreading information.	48	49	46	50	46
My most important job is to allocate resources.	47	52	51	50	53
My job involves managing the workflow.	45	47	52	53	54
Many of my working hours are spent negotiating.	54	50	49	48	48
One of my principal duties is to promote innovation.	67	65	66	65	64
My plans are thrown together on a whim.	36	41	40	39	37
Much of my time is spent checking that decisions are implemented.	40	40	41	47	45

The data presented in Table 6.1 were derived from surveys of municipal managers in Sweden carried out in 1995, 2000, 2005, 2010, and 2015 (previously unpublished data). Obviously, we do not claim that M is reminiscent of a municipal manager, but the data capture something relevant to our presentation. We shall return to this study in our analysis.

Before Hales, one could of course go further back in time to the ancient Greeks, but as this is a modern book, let us stay in the modern era. In her thesis, Lena Andersson Felé (2008) listed the principal duties of staff managers in the homecare services sector (Table 6.2). Admittedly, there are not that many similarities between the British Secret Service and our own homecare services. Who would want to swap their secret agent job for emptying bedpans? The duties, glamour factor, organisation – everything is different. Or maybe not everything: the daily duties of the managers are probably the same.

Table 6.2 Managerial duties and their time allocations (Felé 2008, p. 200).

Managerial duties, time allocations
Contact with subordinates, 1 hour per day per 15 people
Contact with clients and their relatives, 1 hour per day
Ongoing personnel matters, 1 hour per day per 15 employees
Operational management, 1 hour per week
Financial management, 1 hour per week
Long-term operational planning, 1 hour per week
Long-term personnel planning and recruitment, 1 hour per week
Operational development, 2 hours per week
Personal competence development, 1 hour per week
Personnel meetings, 2 hours per month per maximum 15 employees
Meeting with top-level manager, 2 hours per month
Meeting with same-level manager, 2 hours per month
Conflict management, 1 hour per month per 15 employees
Performance review, 1 hour per annum per person
Rehabilitation talks, 2 hours per 15 employees and week
Salary review, 1 hour per annum per person
Holiday planning, 2 hours per annum per person

We can already hear you protesting. Nevertheless, let us for a moment assume that M too has to discharge most of these and other trivial duties. The question is what specific problems one would encounter in one's daily work leading an organisation whose field staff consist of secret agents.

M as a leader and the theory of theories

What does it mean to be a manager of secrets? What is different from and similar to what we perceive as normal for managers? How M's leadership has changed over time is something that we discuss in the next section of this chapter. Let us pick up where we left off in the previous section. We have used the method of reflection through observation, with three observations forming the basis of a reflection.

The first observation based on Fayol

Why not start with Henri Fayol's 'qualities and skills' as a basis for our first observations?

1) None of the Ms seem to be in particularly good health or condition, especially not the first one who smoked like a chimney and hardly moved from his chair. Here our data fails us.
2) We can probably not blame this poor health on the lack of intelligence of the boss: after all, M seems to know a thing or two. However, we would like to know how things are with M's intellect. M has very clear opinions and beliefs that he/she finds difficult to change, and M can become quite irritated even though Bond manages to solve the problems assigned him.
3) According to Fayol, leaders should have a high level of morality. M certainly possesses a high level of morality, but it is not quite in line with the morality of others. M has his/her own morality in which life, property, and anything else that generally represents moral content has little value. The real issue and one's own moral perception is what counts.
4) General knowledge usually refers to a broad knowledge of universal topics. Bond nearly always beats M when their general knowledge is put to the test in the films. Bond knows a lot about wine, diamonds, and women (at least those who like Bond for what he is), while M is virtually a novice in these areas. The question is whether M would perform well in certain other general knowledge categories.

5) As regards the administrative capacity described by Fayol, M
   seems to perform less well. M's plans hardly ever work out, and
   it usually falls to Bond to sort things out. However, most plans
   never go according to plan.

The organisational capacity of M is also debatable. On one hand, the
organisation, seems able to solve most of the problems that confront it;
on the other hand, we never see anyone other than Moneypenny and Q
even though we know that there are other agents. The organisation for
which M is responsible does not seem very complicated and uncompli-
cated organisations are easy to coordinate.

M is definitely good at leadership – everyone except Bond seems to
comply with M's orders.

Control, however, is not M's strongest point. M is usually asked to
take control when everything else has failed. It is, however, worth noting
in this context that there have recently been some improvements: M
now uses satellite surveillance to reinforce control.

M seems to know the organisation well, at least well enough to lead
Bond in the right direction. In this respect, we must give M credit,
especially in the films in which he/she actually leaves the office and takes
control of a command centre or operates in the field.

All things considered, it is certainly possible to describe M on the basis
of Fayol's terminology. However, if Fayol were M's teacher, then M
would likely have had to re-sit his/her tests before achieving a pass. M
would find it particularly difficult to pass tests on health, fitness, intellectual flexibility, and morality.

The second observation based on POSDCORB

POSDCORB (planning,organising, staffing, directing, coordinating, reporting, and budgeting) is what M is expected to do and is the basis of
our second observation.

P) Planning is something that we discussed in our first observation
   and, as we know, not much goes according to plan for M, even
   though he/she makes a lot of plans.

O) Organisation is also something that we have discussed already.
   The need for organisation seems limited in M's world, in addition
   to which it is not one of M's strengths.

S) There is a lot for M to do when it comes to staffing. Bond appears to be chosen only for the more difficult missions. He often takes over when another agent has failed (which, incidentally, means that the agent is dead). M's ability to select employees, and not just agents, is impressive. Moneypenny must be the best secretary of all time, and what she cannot sort out is not worth the trouble (Westbrook 2005, 2007, 2008). Q seems to fit very well into his role too.

D) Directing is about getting others to do the job. Once again, we must compliment M on her/his ability to direct. The job gets done every time, albeit with methods that M does not always agree with, though the end results are to M's satisfaction. Performance management is one of M's strengths, while process management is something that M should not even attempt – it has the same bad effect on Bond as on university professors. *Lean production* means nothing to MI6.

CO) Coordination is closely linked to staffing in the films. M always makes sure that there is someone who can assist Bond on his missions.

R) The system of reporting is simple. Bond reports to M and M reports to the Minister. Notably, however, we never see M reporting on the successful completion of a mission. M only appears to report to the Minister when a mission is not going according to plan.

B) Budgeting is something that M appears to be good at – good enough to be entrusted with a nearly unlimited budget. Q is the one who gets most upset when Bond manages to break things.

All things considered, Luther Gulick would probably approve of M as a leader. After all, Ian Fleming lived in the days when the concept of POSDCORB was formulated, and if there is anywhere we portray leaders as we would like to see them it is on film.

The third observation based on Hales

Our third observation is based on the literature review of Colin Hales (1986) and the empiricism that we have associated with it. In this context, we have asked several people with good insight into the Bond films to assess how well the variables of Hales apply to M.

Table 6.3 Mean values for Swedish municipal managers and assessments of M according to the variables of Hales. Values range from 0 'strongly disagree' to 100 'strongly agree'.

Hales' variables	Municipal managers	M
	1995–2015	1962–2015
It is my duty to act as the front man.	55	50
My main job is to coordinate the work of others.	72	68
Most of my working hours are spent supervising, filtering, and spreading information.	48	75
My most important job is to allocate resources.	51	55
My job involves managing the workflow.	50	53
Many of my working hours are spent negotiating.	50	30
One of my principal duties is to promote innovation.	65	20
My plans are thrown together on a whim.	39	20
Much of my time is spent checking that decisions are implemented.	43	35
MEAN VALUE	52	45

The values relating to municipal managers in Table 6.3 are identical to those shown in Table 6.1 except for the addition of a mean value for the entire period. There is no point in discussing the accuracy of the values assigned to M, as it would be impossible to ask all the different Ms for their opinions. However, they do give us an indication of how M performs in comparison with other leaders. Although municipal managers do not score very highly on the scales for Hales' variables, they do score better than M. M would probably not be very good in the role of a municipal manager, while a municipal manager, on the other hand, would likely perform very well in the role of M!

The point is that M does relatively little of what managers are supposed to do according to Hales. Putting Table 6.2, Felé's list of managerial duties and their time allocations, into the same context, it becomes evident that the M we know is busy doing other things that we never get to see.

On reflection

Overall, M is not a typical manager or leader. He/she does some of what we expect according to concepts such as POSDCORB. Although M does not fit particularly well with our other two observations, few people are oblivious to M's role in MI6. We therefore conclude that there is less wrong with M than with the theories of leadership.

M simply does what he or she must do, just a little differently from what managers are generally taught to do. Maybe M's leadership style is not that strange after all. Leadership theories are good references when talking about leadership, but they should not be confused with what it is that managers actually do.

Therein lies the paradox. Things that, in theory, a manager does not have time for, such as strategy development and contemplation, fit easily into M's schedule. However, things that, in theory, ought to be easy to fit into a busy schedule, such as negotiating and controlling, M finds difficult. The easy becomes difficult and the difficult easy – perhaps it is not just the theory that is wrong.

Another reflection in this context is that the mean value for managers in general or for a certain type of manager (*i.e.* municipal managers) does not seem to apply to managers in the real world. Everyone is different. The managers referred to in the theory of leadership simply do not exist.

The question is whether our dissatisfaction with leadership theory is because we have looked at only one theory. Perhaps we instead ought to be looking at many more theories of leadership. Not more theories as in one theory for municipal managers and another for other managers, but leadership theories concerning entirely different aspects of leadership – not one about apples and another about pears, but about the cultivation of pears and fermentation of apple cider. We hope you can follow our reasoning here. If we can refrain from combining theories into an ideal for the typical manager or leader, we will progress even further. Let us take a step back and start afresh.

Change and stability

Our time series is unique and quite long, prompting the question of what happens to M's leadership over time. What has stood the test? What has changed or been added?

The first question is what we should be looking at. Stability and change always refer to something. Take the soundtracks to the Bond films, for example. According to someone with the right expertise, the Bond film soundtracks have developed as follows:

In the 70s:	Funk and disco fever
In the 80s:	Guitars and synthesisers
In the 90s:	Electro and techno

> In the 2000s: Sampling and more techno
> (agent007.nu/bondmusiken.htm)

You can hear the change in the music. At the same time, *the 'James Bond Theme'* by Monty Norman (and possibly John Barry) has remained the same over the years. There are, of course, some 'famous Bond sounds' that, according to Jimmy Gerdin, are sometimes missing from today's Bond films (agent007.nu/bondmusiken.htm). The theme tunes usually played during the opening credits of the films are still played, though few films have opening credits these days. There is both stability and change. More could be said about this, but the Bond music is not the core and focus of our analysis.

A solid foundation of values

Let us leave the music and move on to values. What do M and James Bond stand for? We will seek the answer to that question among the Seven Deadly Sins and Seven Holy Virtues. Others who have written about the Deadly Sins have argued as best they can that they are still relevant (*e.g.* Strohmenger 2010, p. 22). Surely, the best indication that the Deadly Sins are still relevant as themes in popular culture is a crime novel entitled *The Seven Deadly Sins* (Raine 2010), three or so films on the subject (see reference list), and a best-selling wine.

We could have done things differently, of course. But first two 'nevers': We would never attempt to find more than seven deadly sins, even though our bookcase includes authors who have found *24 Deadly Sins of Software Security* (Howard *et al.* 2010) and *The 77 Deadly Sins of Project Management* (Management Concepts 2009). *Ten Deadly Marketing Sins* (Kotler 2004) constitutes a fairly modest collection as compared to other works by this vocal force among marketing authors.

Of course it goes without saying that we would never have tried to identify our own seven deadly sins. If we have managed to keep the same seven deadly sins since the advent of Christianity, then there is no reason to try to outdo them now. David Schmier (2009) looked for 'deadly job search sins' and managed to identify seven sins exactly, albeit all brand new. Worth noting too is that Schmier's sins are not particularly deadly – how about 'Deadly Sin #6: Quit acting like it's 1999' (Schmier 2009, p. 69ff.).

We shall not elaborate further on the genealogy of the deadly sins (Johnsén 2010) or what they actually stand for (see, *e.g.* Rogers 1907 or Schimmel 1997). Nor shall we waste our time deliberating on how these sins have been alluded to in the management literature cited above. We simply refer to the elementary definitions of the terms.

The same applies to the virtues. We use them in the simplest way without a second thought, despite being well aware that virtue is a complex phenomenon. Those who think about things a little bit more will soon find more than seven virtues. A wide-ranging review of 18 virtues can be found in the book *A Small Treatise on the Great Virtues* by André Comte-Sponville (1996/2001). It should be noted that some of the virtues mentioned in this book are minor and therefore of no great importance. As regards the number of virtues, we come to a roadblock: if we have Seven Deadly Sins then we cannot have more than Seven Holy Virtues.

André Comte-Sponville's (1996/2001) starting point, 'every virtue is a high point between two vices, a ridge between two precipices' (p. 11), is worth some thought. Expanding the number of sins, however, in no way advances our analysis. Replacing sins with vices feels closer to home, not least because this seems more timely than the concept of 'deadly sins'. Regrettably, the term 'vice' loses some of the dark drama that otherwise contrasts so well with the whimsy of the Bond films.

This brings us to our friend Stellan Malmer's favourite quotation from the crime novel *Statsrådet sitter kvar (The cabinet minister remains in office)* by Bo Balderson (1978). The minister is talking about his favourite dinner, and when having to choose between apple pie and custard, chocolate cake, or ice cream with chocolate sauce for dessert, he exclaims 'No, I can't choose! I'll have it all! That will make a nice contrast with the sweetness of the custard and the added sweetness of the chocolate cake' (Balderson 1980, pp. 148–149).

The positioning of M and Bond according to the Holy Virtues and Deadly Sins (Table 6.4) is as balanced as it possibly could be. Bond is far more humble, generous, and compassionate than M. It is true, of course, that Bond kills people and exposes others to danger, but he is never too proud, greedy, or jealous. However, he is often driven by lust and anger when a mission becomes personal. He sometimes devotes himself to gluttony and can be quite lazy at times.

M, on the other hand, has a strong sense of pride. The biased would say that this is an innate sense of pride. As to greed, this is not something that applies to M in person. Not at all, in fact, and although nothing seems to be missing from M's private life, most of what is there would have been obtained at someone else's expense. No, M's greed relates to Britain: what Britain wants, what it should have. The jealousy that M

Table 6.4 M and Bond, rated according to the Seven Holy Virtues and Seven Deadly Sins.

The Seven Holy Virtues versus the Seven Deadly Sins	
humbleness = James Bond	pride = M
generosity = James Bond	greed = M
chastity = M	pleasure = James Bond
compassion = James Bond	jealousy = M
abstinence = M	gluttony = James Bond
patience = M	anger = James Bond
diligence = M	indolence = James Bond

sometimes displays has to do with Bond. M can certainly, from time to time, feel compassion towards Bond. However, there is still a deep-seated jealousy: M really wants to be Bond. Chastity, abstinence, and patience (not least with Bond) are other characteristics of M.

Interestingly, these core values remain stable over time. M has changed quite a lot, but not at all when it comes to his/her core values.

A changeable behaviour

When trawling through the empirical data for possible changes, we find 10 areas of change (Table 6.5). M's way of behaving and leading has undoubtedly changed over the long time that the Bond films have been in existence. As to categorisation, it is definitely a bit tricky. If we had thought it beneficial, we could have referred to Wittgenstein, Plato, or Aristotle. As usual, conceptual definitions present a problem. However, since we are trying to see the bigger picture, some imprecision can probably be permitted.

At first, it seems very obvious: M evolves from an old-fashioned authoritarian type of leadership to modern democratic leadership. But is that evolution really that unproblematic? What is clear, however, is that there is a marked change in the behaviour of M as a leader.

Disengagement of values and behaviours

What is interesting in terms of stability and change is not the stability of values or the behavioural changes in themselves; rather, the two concepts together are what is interesting. The deep-seated values of the leader remain unchanged: the virtues remain, as do the deadly sins, but no other major changes take place.

Table 6.5 The development of M's leadership over time.

M goes from ... to ...
1. Natural legitimacy to professional legitimacy
2. Statesmanship to service orientation
3. Integral overview to technology-dependent surveillance
4. Distance to control
5. Slow follow-up to quarterly capitalism
6. Target management to micromanagement
7. Performance accountability to coordination responsibility
8. Public officer to leader
9. Linear efforts to nonlinear efforts
10. Irritated by subordinates to considerate towards other employees

However, major changes in the behaviour of the leader can be found in certain key areas. The question of superficiality and profundity is a tricky one. One would assume that his/her core values would have some influence on the leader's behaviour. However, when behaviour becomes disengaged from core values, it is a matter of what might lie deeper. Is it really reasonable to suggest that what we actually do in practice should be referred to as superficial? The behaviour of managers and leaders is often seen as rather superficial. We do not agree. Superficiality is indeed a behavioural trait, but this superficiality, as we see it, may also hide behaviours that need to be hidden, for example, by using rhetoric about values greater than those of the here and now.

If a leader's behaviour, despite dramatic changes, can be said to be based on constant values, the question of superficiality versus profundity is of little or no interest. Consequently, it is impossible to draw any obvious conclusions about values on the basis of behavioural studies. From a normative perspective, efforts to improve basic values in order to influence behaviours seem misplaced: the risk is that only the values and not the behaviours may change.

Leadership studies can be divided into two *major* categories – there are many more minor ones, of course, but let us not go into that now. In the first category, leaders talk about their own leadership. Most of these leaders see good values as a basis of good leadership. The second category is about behaviours, often desirable ones, and behavioural observations. In such research, the explanations are often more practical in nature – it is what it is because it was what it was – though explanations are also sought in the values forming the basis of behaviours.

We believe, whether rightly or wrongly, that the theory of leadership should be complemented with a theory of leadership practice that is not based on core values.

And now?

Our point has been made. If you have ever seen any Bond film, then you know how it ends without our having to remind you. If you were to ask, which one of us is Bond and which one is M, the answer is ... we both want to be Q, but in a social scientific kind of way.

CHAPTER 7

Virtual leadership

Johan Berglund

Dinner – the whole family is gathered. On the menu today is Dad's 'sausage stroganoff'. Everyone has a good appetite (which in itself is a success with a nine-year-old son and a two-year-old daughter) and chats a little between mouthfuls. Sausage for dinner makes the tummies of most kids happy and eradicates any protests over the dinner table. I keep a constant eye on the time, which is fast approaching seven o'clock in the evening. Why am I always late preparing dinner?

The guild competition starts at seven and we are still at a delicate stage of our diplomatic negotiations with our arch enemy – *the Camorra*. I am trying to reach an agreement that will regulate the frequency with which members of our respective guilds attack each other in the arena, because our less experienced members stand little chance against the members of the Camorra. They are beaten all too often and, as a result, end up losing a lot of gold and, more significantly, their motivation. Less gold means fewer training opportunities and less chance of buying the equipment needed to succeed in the arena. In short, our members will not develop as well and as quickly as we would like, making the guild relatively weaker than the Camorra. It would be good to reach an agreement with the Camorra to gain some breathing room and give the weaker members of the guild time to develop. Our negotiations with the Camorra are going well and we are now close to an agreement. However, it is more difficult to sell the idea of an agreement to the guild members who would benefit the most from it – they appear the least interested.

'Daddy?' My thoughts are interrupted by Benjamin's question: 'What is the largest city in the world?' Many of Benjamin's questions at the moment are about what is the largest this or that in the world. I hear myself answer with a question: 'In terms of surface area or population?'

Not that I necessarily know the answer to either question. 'Where most people live', Benjamin replies. 'I'm not completely sure', I answer, 'but we can Google it later'.

Back to my thoughts about guild diplomacy. How can we get the members to see that it would be in their best interest to follow the rules of a possible agreement with the Camorra? Providing factual information on the benefits of such an agreement would not, I fear, have much of an impact. Instead, some of our more vocal members believe that we ought to declare war against the Camorra. Other members write angry and sometimes insulting messages to those individual players in the Camorra who have attacked them in the arena. These messages, written in anger, do not exactly help the ongoing negotiations. It is understandable why the players send these and similar messages to one another, but at the same time, as a gladiator, you must be prepared for fights and battles in the arenas. After all, this is a central part of the game. The problem is that if the e-mails with the messages are reported to the game administrators and are deemed offensive or threatening (which they often are), the players risk being banned from the game. And a ban would give the Camorra a legitimate reason for declaring war, which the guild could really do without. In the event of a prolonged war, there is a high risk of losing members as the joy of playing is undermined by constant poor health and loss of gold from all the attacks.

A quick glance at the clock tells me that it is now five minutes past seven. As the new guild master of *Centurion-Progressus*, I should be online and active in the guild at the start of a competition; otherwise, I'll send the wrong signals. This was something that I learned early on in the game when, as a new guild member, I saw how the guild master and the other leaders in the management team behaved.

I get up from the table and put my plate and cutlery in the dishwasher. I realise that I am the first to leave the table, which is very rare. I hear myself making the excuse that I am now a guild master in Centurion-Progressus and that I have to set this weekend's competition in motion and sort out a few things in the guild. 'Master? Guild? Centurion?' my wife asks, emphasising the seriousness of my attempt to leave the kitchen in favour of the computer in the next room, 'On a Friday evening?' Benjamin, however, lights up and jumps down from his chair, asking if he can come along and watch.

The game that I am playing is called *Gladiatus* and is a massively multiplayer online game (MMOG) created by the German company Gameforge, which is also the creator of several other MMOGs. It is a browser game following the usual logic of 'levelling' (*i.e.* advancing your character to progressively higher levels) so common in these games. The objective is to make your character grow and develop into a much greater and stronger character, which brings with it new opportunities and missions (*e.g.* the dungeon missions only available to higher-level players). Achieving success takes time – and money, for those who want to take shortcuts.

The most famous MMOG is probably *World of Warcraft* (WOW). There are many similarities between the World of Warcraft and Gladiatus as well as many differences. In WOW, you are moving within graphically rich virtual environments. Before you can play WOW, however, you have to buy the game and then pay a recurring subscription fee. WOW is also more detailed and elaborate and has significantly more users. Gladiatus, on the other hand, is 'free' of charge: simply download and start playing straight away. However, you have the option of paying a fee to get ahead in the game, a necessity if you want to make any progress (hence, 'free'). Gladiatus is also not as graphically advanced as WOW. It is a browser game. You do not move within a graphically rich 3D virtual world, instead being presented with various menus and static images. In addition, all fights and battles are over at the click of a button – no moving monsters or characters to defeat with nimble mouse movements and keyboard shortcuts. Yet it is surprisingly easy to get drawn into this seemingly simple virtual world, which can probably be explained by its social dimension. When playing the game, you interact and play with, and against, other people.

Not just a game

Some might object that it is just a game and recreational pastime and, surely, very different from the (harsh) realities of life: 'What is there, if anything, to learn from this game that has to do with organisation or leadership?' However, many have in various ways problematised this and similar dichotomies, such as play–work and virtual–real. It is becoming increasingly difficult to maintain the boundary between our virtual and real worlds, as more of us seem to be spending a lot of our lives on social media. We live in an ever more mediatised society (Hjarvard 2008) where many of our experiences of the world and interactions with people occur through various forms of social media. Perhaps the activity of playing computer games does not separate us from the 'real' world that much, but rather gives us a glimpse of a world that is increasingly becoming our future?

In the world of MMOGs, standard organisational forms are problematised and new forms developed. For example, the games industry has invented a new category of employees: playbours (Kücklich 2005). Playbours are players who in their spare time and free of charge help develop games by creating various 'mods' (*i.e.* modifications) or add-ons. These can be anything from tools that facilitate the playing of a game, in various ways enhance the game experience, or make you play more efficiently or effectively. This increases the longevity of many games, as they are continuously developed by the players themselves. In addition, devoted fans use various internet forums to report errors (bugs), as new game releases are never without their faults. This is not necessarily a major problem seeing as so many players are happy to help test new games and report on errors or bugs they come across when playing, which hopefully the game manufacturers will address in the next update. In fact, game manufacturers usually provide special forums for reporting errors and bugs on their game websites. These forums are also used for discussing tactics and strategies.

Players also set up 'unofficial' websites where the experience of playing a game is discussed, advice on tactics and builds is discussed, and gaming guides are provided on different topics. They share their 'mods' and come up with strategies for getting the best out of a game. Problems in completing certain tasks/missions/quests are also discussed together with possible solutions, called walkthroughs. Many games are supported by series of websites that are important parts of the gaming community and add further dimensions of value for the players.

Not always does the gaming industry see these players as active co-producers, despite being very quick to benefit from their labour. According to T. L. Taylor (2006a), game manufacturers tend to have a fairly narrow view of game players as consumers who pay for their leisure-time entertainment. Another rather common view of players is that of potential troublemakers who sometimes ruin the design of a game by cheating, hacking, or otherwise behaving inappropriately in violation of the rules and conditions of the game. Yet another view of players is that they are relatively ignorant and non-technical, not understanding the complexity of and expertise involved in designing a game. They simply need to be firmly steered onto the right path. A final view of players is that they tend to be fairly selfish and calculating, always pursuing their own self-interests when playing a game.

These views, despite signs of possible tensions and conflicts among them, fail to take account of some of the key aspects of various game communities, according to Taylor (2006a). Game players are not merely passive users of games but active co-producers of lifeworlds through their commitment and continuous playing. The cultures and behaviours that grow and develop out of these games might often differ from how their designers imagined that the games should be played. MMOGs can be seen as evolving communities in which the games emerge from long-term interaction between game designers, players, and comprehensive social norms (Steinkuehler 2006).

Although there are those who like to destroy and cheat in the game world and always seek their own advantage first, the socialising that takes place in these games and the cultures that evolve constitute relatively unexplored and rarely noted phenomena (Taylor 2006a). Norms on how to play a certain game are communicated between players, and there are many examples of self-regulatory activities being put in force when someone does not follow the norms. These norms are often in keeping with the values and rules explicitly expressed by the game manufacturers and incorporated into the game design. Players are often knowledgeable about the underlying logic of a game (in contrast to the image of ignorant and passive game users) and usually have ideas about how it can be developed and improved. This is channelled into various tools and 'mods' that the players develop and sometimes through making criticisms or suggestions in game forums to express dissatisfaction with the development – or lack of it – of a game. Sometimes collective critiques take place in-game. One example of such a players' protest was *the WoW Warrior Protest*, which was carried out in the game wow and involved hordes of players meeting at a predetermined place on the server to express their dissatisfaction. In short, it was a virtual demonstration. The dissatisfaction of the players related to the status of the Warrior class in the game, which had noticeably deteriorated as a result of various game updates. The game manufacturer responded by threatening to ban the players unless the demonstration was immediately dispersed, using a tone not unlike that of a police force trying to disperse an illegal demonstration in real life (Taylor, 2006a).

Furthermore, these games often problematise copyright protection (*i.e.* intellectual property) since the law essentially applies to a reality that is without virtual assets and the accompanying unique ownership issues. One frequent question is who should be deemed the lawful owner of a character (*i.e.* account) and the symbolic fruits (*i.e.* artefacts) of a game (Taylor 2002; Grimes 2006). The simple answer, according to the game manufacturers, is that they own the copyrights. Taylor (2002) has argued, however, that players should be seen as at least co-authors of games, since their input and efforts in terms of time, commitment, and creativity are central to the creation of the (life)worlds in the games. The problem is that players are seldom seen as creative co-authors who, together with the game manufacturers, are involved in the design and creation of games. The difference between the case of online games and, for example, the earlier debates on illegal file sharing in the music industry is that, in the case of gaming, the issue is not illegal copying (Grimes 2006). Instead, it is often seen as a form of creativity when the players use the raw material provided by the game manufacturers to create their 'own' characters. Because the players themselves are creators of characters, it has been suggested that they should be allowed to sell the characters (*i.e.* accounts) they create if they wish to. Even though the game manufacturers with their superior resources are the ones to set the agenda in terms of the virtual assets and who owns them, debate on this issue is ongoing. Even in the USA – a world leader in corporate copyright law – lawyers' opinions are divided on who are, or ought to be, the lawful owners of the characters in virtual game worlds (Grimes 2006). I doubt very much that the last word has been said on the subject.

Game manufacturers usually choose to strictly enforce their copyrights and prevent online auction sites from popping up, where artefacts, games, currencies, and even characters (*i.e.* accounts) are sold for real money (Grimes 2006). However, the success of the game manufacturers has been mixed, as there will always be unscrupulous sites where such trade continues to flourish. One phenomenon where many players seem to support the strict enforcement of the game manufacturers' copyrights is 'gold farming' (sometimes referred to as *Chinese farming*). In many of these games, it takes considerable time to play and develop a character, time that middle-class players in the Western world do not always have or do not want to spend to gain success. This creates the prerequisites for a lucrative market in which players are prepared to pay hard cash for pots of game gold or ready-made high-level characters in order to progress faster in the game. As a result, there are companies in, for example, China (hence, *Chinese farmers*) in which organised groups of employees take turns playing the same game character over the course of 12-hour shifts for the purpose of simply collecting as much gold as possible, which is then sold via various auction sites (Steinkuehler 2006). In other words, these are professional players whose job is to play. Depending on your opinion of this phenomenon, and whether or not you are part of the value chain, these organisations are called either *virtual sweatshops* or sometimes the slightly nicer term *mining studios*. However, the estimated salary of those working in these organisations is relatively high in comparison with the average salary in China (Steinkuehler 2006).

The phenomenon has led to strong reactions from the gaming communities because, as they see it, it ruins the entire concept of gaming and contravenes the established norms of play. Apart from the ethical problems and the injustice perceived by serious players who have invested a lot of time into developing their characters, the gold farm industry also helps create imbalances in the game, ruining the gameplay experience of ordinary players as well. Players of games such as *Lineage 2* and wow have been known to organise themselves into groups, a kind of virtual posse, with the aim of 'farming' the farmers. That is to say, large groups of players set about, in an organised manner, to attack and kill those players they think are gold farmers (Steinkuehler 2006; Taylor 2006b).

Although these posses illustrate how game communities can stand up to what many see as unethical and game-destroying behaviour, the other side of the coin is equally alarming (Steinkuehler 2006; Taylor 2006b). If your English language skills are fairly poor and you are hunting in certain areas, you risk being taken for a Chinese gold farmer, regardless of your ethnic origin. Moreover, it is not just players from China who are guilty of gold farming and *real money trade* (RMT) – far from it. However, this type of game behaviour can become linked to ethnicity, reinforcing the prejudice that already exists between, for example, Americans and Western Europeans, on one hand, and the Chinese and other Asians, on the other. This type of virtual racism sometimes shows its ugly face, bringing underlying ingrained stereotypes to life – another example of how real and virtual worlds intertwine.

Gladiatus

As mentioned above, my main focus is a game called *Gladiatus*. The game is available in 30 countries, from Argentina to Vietnam, with a number of worlds (*i.e.* servers) in each country.

When playing the game, you move around in your own world or province (*i.e.* server); you are not allowed to move between provinces. Also, in order to prevent players from cheating by using 'support accounts' where, for example, one character is used to get another character more gold, only one account (*i.e.* one character) per player and province is allowed. You can, however, have multiple accounts and characters in other provinces and countries, but only one character per province.

The objective of the game, as in so many similar games, is for your character to grow and develop, *i.e.* advance in terms of character level. This is achieved by winning battles in the arenas, going on expeditions, and completing *dungeon* missions. A win in the arena is rewarded with gold and experience points. The gold is then used to pay for training or better equipment, ranging from weapons and armour (*e.g.* helmets, gloves, shields, and boots) to jewellery, food, drink, etc. These objects bring various bonuses that, in turn, can be used to improve various skills. There are also negative effects, such as other skills being impaired by the use of certain objects. It is a constant balancing act to equip your character in the best possible way so as to optimise desirable skills. A successful expedition or the completion of a dungeon mission will also result in more gold and sometimes weapons and other equipment (*drops*). The higher the level of the monsters you defeat, the greater the reward.

Gladiatus can be played by single players, although many players choose to belong to a guild. There is safety in numbers, as the saying goes, in this type of game. There are many advantages to being a guild member. One such advantage is that you can get a lot of help and advice from other more experienced players. Another is the training. As a guild member, you can build and upgrade buildings, which makes the training cheaper and the healing more effective, etc. The social aspect of guild membership is also important. In addition, each guild has an internal market where you can sell and buy equipment from other guild members, usually at a much better price than on the open market. However, the internal market is primarily used for packing gold, a central component of the game. You pack gold for the purpose of losing as little gold as possible if someone attacks you in one of the arenas and you lose the fight. If you lose a battle, your winning opponent is entitled to a certain percentage of the gold owned by your character (around 10 per cent). You can see how much gold you have lost in the relatively large amount of statistics available for each character.

There are also leaderboards where players are ranked according to ability. This allows you to quickly see which player is the best in a certain category (*e.g.* level, honour, fame, winnings, achievements, and looted gold). The leaderboard listings can also be filtered by category so that you can see how well you are doing in comparison with other players. Another similar posting of statistics from the past seven days can be used to quickly find out who is currently ranked the best player. By filtering the seven-day list down to the category of looted gold, you can also find out which opponent you should attack next. Players who have recently been very active and looted the most gold are possibly your next looting victims should you manage to win in the arena.

Apart from achieving higher status, losing as little gold as possible (and, of course, looting as much gold as possible) also signals to other players that you are in control and probably an experienced player. High-status players should be avoided when you search for your next victim in the arena. Instead, you should target players with a history of losing gold who are clearly weaker than yourself. Keeping track of your own gold is a good long-term strategy if you want to avoid becoming the target of other players. Another more experienced player once advised me that to maintain the image of a player who has everything under control, I should, after losing a battle and a large amount of gold in the arena, immediately message the winner congratulating him or her with something along the lines of: '*You were lucky! The gold was only out for a few seconds when I was about to go training ...* ☺.' I now follow this advice (as do others who have fallen victim to my own looting). And we all try to pretend that it was just a one-off looting: '*There is no gold to loot here.*'

Packing gold means buying useless things (*e.g.* jewellery at a lower level) for a lot of money. To cover the gold packing requirements of major and minor characters in the guild, different denominations can be used for buying jewellery. Once you have bought a piece of jewellery, you offer it on the market again for the same asking price. You get your money back as soon as another guild member buys the jewellery. The money is then 'packed' and can be placed in the backpack of your character. Once the money is in the backpack, it cannot be looted by others should you lose a battle in one of the arenas. Hence, you keep packing your gold. A rather irritating occurrence is when guild members fail to correctly pack their gold (*e.g.* forget to put the jewellery back on the market, do so for less than the stipulated 24 hours, or attach the wrong price tag). It is very important that new guild members be taught the ins and outs of the packing system, since it is vital that this work properly and that jewellery be constantly in circulation.

When you want to go training or buy something from the auction house (*i.e.* one of the open markets available to all players on the server), you must once again redeem the money, *i.e.* move the gold from the backpack to the pockets of your character. This is one of the times when you are most vulnerable to attacks. You must also keep an eye on the time. The packed gold must be used within seven days or it will automatically be redeemed and put back into the pockets of your character where it is at significant risk of being looted. Therefore, if you are inactive for more than seven days, you must log in and re-pack from time to time or give a so-called sitter authorisation to log into your account and look after your character for a limited period of time. However, such authorisation must be approved in advance by the game administrators.

Battles are carried out by the simple click of a button. Straightforward one-on-one battles are decided by damage points and the amount of gold looted. The player who causes the most damage wins, unless one player's health level drops to zero, as a result of which that player will lose, despite having possibly caused more damage than did the opponent. There is also a battlelog where players can check the results of different battle rounds, for example, what damage was caused by whom and the number of unsuccessful attacks (and successful defences). A more extensive battlelog covering additional rounds is generated in conjunction with complex battles in the Turma arena (where you battle with troops of four) and in conjunction with fights against a monster (especially dungeon bosses). Based on these logs, you can decide whether or not you ought to change tactics and/or upgrade some of the weapons and combat gear you are using. However, the battlelogs are not entirely intuitive and you have to learn how to interpret them through personal experience and advice from other more seasoned players.

When it comes to launching an attack on another player, there are restrictions on how weak a player can be for you to be allowed to attack him or her. Gold can only be won in attacks on players who are in the same arena league as yourself. Levels 1–10 constitute one league, levels 11–20 another, and so on. There are also rules governing *bashing*, which is when you attack a player at a level well below you. If you bash another player more than once during a 24-hour period and this is reported to the game administrators, you will be banned from playing the game. The length of your ban depends on whether you have violated this or similar game rules before. In the worst-case scenario, you could be banned forever. Another form of bashing is when you attack an opponent in your own league more than five times during a 24-hour period. Thus, there are rules on who you can attack and how often. The only exception to the rule is during a state of war: no bashing rules apply when you are at war with another guild and you can attack or hit members of the opposing guild as often as you like. However, a restriction is built into the game that cannot be bypassed: an attack is always followed by a grace period of one hour during which no further attacks can be launched on that player in the arena. The grace period is often used to protect one's own gold. A common tactic is when you launch 'friendly' attacks on members of your own guild. These attacks are often 'naked', *i.e.* with all weapons removed in order to avoid losing much health. Another advantage of 'naked' fights is that they usually end in a draw, which looks better in the statistics. This is particularly important for some players. After a friendly attack, you are protected in the arena for one hour, allowing you to quietly unpack your gold for the purpose of training or trading. This is an example of players creatively applying a game rule in a way that was not initially conceived by the game's designers.

There are similar examples of players creating new strategies for how, without violating any rules, best to play the game within the terms and conditions stipulated by the game's designers. Another example of this is the packing system used by players to protect their gold through the internal guild market, which is a play-generated solution to the perceived problem of how best to protect one's gold. There are other ways in which to pack gold, for example, by buying worthless jewellery at an auction house (worthless in that it is not especially attractive or useful – nothing that people would normally want to bid on at an auction – merely serving the purpose of improving a player's chances in the arena). However, this jewellery is worth its weight in gold and is usually the preferred category of objects that players bid on at an auction. It is widely recognised that if a piece of jewellery is priced at no less than 42 rubies then you will, if and when required, get your money back in gold when you sell the jewellery to a trader. As long as the piece of jewellery is in your backpack, your money is safe and no gold can be lost.

Defeating other players, non-player characters, and monsters will give you gold and experience points so that your character can grow and obtain more health points (and, as a result, take even more of a beating in the arena). As a new player, 'levelling' goes pretty fast, but the higher the level you attain, the longer it takes to advance further. However, climbing levels does not automatically mean that you become a better fighter in the arena. This requires training, which costs gold. The skills that you can train and improve on include strength, agility, ability, constitution, charisma, and intelligence. Also, the more you train a specific skill, the more expensive the training becomes. The type of skills you possess will have an effect on various aspects of the game and on your chances of winning a battle, whether as a defender or attacker. The standard advice to all new players was previously to invest as much as possible in training your charisma, as this would increase your chance of a critical hit and thus your chance of winning. However, following a major upgrade and rebalancing of the game, training charisma became less crucial while training other skills gained in importance.

This and previous upgrades were points for discussion, particularly among the more experienced players, and nearly always subject to criticism. The reason for the criticism is that the range of strengths of different players has decreased. New weapons and types of equipment were introduced in addition to new skill bonuses, which are more in line with the current game balance. This has meant that players must effectively start from the beginning and rebuild their characters in terms of training and equipment. My own character had pretty much everything a character could ask for at his level, but I had to sell most of his old equipment and look for new.

It is understandable that the game manufacturer would want to attract new players (preferably paying ones) by constantly developing the game and reducing the differences between seasoned and new players, to induce new players to stay with the game. New players will likely be more inclined to continue playing the game if they see that it could be possible to reach the same levels as the more seasoned players. However, the risk is that the older players may leave the game if the game's rules (and therefore balance) are changed too much. In fact, this is exactly what has happened. There is constantly a potential conflict between how the game manufacturer would like the game to develop and how the players (especially the more experienced ones) would like to reap the benefits of the time invested in the game and in their own characters.

The problem is, however, that the equipment you need is not always that easily obtained. It is not just a matter of having enough gold to afford the purchase; rather, there is very limited availability. Occasionally, you have the opportunity to buy a sought-after weapon or other objects at the auction house (one of two open markets). The auction house is regularly updated with new products at different intervals throughout the day and night (to make it more difficult to predict when the current auction ends and the next one begins). Once a desirable object becomes available, it can be bought by only one player. The player making the highest bid gets the object once the auction ends. One way of avoiding the bidding and the risk of not getting the object you want is to use *rubies,* which you can buy in the game using *real money*. Another way of acquiring the object of your desire is to win it as a reward for defeating a monster in what are known as *drops* – although these are fairly rare. Drops are awarded all the time, but usually not for the most sought-after objects. Most of the drops are sold to the merchant for gold.

The game is free to play, but there is a catch: you will level up and become successful much faster if you buy rubies. You can use your rubies to gain a number of advantages over those players who never pay for anything. For example, you can get various kinds of blessings that will cause greater damage and improve your performance in arena battles. There is also the added advantage of being able to buy objects outside the auction house bidding, which guarantees that you will be able to get certain very desirable weapons or equipment. When using rubies to pay for a certain object, you are guaranteed to get the object immediately without having to wait until the auction ends. You also have the option of buying more than one of the desirable objects (at the cost of additional gold and rubies, of course). As with similar games, time is crucial for success (whether using rubies or not). To reach the higher levels (accumulating experience and skill), you must not only invest a lot of your time, you must also do a lot of training, for which gold is needed. You have to spend much of your time online waiting for desirable objects to become available at the auction house, which occurs randomly and infrequently. Time is of the essence.

Keeping up the morale

The disappointment is immediate: 'What!? There was no battle, nothing happened! Is that character you, Dad?', says Benjamin, pointing at the image of my character. It is not long before I am left alone in front of the computer. My game did not make much of an impression on a nine-year-old boy whose own computer games offer so much more in the way of colours, animation, hustle, and excitement (*i.e.* blood).

For my own part, I barely notice that Benjamin is leaving me while I read the message that I have just posted in the guild chat. This will hopefully teach our less experienced players in the guild to pack their gold better and that it is always good to keep up the activity with a few competitions, I think to myself, while quickly reading through my message:

****COMPETITION!!!!****

A competition open to both our guilds starts now. This partly a defensive competition, the purpose of which is to lose as little gold as possible for a period of one week. Fantastic prizes await the three best performing players!

However, it is important to remain active, you must not be idle.

The competition has taken some inspiration from the game of poker. To participate in this competition, you must either loot pairs of numbers (for a double-digit result), such as 11, 22, 33, or double pairs (two of a kind) of numbers, such as 1122, 1133, 2244, or triple numbers (three of a kind), such as 111, 222, 333, or quadruple numbers (four of a kind), such as 1111, 2222, 3333.

A three-digit result can also be made up of sequential numbers (a straight) such as: 123, 234, 345, and so on (or 1234, 2345, and so on). The numbers must be sequential, so 1235 is not a valid number for participating in the competition.

The competition rewards those who are active and protect their gold well – two crucial factors in the game of Gladiatus.

Mail me in-game once you have achieved the correct poker result. The competition ends at 00:00 on Saturday the 22nd of May.

Good luck!

During this period, there were two minor guilds – or farm guilds – in which less experienced players at lower levels could grow and progress within the guild structure: first to the mid-level guild, *Centurion-Progressus*, and then to *Centurion-Primus*, the main guild. The idea was for the players to learn the game and develop and grow before advancing further. Moreover, it was a way of ensuring that players recruited to the main guild had the experience required as well as the ambition to remain active players. Many players start the game with a lot of enthusiasm and energy and spend a lot of time playing. However, they soon get bored and stop playing, either completely or partially. These players are largely sorted out by the system of farm guilds. It was also a good way to test new members, whose characters admittedly had the right amount of experience but were less known. New members always have to start in one of the lower guilds before being allowed to move up. A new member completely unknown to the guild and with no one to vouch for him or her would usually stay a little longer in one of the lower guilds until it could be established whether he or she was a good match for the guild community.

The main reason why we started the farm guild system was that the original founder and master of our guild – *Caesar* – following negotiations with the guild master of another large and well-established guild on the same server – *Slayers of Thunder* – had agreed to a merger between the two guilds. Our ambition of becoming the largest guild on the server led to our entering into a merger agreement. As a result, we had too many players. Making room for everyone in our guild (which then only had 38 membership positions, all of which were filled) was impossible. Increasing the maximum number of members would entail upgrading the guild in several stages at a very high cost in gold. Consequently, it was decided that the most experienced players should move to *Centurion*, which changed its name to *Centurion-Primus*. At the same time, *Slayers of Thunder* changed its name to *Centurion-Progressus* and became the guild for the medium-level players. It was also decided that another lower-level guild should be created, *Centurion-Novice*, for newly recruited and inexperienced members.

The guild masters of all lower-level guilds were fairly experienced players, though not the most experienced ones, who prefered not to leave the main guild for missions elsewhere. However, the more experienced players from the main guild visited the lower-level guilds to help out with gold, tips, and advice. In conjunction with establishing new guilds, I was asked if I wanted to become the master of the mid-level guild – Progressus – which I accepted (happily unaware of the extra time this would involve).

Following the merger, the idea of using the farm guilds to develop and produce good and active players began to take shape. What constituted a good player was not defined at the time, but having been an active member and player for quite a while, I had gained a fairly coherent sense of what a good player was through various discussions and events. A good player is first and foremost someone who is active and plays often. Because how much time you spend playing the game is important, a good player is also someone who has experience and plays at a *high level*. However, there is more to the game than just character level. To have a chance of winning in the arenas over other players and of defeating monsters and bosses that are at a higher level than yourself, your character needs to be well trained in important dimensions (*e.g.* charisma, skill, agility, and strength) that command respect. Most important is your level of activity: players who have been out of the game for a long period of time are usually kicked out of the guild to make room for new, active players. As time went by and some original members stopped playing, the level of activity started to become even more important than the level of the character. The social dimension of the game should not be underestimated. It is more fun to play when multiple players are logged in, actively engaging in various discussions in the guild chat.

To develop players, more formalised attempts were later made to create a certain culture of and identification with the guild. Some guild masters took the opportunity to role play by communicating the values of the guild through narratives using Latin terminology and more or less ahistorical references to the Roman Empire and gladiators, to emphasise values and behaviour befitting a member of Centurion. For the most part these values and expectations were implicitly communicated through leading by example and communicated in smaller discussions advising less experienced players on how best to develop their character and what tactics to use. At one point it was decided to more formally communicate these values that had been established in the guild over time. The following message was posted in Vox Logus – where permanent messages are posted:

To have a chance of levelling up to Centurion-Primus, you must clearly demonstrate that you possess the qualities that we in this brother/sisterhood value the most:

- Loyalty
- Honour
- Bravery
- Glory

Hence, you are expected to stand up for your guild at all times. If you have armour or weapons that you do not need yourself (and do not want to sell on the market), you can offer these to your guild comrades for a friendship discount. Or you can put them into the guild warehouse for anyone to help themselves to for free. While trying to improve your own gladiator through training and adding equipment, you should also try to help other members of the guild, as this will benefit not only you but the entire guild.

There is a lot of experience in the our guild, so make sure you take advantage of it. Learn from the experience of others and you will get better faster. If you have any questions about the tactics used in Circus Turma or the dungeons and arenas, please feel free to ask. Also, be sure to read Vox Logus where you can pick up a lot of tips and advice. We all listen to one another, regardless of character level and experience. Your opinions, ideas, and participation in discussions are vital for the future of our guild. Also make sure you keep yourself up to date by reading guild messages and messages in Vox Logus. And last but not least – do not forget to have fun!

Always try to behave respectfully towards other players inside and outside our guild, though this is often easier said than done when everyone's emotions begin to flow. However, try to maintain straightforward and polite communication, even with your worst 'enemies'. Please contact the guild administrator if an individual player is causing you problems.

The descriptions above are meant to give a little bit more 'flesh and blood' to the qualities that we value in the guild. Before you can level up to Primus, you must prove that you have the characteristics described above and have reached the highest level in Progressus and at least defeated the boss Frank N. Stein in the dungeons. You must also be an active player. Once the requirements above are met, you will be moved up to the main guild – Primus – as soon as a member-ship position becomes available.

Some of the values considered important by the guild, and that also consti-tute key norms in the game community as a whole, are highlighted here. In other words, making contributions, being active (and preferably socia-ble too), and treating other guild members and opponents with courtesy. The last value is of particular importance to the lower-level guilds and is handled through the appointment of diplomats among the leaders of each guild. It is their responsibility to communicate with representatives of other guilds, if and when required. The main reason for this is to avoid a war, often instigated by member players behaving badly towards play-ers from other guilds, whether in words, deeds, or both. These values are fairly similar to those seen in guilds in other games (Taylor 2006c), where values such as trust and responsibility are highly regarded.

Playing seriously

What type of leadership is it that I and other leaders in the guild's man-agement team try to enact in the game of Gladiatus? Does it have any bearing on what we usually refer to as reality? Jonas Thente, journalist at the Swedish newspaper *Dagens Nyheter*, seem to suggest that it has everything to do with what happens in real life:

> These days – at least in the US – being the leader of a guild in an
> MMORPG is often mentioned in people's CVs when applying for a
> job. It is considered to be a truly excellent experience. Personally,
> I cannot think of more valid experience than having successfully
> managed and led a guild in World of Warcraft or any other of the
> role-playing games currently available. I would even go as far as
> saying that it beats more than a thousand years of studying at the
> Stockholm School of Economics. (Thente 2010)

I am probably not quite as inclined to dismiss practical work experience
and education in favour of computer game experience. However, Jonas
Thente has a point and is not alone in this opinion.

At first glance, the leadership of a guild seems more bureaucratic and
formalised than expected. The only communication is in writing and
important rules and policies are documented just as in any other bureaucracy. This is of course not the way things really work. As in other 'real'
organisations, the informal work, *i.e.* what one actually does, is usually
different from what one ought to be doing according to the more formal
rules and regulations.

As demonstrated by a number of organisational researchers, it is
difficult to lead on the basis of rules alone, so more emphasis ought to
be put on the role of the informal organisation (alongside the formal).
This does not, however, hinder attempts to organise or rationalise – on
the contrary. It is easy to be drawn into and captured by this desire
to formalise things, especially when you yourself, in your capacity
as a guild master or leader, try to drive the development forward. At
the same time, it is surprisingly difficult to get everyone to follow, or
perhaps even understand, even the simplest rules. Communication is
difficult. Despite the fact that I, as an organisational researcher, am well
aware of the loose coupling between the formal organisation and the
informal one – between what you say that you do and how you actually
behave – I still end up having functionalist thoughts about the best way
to effectively improve the formal organisation. Even a somewhat jaded
organisational researchers like yours truly have often been captured by
this strong desire to formalise processes in the guild: Surely, we should
be able to control this better? Is it not possible to standardise this process
to ensure that we all do the same thing? This could be improved if only
we had certain criteria in place ...

What struck me when I began thinking about leadership in multiplayer online games, in this case, Gladiatus, was their many similarities

with actual real-life organisations. Many of the ideas about leadership and organisation in Gladiatus seem to have become institutionalised (*i.e.* taken for granted), giving rise to similar activities in different guilds and being seen as the obvious way to organise a guild (at least by those in the management team). Work tasks are allocated, various leadership roles, criteria, rules, titles are defined, and reward systems are instituted – just as in any other modern organisation. Different leadership functions are established in a guild to meet the perceived needs of the organisation, just as in any real-life organisation, although the functions and titles may be different. Someone is responsible for recruitment, another for diplomacy and negotiations with other guilds, a third for warfare, and so on it goes. In addition, all guilds have a competition manager whose responsibility it is to organise internal competitions and games. After all, your guild members ('employees') need to be kept both motivated and happy.

Like any other online game, Gladiatus is not just about play and playfulness, it is also about the production of seriousness (Gustafsson 1994). According to Sara Grimes and Andrew Feenberg (2009), online games can be seen as:

> systems of social rationality operating within the larger sociohistorical context of modernity, and by providing a framework (ludification) for a more comprehensive exploration of the processes through which game rules become technically mediated, play practices become institutionalized, and players become rationalized (and professionalized or commodified). (p. 116)

Björn Rombach *et al.* (2005) have demonstrated that economic thinking and parlance is spreading throughout society in areas where such 'management speak' was never before heard. Gladiatus does not seem to be in any way exept from the dominance of such thinking. A number of rationalisations were taking place throughout the guilds of Gladiatus, as players were very much playing the part of being in modern organisations, especially those players in management positions. Several researchers have observed this phenomenon and argued that games could be seen as a hybrid of play and work (Rowland 2012; Vesa *et al.* 2017). It is a two-way street, however, as real-world organisations also draw on discourses and practices from the gaming world. 'Gamification' is a concept used to describe practices in real-world organisations that attempt to create the sort of enthusiasm and energy in the workplace that people have for games – in other words, attempting to disguise work as a game (Vesa *et al.* 2017).

In addition to the ongoing work on the formal organisation, attempts were also made, as we have seen, to create a guild culture. This was done both formally and informally, though perhaps mostly informally (not unlike what happens in real-life organisations). Culture evolves regardless of whether or not you try to manage it. As a new player, you quickly get to learn the essential values that characterise the game, *i.e.* what you are expected to do and not to do (much of which is not regulated by the game manufacturers themselves). Taylor (2006a, 2006b, 2006c) has often to tried to highlight the culture that develops in these game communities in an attempt to understand their worlds. Many values are common to a game as a whole, but the individual guilds hold certain specific values too. Our archenemy – *Deus* – (which we always fought for the top position among all guilds on our server) prioritised the arenas and looting gold from other players, which was obvious from its members' behaviour and was communicated on the guild's in-game page. The Deus players were also ranked among the highest when it came to looted gold, though not necessarily when it came to other categories in the ranking list (*e.g.* experience). Other guilds, like ours, tended to prioritise experience, which is used to help characters grow and develop faster (you get the most experience points from participating in expeditions and in dungeon missions, not in the arenas).

Values were generally conveyed by means of communications and examples. You always tried to lead by example in both words and deeds. The guild chat was used for communicating explicit values, while more implicit values were communicated in individual chats or by individual game mails to specific players. This type of communication was common during my time as a master of the mid-level guild, Progressus, at the same time as there was, at least initially, a clear role-playing dimension in the references, often in Latin, to the Roman Empire. This aspect of the game was important to Caesar, the founder and master of our guild. He was very happy to take on the role of Caesar and gave passionate speeches to us all, trying to get us (*i.e.* masters of the lower guilds) to communicate in a similar manner, using our Latin titles when, for example, posting a message in the chat. Once Caesar stopped playing and I was moved up to the main guild, this role-playing dimension decreased significantly. Among the more experienced players, who all know one another fairly well (some even out of play), more sociability crept into the discourse, with jokes about this and that and various mundane details from people's private lives. The game became less and less a role-playing game.

Taylor (2006b) also observed that many online games become cross-generational meeting places where older and younger people play side by side. This was also the case with Gladiatus. However, most players, as far as I could gather, were around 30 years of age or older. For example, the members of the management team that I was part of towards the end were all aged 40 years or more. Although these games are an arena in which young and old can socialise and play alongside one another, there is still a certain amount of age discrimination, which is something that Taylor (2006b) noticed. None of the Guilds that I knew of had a leader under the age of 18 years, most leaders being aged 30 or older. The younger players were normally considered too immature, and older players would sometimes joke about their youthful ignorance. However, our youngest players would occasionally go a step too far and ask to become leaders (*i.e.* become part of the management team), breaking what was generally seen as an unspoken but powerful norm. None of those who asked to become a leader ever became one.

It is not unusual for these online games to be fairly rationalised – they are, after all, both work and play (Rowlands 2012) – with certain rules and values that you are supposed to follow. In this respect, online games are no different from real-life organisations. One aspect of online games that appears to differ from real-life organisations is that their social responsiveness (Asplund 1987) is sometimes less self-regulated, as expressed in behaviours that you would not normally expect to see in a modern organisation.

These game environments create a certain type of anonymity (as seen in other social media). Here, players can have tantrums and say and do things that would not usually be accepted (or done) in public at one's workplace. You encounter more trolls and griefers in the virtual world; in real life, people try to restrain themselves. On many occasions I have found myself engaging in verbal altercations with other players (it is all too easy to get pulled into this type of social responsiveness and fight fire with fire). It often starts with someone asking why you are attacking the player in the arena, which is then followed by a number of more or less well-worded insults. The fact that the game is all about attacking one another in the arena seems to have been completely forgotten. These altercations are also expressed in other ways, such as attacks in the arena and acts of revenge, often involving other much bigger and stronger players. Once started, these situations can escalate quite quickly.

I have also seen a leader in my own guild, in full view of everyone else in the chat and after a long period of constant heated arguments and discussions with another guild member, simply kick that member out of the guild because he thought that the member was an idiot – not because the member in question had committed a disciplinary offence. This kind of action was completely against the established culture of open (and sometimes democratic) decision-making that usually characterised the leadership. As one would expect, the altercation carried on in full view of the other players had arisen from earlier less intense discussions and arguments. The players in question had disagreed on many issues before – mostly outside the game – from football teams to political views and values. The leader remained in the game, probably because the member he kicked out was not particularly liked by anyone. In this case, our guild principles counted for little.

In comparison, in games such as World of Warcraft the leadership is even more direct. A group member, for example, in a dungeon mission or a raid, who does something wrong risks being quickly kicked out of the group or, as a minimum, being severely reprimanded. Here, the game culture is communicated much more directly and you learn the hard way what cultural rules apply. For example, you are not supposed to pick up any drops (*i.e.* weapons or other equipment, which can always be exchanged for gold) from the monsters you defeat unless your character is in immediate need of them. One must not be greedy. In addition, you must make contributions that are normally operationalised and measured in *damage per second* (dps), at least for those group members whose mission it is to 'deal damage' (other roles are receiving damage – tank – and healing others). There are a number of play-generated add-ons that you can download to measure the damage and healing done (and received) in a group and to rank individual players after each battle. This allows individual players and group leaders to quickly obtain information about the individual contributions of other players. Some group leaders choose to communicate this information to everyone in the group so that any underperformers can take note and shape up. After a number of taunts, reprimands, and, at times, quick dismissals, new players soon learn how they are meant to behave in a group.

Finally, it ought to be mentioned that the leadership of online games is serious business characterised by social rationalising, not unlike the way most of today's organisations are managed and organised. It seems that the *system world* is also, to some extent, colonising this virtual world (or existence). In other words, everything remains much the same. However, the aspect of play (*e.g.* social responsiveness) is present here in a different way, under the surface of the virtual world, and sometimes manifests itself at a more emotional level. The anonymity in these games offers a quick and welcome change from an otherwise tedious way of life, allowing people to say and do things that they would never say and do unless so protected. People tend to exhibit less restrained behaviours in these virtual environments. Perhaps it is easy to forget, if only for a moment, that a virtual reprimand is still a reprimand like any other, and that behind the avatar and the user name is a complete person. If these virtual and real-life worlds were to become even more intertwined and influenced by each other, which is the trend, let us hope that some of the behaviours we see in these games is not what the future holds for us in our real and working lives.

CHAPTER 8

Leading in crisis

Iréne Lind Nilsson

Even though our everyday lives seem to plod along nicely, with the same routines day in and day out, we sometimes find ourselves in situations characterised by the complete opposite to the habitual and familiar. What might start as an ordinary day can suddenly become unexpectedly extraordinary in a stimulating or very disturbing way. What, then, is normal? For some, constantly handling unexpected events forms part of their normal routines. Leaders are probably one such group. But even for those whose everyday lives are quite unpredictable and contain much turbulence, some situations are clearly beyond the ordinary. Such situations may arise through natural disasters, armed conflicts, or terrorist attacks. They may also arise from less disastrous though still turbulent organisational events such as decommissioning processes, power struggles, media scandals or decisions to fire someone. In this chapter, I refer to these situations as crises. The examples given differ considerably from one another, depending on the character of the various incidents in the surrounding world or within the organisations. However, they all represent situations that deviate from the normal and are exhausting to handle as they cause organisational chaos and strong reactions from the people involved. My aim is to explore leadership in such extraordinary situations.

Crises and chaos

Some people occasionally choose to expose themselves to extraordinary situations incorporating elements of positive tension and excitement that other people would find unthinkable and risky. Adventurers are individuals who, based on their own drives, put themselves in extraordinary situations, such as trekking through the jungle, rock climbing, or sailing around the world. The Red Bull X-Alps is one of the toughest adventure competitions in the world (redbull.se) in which the participants must be both skilled mountaineers and paragliders. The objective of the competition is to cross the Alps in the shortest possible time, from Krippenstein in Austria to Monte Carlo, with a maximum of three hours sleep a night. Apart from a parachute, the only other aids allowed are a safety helmet, a GPS system, and three flares for possible emergencies. Such an adventure requires extreme mental and physical strength as well as an ability to be creative, as it stretches the limits of what is possible. For Göran Kropp, a Swedish mountaineer and lecturer who climbed five of the world's highest mountains (and sadly died in a climbing accident in 2002), it was all about the challenge of throwing yourself into the unknown. When actually dealing with such a situation, you can learn something about yourself and the surrounding world.

A significant change at the workplace can also lead to what might be seen as an extraordinary situation for both leaders and employees. Leaders are sometimes unwillingly drawn into these situations; sometimes they are the ones instigating them. In these situations, the fundamental human need for security and continuity is set against the organisational need for change that so often arises in conjunction with global changes (Lind Nilsson 2001; Lind Nilsson & Gustafsson 2006).

> The concept of order always seem to give us a sense of security.
> The importance of this cannot be denied. However, one of the key
> challenges in human life is to resist hegemony. Every time we fall
> victim to the principles of arrangement and its illusions of peace and
> harmony and deny or ignore the concept of chaos, we are trying to
> escape the realities and, inevitably, the uncertainties of life. Always
> with disastrous consequences. Once we start clinging to a compensa-
> tory order, we ruin all possibilities for development and deprive
> both ourselves and our society of liberty and freedom. (Wieland-
> Burston 1991, p. 13)

In this chapter I tell five stories about leadership that all involve crisis situations caused by unforeseen critical events. The first four stories derive from my dissertation (Lind 2001) and illustrate critical situations handled by a UN colonel in a war zone, an airforce commander dealing with aircraft accidents, a hotel manager handling a critical economic situation in addition to a computer sabotage, and a guest conductor who tries to lead an orchestra characterised by major conflicts and power struggles. The fifth story is taken from the autobiography of Bengt Ericson (2007) entitled *Antonias revansch* ('Antonia's revenge'). This book gives so many perspectives on critical events that it almost constitutes a summary of the entire chapter. Together, the five stories presented here are used in examining and analysing how leaders deal with crises and what they learn from this experience. I also discuss what we can learn about leadership from them.

The perspective of this chapter is that leaders are significant participants in working life, whose function (or intended function) is to act as buffers between employees, colleagues, elected officials, and administrative boards. Although some researchers distinguish between managers and leaders (*e.g.* Kotter 1988), I use these concepts synonymously as both formal and informal roles are touched upon in the stories.

UN mission in the Balkan war zone

This first story illustrates an act of war in modern times. The story was told by a Swedish colonel who, during his service with the UN, was assigned to the civil war that raged between ethnic groups in the Balkans in the 1990s. The story illustrates how the colonel and his troops found themselves in an extremely critical situation in which they risked having to use their small arms.

> They could not understand how the situation had escalated into a full-blown war. In my opinion, it was not an ethnic war but a war about power, money, and property – just like any other war. Many people could not understand how the heck they had ended up in a situation of war. It all kicked off when the leaders wanted more control and used military units – in particular, special forces and gangsters. That is how they created this war. The toughest incident took place around three weeks after we had arrived. We had positioned in a city that was Croatian and where there had been a massacre in a nearby Muslim village. Around 250–300 Muslim men had been incarcerated in a school building under conditions that were no better than a concentration camp. We tried to mediate between the two groups. The Croats were very irritable, to say the least, and their commander said that the UN should leave. But we did not

move. The question was whether to force the roadblock they had set up or not, should they decide not to let us through. In other words, whether to say 'go' or 'stop' and risk putting us all in a life-or-death situation. When you are faced with a crisis, you have to make a decision. I said, 'the UN has a clear mandate to do this, and if you so much as move, this machine gun will be used'. And it would have been used. You then fire warning shots. If you then have really motivated and self-disciplined soldiers against a bunch of poorly trained guys who lack discipline and whose motivation is questionable ... to conclude, they got scared and let us through.

Communicating is one of the hardest things to do, as words mean different things to different people. Your body language speaks more clearly but, of course, cannot be seen at a distance. There is a basic rule: your subordinates do what you do and not what you say. I took the same risks as they did. It made them think: 'What the hell ... if the old man can do it, then I can too.' I should think it is the same in any other organisation. Your body language is extremely important and, for example, your eyes. They are the only things that give you away. Your eyes say a lot. One reason for threatening to shoot in order to kill was that the Croatian commander was scared. I could see it in his eyes. He did not dare look me in my eyes. You can usually see when another person is a bit uncertain. It is also a matter of intuition. It is something in the air. I firmly believe in intuitive decisions in situations when a quick decision is needed. If you wait too long, it could be too late.

However, after two days, our units positioned in the city were ambushed and subjected to hand grenades and shelling. But as we had armoured vehicles, no one was injured. However, we decided to bring matters to a head and told the Croatian commander that 'from now on, we will shoot to kill. There will be no warning shots. A number of cars have tried to run over our patrols in the city, so I have now instructed the drivers of our tanks to run over these cars without hesitation'. 'You cannot do that', responded the Croatian commander. 'Of course I can. If you can shoot, I can shoot.' I was completely convinced that it would work but I could never be hundred per cent sure ... It was a tough ten-day period, but once we had put our cards on the table, we did not need to fire one single shot.

Yes, it is a long-term task building up your knowledge about leadership and the organisation. As a leader, you should be out in the field, motivating and communicating with your subordinates. There is no difference between military and civilian leaders. You must communicate the reasons behind your action. You may falter but then you say, 'I'm not sure what to do now, so let's have a think'. Whether in peace or in war, there will always be an infinite number of leadership situations like that, [requiring] leadership that adapts to the current situation. Sometimes, in a crisis or emergency situation, the leader has to quickly decide what to do based on his or her knowledge and experience. Then, only one person makes the decisions. In other situations, however, including war, you can allow your subordinates to get fully involved. It is the situation that determines what you say and do. Regardless of whether you are a commander or manager of an employment agency or whatever it may be. You may lose your authority if you are not knowledgeable enough, but I built up my authority in the field ... I would like to think that I have authority but I am not an autocrat. I have a solid knowledge and experience base. I know my field. It helps in getting people put their trust and belief in you, but in order to get that, you also need to listen to your subordinates. I will happily change my decision if new input values come to light. If someone says, 'this wasn't very good', then you must reconsider your decision. Failing to do so will undermine your credibility.

There are two ways of organising an army. First there is the traditional organisation with a hierarchical leadership whose main responsibilities are to prepare, plan, and organise in times of peace. In wartime, there is another, flatter type of organisation in which the leadership engages more directly with the soldiers, influencing their actions and behaviours. This type of organisation facilitates the handling of urgent situations in which those involved put their own lives at considerable risk. From a social and organisational perspective, the UN force in the above example acted along the lines of a flat organisation. The unit had the authority to take direct action in order to achieve long-term peace between the conflicting parties in the Balkans. The concrete mission implied seeing to the humanitarian aspects and concerns in order to neutralise and reduce violence among ethnic and communal groups. In this story, the mission was eventually completed although the path to achieving this was both arduous and extremely sensitive.

Reflecting on this story from the group and individual perspectives, one sees that the UN colonel immediately realised how volatile the situation was between him and the Croatian commander when meeting face to face. A critical situation like this is a matter of balancing on the line between life and death. When the UN colonel challenged the Croatian commander at the border checkpoint, the situation became very tense and almost anything could have happened. There was no time to reflect on various options. The UN colonel was forced to make a quick decision and had to rely on his intuition ('it is something in the air'), experience, and his soldiers' trust that he would make the right decision. His courage to challenge the 'enemy' was based on the strong belief that he had a mission to accomplish, *i.e.* save the incarcerated Muslims. Determination, persistence, and a clear message were the decisive factors in resolving this critical situation.

The UN colonel described the significance of words and actions interacting in situations in which your words and body language clearly communicate the message. As a result, both parties refrained from using violence. Furthermore, the UN colonel stressed the importance of knowing your own organisation, your soldiers, yourself, and the role of your leadership. He pointed out that even though he has authority, he is *not* an autocrat. The colonel further believed that the attitude and actions of a leader have a direct impact on others' reactions and actions. The leader becomes, according to the colonel, a role model for others – 'your subordinates do what you do and not what you say'.

Airforce crisis

Story number two is about the organisation of a Swedish Air Force division with around 500 employees, which, over a period of some years, was exposed to considerable stress and pressure. At the same time as this division's entire field of operation was to be decommissioned, two unexpected and inexplicable fatal accidents occurred. This is the story as told by an Air Force commander:

> Well, together with the threat of closure that was hanging over us, we had two fatal incidents, two aircraft accidents. The second one was especially chaotic. I really thought that I was completely losing my grip. You did not really know what was going on or what was going to happen. It was probably as close to chaos as you could get.

... Everyone was shocked and upset. After the first accident, we had a fairly long and drawn out crisis management. We began asking ourselves if there was anything in our operations that had led to our being in this situation. ... We held a number of meetings in which we tried to assess whether there was anything in the way we operated our aviation activities that could have led to the incidents. We had flown for 16 years without one single accident and then had two accidents in the span of only three months. And they happened in pretty much the same way. It was a real eye-opener for everyone flying at the time, especially as one of those killed was a very experienced guy. If it could happen to him, then it could happen to anyone.

In hindsight, the most important thing was that you were part of the process of handling the crisis and were kept informed. You spent time with the relatives and you also became involved at the division, when you felt it was needed. There was also the possibility of moving forward with the help of our Staff Welfare Officer. After the first accident, we quickly found out where the parents of the pilot lived and, therefore, were the first to tell them about the tragic accident and loss of their loved one. Help also came from two external professionals. It was also we who ended up giving the parents support and helping them with this and that. We were able to keep them informed and up to date on things. They seemed to have confidence in what we were doing and seemed comforted by the fact that we had been there from the start. Once again, after the second accident, we were the first on the scene, which I believe helped. The wife understood immediately what had happened, and we stayed with her throughout. We are still in contact with these people and talk to them.

When the first aircraft accident happened, the entire organisation was already in turmoil, facing decommissioning. All employees had been informed about the situation. The work on mobilising support functions, based on an already established policy for the humane handling of crisis situations, was ongoing. At the same time, the organisation was also busy participating in the rescue work with crew members and helicopters in connection with the Estonia disaster in the Baltic Sea in September 1994, in which 852 people died. Consequently, the situation was already chaotic, and with the aircraft accidents the level of crisis became extremely high. Everyone was emotionally involved and shaken. The Air Force commander said that he was almost losing his grip on the situation. At this point, the organisation drew on help from internal resources and also obtained external advice. It became extremely important for all employees to feel that they were part of the process and the information exchange. Mutual debriefing was organised at the workplace to help everyone deal with the situation and any possible issues that might arise from the effects of the accidents. When the accidents happened, the leadership focused on contacting the relatives as soon as possible and providing them with needed information and support in addition to always being there for them (also as a way of showing respect).

Computer system sabotage

The third story describes how an individual employee caused great frustration for his colleagues and manager at work. The background to this story was that when a hotel manager assumed her position, she discovered that the company was in dire straits financially. To save the company from bankruptcy, a major reorganisation was necessary in addition to dismissing a number of employees (including middle managers) from their positions. Consequently, a lot of anxiety and stress was felt in the workplace, with most personnel, including the new manager, being shocked at the poor financial state of the company. No one had been made aware of the situation while the former manager (who had resigned with only one day's notice after a disagreement with the Board) was still in charge:

> There were days when you were wondering what you were doing. Why go to work? To sit and tell people of your own age that they no longer have jobs. It is terrible really. It sometimes felt as if I was entering enemy country when I walked into the office in the mornings.

Having to inform everyone of forthcoming redundancies was not the easiest of situations for the hotel manager to handle. Nor was it very easy for her to anticipate and deal with the different reactions of people when there was more than one critical situation in the organisation at the same time. It was apparent that a constructive solution was crucial:

> Perhaps I should not have suggested a reorganisation as soon as I did and instead, listened more to the others ... and got them involved.

But I was obsessed with the thought of trying to save the company from bankruptcy. I saw it as my duty.

When information about possible forthcoming redundancies reached all the employees, just as the summer holidays were about to start, the following happened:

One of our employees, a salesman, was dismissed from his job. The same employee then proceeded to destroy our entire computer system, records and everything. This happened in the summer, when a lot of people were away. He erased everything. He then sent a letter to all our customers, saying that the new manager was dismissing a lot of people. He advised them not to have anything to do with us. He also told them that, as a result, the quality of our services would suffer, that he had no confidence in the new management, and that some of the middle management had been asked to leave, too. One of our receptionists showed me the letter. By that time, however, the letter had already been sent out. There was nothing you could do. What happened next was that I managed to get the support of some of my staff, since those who were still employed felt that the salesman had let them down too. Some of our customers wondered what was going on ... but most of them did not react much to the letter. I do not think that the salesman in question was very well known to our customers. Understandably, he was very angry about the situation he had found himself in. I was obviously very upset, but somehow I think the rest of the staff was even more upset. I do not think that the salesman had planned on that effect as a result. Our only alternative ... he lost in court ... was to take his holiday pay as compensation for the damage caused.

Erasing all the data could be deemed an expression of despair as well as 'punishment' of the main 'culprit' – in this case, the new manager. It is difficult to determine exactly the reason for the conduct of the salesman. Perhaps the manager in this example had failed to follow up on how this particular employee reacted to the new situation. The manager, on the other hand, said that she fully understood and sympathised with the desperate measures taken by the employee who, in the end, was the one who lost out, not the company.

Reflecting on the situation, the manager said she learned that it is important to keep employees informed about various problems facing the company. Here, this meant the difficult financial situation of the company, which no one initially believed due to the lack of communication from the former manager. The alternative, she argued, would have been to put the company into bankruptcy, which would have led to all employees losing their jobs.

A conflict in the orchestra

The fourth story describes the experiences of a guest conductor working with an orchestra in preparation for a concert. This story incorporates a number of strange behaviours, both in the group as a whole and among the individuals with whom the guest conductor rehearsed many times. The situation is illustrative of a complex and collaborative project that, at best, could have been characterised by driving forces such as professionalism, job satisfaction, and a common goal (*i.e.* the concert performance). The story raises questions about conscious and unconscious behaviours, power struggles, ethics, and attitudes.

> I can tell you about the worst 'hit the wall' experience that I have ever had with an orchestra when rehearsing for a concert. The rehearsal hall was absolutely freezing. I kept working and gave all I had but got nothing back in return. As soon as I opened my mouth, the concertmaster looked at me as if I was a complete idiot. Or he did not look at me at all – just across the hall while sighing. I had never before heard so much sighing in an orchestra. Even at the actual concert, I only felt a musical connection with perhaps five or six of the 45 musicians in the orchestra. I lay sleepless the entire first night of the rehearsal week, going through my work in detail, what I had done and said, and how I had behaved. I actually had to tell myself that this was not my problem. It was the orchestra's problem. This was confirmed to me the following day when a soloist, a very fine musician, told me exactly the same thing. We got to talking about it over lunch. I approached the subject very carefully, as it would not have been correct if the conductor was found talking behind the back of the orchestra. I asked him how he felt, and he then told me that they were not cooperating with him either. I have since met other people who have had the same experience with this orchestra, which made them feel really bad.

In retrospect, I have also learned that the orchestra was not at all happy with their orchestra manager, an administrative manager, who did not have the ability to make people feel comfortable about themselves. In addition, the chief conductor also seemed to have failed in his role, seeing as the musicians were apparently unable to cooperate or play in tune together. They did not listen to each other. I could feel this from where I was standing. There were nasty glances, especially between the concertmaster and the first oboist – yes, that is how it was. When the concertmaster started on his piece, which admittedly did not sound that brilliant, I saw how the first oboist made a sign. I had never before seen or experienced this in an orchestra, such disloyalty to your colleagues. Another man, who had probably been a member of the orchestra for at least 30 years, was constantly joking, whereupon the others would sigh. He had probably been telling the same jokes for the past 20 years. The first trumpeter suddenly said something out loud and everyone laughed. Except for myself, who did not understand what it was about. It was truly odd, but I decided there and then that this was not my problem and I was going to do the best I could with the music. I made sure that they played together and had a great time with the soloist. I guess that is what saved my week, that I got to make great music with him.

As for the rest, I felt very sorry for the orchestra. I thought a lot about them afterwards, that I did not take the opportunity. ... As a guest conductor, I am only responsible for the music that is going to be performed. I do not have to take responsibility for how the orchestra is feeling. The orchestra manager once asked me how things were going. 'Good', I replied, but I should have told him the truth, and asked him, 'What type of orchestra do you have?' Go on a course, go to therapy together, do something ... I could have told him how I felt about the orchestra, but he would probably have responded, 'It depends on who is standing in front of it'. Later on, I met someone who asked me how much I, the conductor, should have to put up with and compromise. Could you not have said that, unfortunately, we cannot work together and just have cancelled the concert? Perhaps, I could have told them off: 'What are you doing? Are we going to play music or not?' But, I think that would have made them feel as if under attack. Then again, perhaps one of them would have taken note of what I said. There were actually a few people in the orchestra with whom I had a very good musical connection. They would probably have confirmed what they had known and felt for a long time – that there was something not quite right with the orchestra. Well, I am not so sure. Anyhow, it affects me very badly if I feel that there is a lack of trust or confidence in me – then you end up feeling very lonely indeed.

The guest conductor described this situation as one of the worst 'hit the wall' experiences ever encountered in her professional life. She described the 'iciness' that she felt in the rehearsal hall and how some members of the orchestra behaved in strange ways. Despite working extremely hard and giving everything, she believed that she got little in response from the musicians. Some of the orchestra members behaved in a disloyal and arrogant manner. Later on, this behaviour was also confirmed by other people.

The guest conductor concluded that her unpleasant experience was a manifestation of internal problems that existed within the orchestra and that all she could do was to get on with her job and complete the assignment to the best of her ability. Her salvation was to make music with a great soloist who also happened to be a very nice person. The guest conductor felt sorry for the orchestra and wondered if she could have handled the situation differently, perhaps by talking to them openly about it. However, she did not feel that the orchestra members trusted her, nor that there was enough time. She could only speculate about what would have happened had she tried to be more open with the players.

From crisis to success

The fifth and final story is a synopsis of the book *Antonias revansch* ('Antonia's revenge') (Bengt Ericson 2007). This book describes a number of critical events over ten years in the life of a family-owned company, highlighting the experiences of a leader at a high management level. The story offers a variety of perspectives on difficult situations and strikes a responsive chord in most leaders.

According to the book, one leader who experienced a great many extraordinarily stressful situations and crises was Antonia Ax:son Johnson (hereinafter, 'Antonia'). In the 1980s, the family-owned Johnson Company was divided into two: first, the industrial company Nordstjernan, of which

Antonia was a partner and, second, the Axel Johnson Group, focusing on international trade, of which Antonia was the sole proprietor.

At the time, there were internal frictions within the Group stemming from declining markets in steel, shipping, and fabrication. When Antonia's father suffered a stroke and consequently became less involved in the family business, it was Bo Ax:son Johnson, the younger brother of her father and newly elected chair of the family foundation, who acquired the greatest influence. One day, Antonia found herself excluded from a general meeting in Nordstjernan. The first crisis that Antonia had to face was exclusion that etched into her mind:

> The telephone rang. It was my uncle informing me that there was going to be a shareholders' meeting at Johnson Line that same day. And then he went straight to the point: 'I do not think you should attend the meeting', he said. It came as a complete shock, to be excluded like that. I had been brought up and trained to become one of the owners, to act as a bridge between the two family-owned groups. Instead, I was displaced. (Ericson 2007, p. 73)

Many of the critical situations that ensued derived from, among other things, conflicts of interest and the future distribution of power and ownership in the family group. The Axel Johnson Group was facing a tough transition period during which businesses were to be bought and sold, expanded or scaled down. Bo Ax:son Johnson argued that it was impossible for Antonia to serve on two boards at the same time, seeing as some companies were in competition with each other after the division. 'It was an extremely difficult time in my life', Antonia remembered:

> Both Göran (managing director of the Axel Johnson Group) and I were, at the time, going through difficult divorces. My father was ill and wheelchair bound. Then my mother suffered a stroke too, which led to aphasia. At home, my teenage kids were slamming the doors. At the personal level, everything was total chaos – and at the professional level, there was this constant and tiresome fighting with Nordstjernan. It was as if everything around me had just fallen apart. (Ericson 2007, p. 47)

During the banking crisis of the 1990s, the Axel Johnson Group came very close to being declared bankrupt and having to carve up its companies, as a consequence of the liquidity and confidence crises that arose between it and Skandinaviska Enskilda Banken (SEB). Antonia risked losing the entire Swedish side of the group:

> There were many times when I had my heart in my mouth, petrified of losing everything … it was like a constant near-death experience over a period of several years. … Could I live with a bankruptcy? (Ericson 2007, p. 123)

However, the mass closure anticipated for the Axel Johnson Group never happened. Thanks to successful mergers with other companies and developments resulting in the stabilisation of operations, the worst of the crisis was finally over. Antonia recalled the time:

> It was a fantastic feeling. … All these problems, year in and year out – and then, finally, it turned around! Everything was working and the companies seemed to be doing fine. It was just wonderful. (Ericson 2007, p. 123)

When asked what she had learned from these difficult years, Antonia mentioned, 'never again to be indebted or put all my eggs in one basket. … The greatest reward is that the companies are doing well again':

> It is always easy to be wise in hindsight, but I am actually glad to have had this period of crisis. It has made me a more skilful businesswoman and a stronger human being. I have asked other business leaders, 'Have you ever felt as if danger is breathing down your neck? As if you could be destroyed by fear?' They said, 'No, the only thing that could happen is that I would lose my job'. But for me, the feeling of danger was very real and tangible. In such situations, the question of the meaning of life is truly brought to a head – what is important and what is not so important in life? (Ericson 2007, p. 231)

The above quotations give us insight into Antonia's personal feelings and reactions, which probably only her dearest friends and closest collaborators were allowed to see during those critical years. Her feelings were of shock, fear, and danger against a background of conflicts of interest, agonising quarrels, power struggles, and threats of bankruptcy. Consequently, it was a huge relief for Antonia when the family business could be saved after years of internal conflict and crisis. She believed that her role as a leader became much clearer to her during the turmoil she had to endure, both as a company leader and as a human being. Her beacon of hope in this time of turmoil was to make long-term plans and never give up.

Antonia believed that reorganising the management teams and recruiting new people with similar corporate values and a similar business approach played a key role in the company's recovery. The employees turned out to be significant contributors in analysing the crisis situations, which greatly influenced Antonia's decision-making process. The more tangible and visible activities, however, included selling the worst-performing companies, creating mergers, and developing profit-making activities. Antonia took a lot of initiative in order to influence this development and ultimately came to wield more power and authority than she had in the initial stages. Today, she is the Board Chair of the family-owned group of companies, and confirms that the crisis definitely made her a more skilful businesswoman and a stronger human being.

Attitudes and strategies in crises

The organisations featured in the above cases differ greatly from one another, being characterised by a wide range of activities, assignments, and responsibilities. The extraordinary situations in which the protagonists of these stories found themselves also differed greatly, depending on both exogenous and endogenous factors. However, a common denominator is a complicated course of events that was difficult to deal with, largely because there were no predetermined solutions to the problems encountered. Many people were involved and their reactions were unpredictable, as was the course of events as a whole.

The story of the UN mission involved a face-to-face confrontation between the UN colonel and the Croatian commander, which in the worst case could have led to acts of violence. As such, it was a highly critical event. The colonel's strategy was to act immediately and to believe in his mission. The psychological advantage that the UN colonel felt he had over the Croatian commander made him trust his own intuition. The UN colonel did not see himself as an autocrat, though he believed that he was *authoritative*. For him this meant a role based on well-structured social relationships and a degree of influence acceptable to his subordinates. Being authoritative means (according to Weber 1964; Adorno *et al.* 1950) having social relationships and a degree of influence in one's legitimate professional role that others perceive as rightful. The UN colonel relied on his experience and on his soldiers' confidence in him. In addition, he stressed the importance of verbal expressions, body language, and actions being consistent in order for leaders to be perceived as credible and trustworthy in their communications.

In the case of the Swedish Air Force division, the decommissioning was itself a turbulent process, but the two air accidents represented an entirely different sort of crisis. They were acute events that had to be handled immediately. The story gives us insight into the turmoil and the emotional state in which the leaders, employees, and relatives of those killed in the accidents found themselves. The strategy adopted by the Air Force commander entailed managing the critical events based on established principles of crisis management.

Crisis management theory (Cullberg 1992) describes how people react and cope in crisis situations. According to this theory, a crisis can be described as a process consisting of four phases: shock, reaction, processing, and reorientation. The initial shock phase can last for a few moments or up to a week. The reaction phase may last for a few weeks and is usually characterised by strong emotional reactions. The processing phase lasts for at least a year and constitutes the initial acceptance of the new situation. Finally, the reorientation phase leads to clarity and to the will and strength to live on with the knowledge of what has happened.

These phases should not be seen as entirely distinct from one another but as interrelated and overlapping, sometimes evoking a sense of 'taking two steps forward and one step back'. In the story of the Air Force division, there was clear awareness of this, particularly when it came to internal crisis management. For the Air Force commander, the most significant symbolic act throughout the crisis, when everyone was in a state of shock, was to be the first person to contact and tell the relatives of those killed about the accidents: to him, this was about showing respect.

The 'debriefing' mentioned in the story was how the organisation chose to deal with the accidents, through 'a sort of psychological analysis of events' carried out in organised group talks with the aim of reducing the emotional stress felt by everyone. The idea was to strengthen the group's solidarity and potential to work together in the future without seeking a 'scapegoat'. Furthermore, the debriefing provided a basic understanding of the reactions that could be expected in such a critical and tragic situation, which in turn, reduced the risk of adverse reactions among those participating in the talks. The conduct of the entire division displayed compassion and empathic ability; as a result, the Air Force commander, employees, and relatives stayed in touch for a long time after the accidents.

The story of the Axel Johnson Group describes how the company had fallen on bad times with the risk of going into liquidation and being declared bankrupt. In addition, Antonia's role as a business leader was jeopardised. An ensuing power struggle in the family group of companies turned out to be a very lengthy process. It included all of the phases described in crisis management theory (Cullberg 1992), and in Antonia's case the phases were clearly overlapping, partly because there were multiple crises in the story. Much of the 'debriefing' appears in this case to have been related to the future development of the company. As regards leadership, Antonia's reflections meant that her understanding of her role as a leader became increasingly clear over the many years of crisis. Although Antonia acted purposefully, the protracted crisis seems, based on her own story, to have been an emotionally chaotic ordeal.

In the story of the new hotel manager, the first crises emerged when the manager told the employees about the hotel's financial problems and their consequences, which led to hostile responses. The hotel manager realised she had not made herself well understood, nor was there initially a great deal of trust in her ability. She therefore decided to communicate personally with the employees whom she had to dismiss from their work. In doing so, she experienced how difficult it was to interpret their more or less obvious reactions. When reflecting on this, she regretted that she had not followed up on her talks at a later stage. The reorientation phase began in conjunction with the subsequent business reorganisation, the completion of which took two years. In the end, the manager seemed to have succeeded in her objectives of creating a more efficient organisation and more flexible job roles, making the company less vulnerable to financial fluctuations.

When it came to the sabotage of the internal computer system in the same hotel, no one had foreseen such an occurrence. The hotel manager, who was very upset by the incident, asked the employee in question to resign from his job with immediate effect. She interpreted the incident as a bitter revenge that, in principle, was aimed directly at her. To some extent, the manager could understand why the employee reacted the way he did, as he was frustrated and disappointed. Yet it was the employee who lost in the long run, not the company. The situation was primarily handled in compliance with the recognised principles of employment law.

Having a strategy is usually seen as essential when you want to achieve something. However, sometimes the strategy is *not* to have a strategy at all, which means just waiting and seeing what happens. Sometimes problems may resolve themselves. Unfortunately, this is not often the case in crises.

In the story of the guest conductor, the members of the orchestra had been stuck in a destructive behavioural pattern for a long time. One can assume that none of the musicians was very happy about the situation, but it appeared that the orchestra members were not that good at communicating (compared with the employees of the Air Force division, who were much more skilled in this respect). We are not told, in the case of the orchestra, about the roles of the chief conductor and the concert-master (leader of the first violins). Some of the musicians clearly chose not to act at all, nor to support the guest conductor during rehearsals. It should have been the responsibility of the chief conductor (absent for most of the working week) to identify and deal with the problem – the guest conductor did not see this as her responsibility. Persistence and perseverance was the strategy strictly adopted by the guest conductor, despite the orchestra continuing with its non-cooperative behaviour. Ignoring the dysfunction of the orchestra while emphasising musicianship to achieve the objective of performing the concert required both strength and courage. In this example, it was only the guest conductor herself who, through inner struggle, underwent the various phases of crisis management (according to the theory of Cullberg 1992), probably because she was the only one experiencing the dysfunctional situation as a crisis.

Theories of dysfunctional groups or subgroups can help us understand what happens in a group that is unable to cooperate (Alvesson & Sveningsson 2007; Granström 2000; Maltén 1992; Polsky 1967). Unfortunately, the ambitions and motivations of such groups tend to pull in opposite directions, which we can see in the story of the guest conductor and the orchestra. Dysfunctions are also very evident in the story of the hotel manager when, new in her job, she tried to introduce measures and methods completely at odds with the ingrained work patterns of the employees.

The genre theory of dysfunctional groups includes a variety of stereotypical roles that impede the ability of a group to operate functionally. *Schemers* are empowered by talking behind people's backs while simultaneously lobbying on behalf of themselves and attracting followers through wit and irony. A *clique* is a subgroup of people sharing the same interest in sticking together on specific issues, fostering certain attitudes, and in this way excluding others from their close-knit group. The objective of a clique is either to support or inhibit its members.

In the case of the guest conductor and the orchestra, we can see some of the musicians exhibiting such behaviours. They whisper and exchange knowing looks, whereas others tell jokes that no one, including the conductor, can understand. Another strategy, according to the authors, is to remain neutral, trying not to influence anyone in any way, avoiding confrontation. Examples of this are also evident in the story of the orchestra, in which some players remained silent while others suffered. As a consequence of these stereotypical roles, the existence of certain coteries may lead to conflicts that prevent others from carrying out their work in a professional manner. Accordingly, individual group members may try to exert influence inwardly, towards their own group, and outwardly, towards others. Another stereotypical group formation, according to the aforementioned theory, is the so-called *devitalised group*, characterised by a low level of energy and motivation. Conversations and discussions about feelings and controversial topics are banned in these groups. Because no one is used to any significant competition in a devitalised workplace, all changes are seen as threats, especially if proposed by someone from outside the organisation (as in the cases of the guest conductor and hotel manager).

The situation determines the action

The above stories describe very different crisis situations. They involve difficulties of cooperating, power struggles, decommissioning processes, sabotage, and accidents with a fatal outcome. Each situation must be dealt with in a particular way and there are not always set guidelines or recommendations to follow. Much depends on how critical the situation is, the nature of the assignment, what problems arise and need to be solved, and what advantages and risks are at stake. The difficulty in choosing what course of action to take can also be complicated by not knowing exactly what requirements, expectations, and regulatory systems exist in an organisation or what room there is for manoeuvring. It appears that approaches and courses of action are partly governed by the different personalities and competencies of the leaders, together with their view of how their leadership should be exercised in any given situation. Their sense of duty is also important, *i.e.* that an urgent situation *must* be dealt with. The leaders in the above stories take their responsibilities seriously, despite having different strategies.

However, in a crisis situation, it is not always possible to stop and assess what course of action would be best. The UN colonel chose to complete his mission by confrontation, a decision he presumably based on previous experience, knowing the purpose of his mission, and trusting his soldiers. For him, there was no alternative. The Swedish Air Force commander, on the other hand, chose to deal with his division's internal crises by talking, following up, and debriefing. He also stressed the importance of showing respect to his employees and the relatives of the victims. The hotel manager chose to come to grips with the strained financial situation. Faced with having to dismiss people from their jobs and then having to deal with the sabotage of the hotel's computer systems, she initially followed standard employment principles. After a few years she was able to start working on developing the professional roles of her employees. In contrast, Antonia fought for her professional role and influence on the family business, and eventually succeeded in securing the position to which she felt entitled. She also achieved economic stability throughout the group of companies. Finally, the guest conductor gave up on her lofty artistic ideals for the concert: she accepted the limited possibilities and was simply content that the concert *could* be performed at all.

The UN colonel and the Air Force commander did not talk much about their concept of leadership in the interviews, but seemed to be fairly clear about their roles and what needed to be done in the crisis situations where they found themselves. The UN colonel relied mainly on his authoritative style of leadership. However, a common denominator for the hotel manager and Antonia was that they took over existing organisations with the hope of making changes for the better, using the power of influence conferred by their formal leadership positions. That was not easy, however. The critical events that occurred in succession and manifested themselves as resistance, doubt, and power struggle created shock, confusion, and uncertainty, and the ensuing crises lasted for several years. However, as both leaders dealt with their situations, they grew into and became clearer about their roles as leaders.

According to Antonia, the lesson she learned from this was 'never again to be indebted or put all my eggs in one basket'. Antonia believed that the crises contributed to her own development as a person and businesswoman. The hotel manager also talked about seeking her proper role as a leader. One leader who differed from the others was the guest conductor. She was a temporary leader who came from the outside for one week only and had to exercise her leadership over a group she had never met before. Initially assuming that her assignment would be both professional and creative, she soon became stymied by the peculiar behaviours of the musicians. For the guest conductor, the lesson learned from this was never to assume someone else's problem, *i.e.* that of the chief conductor. She therefore chose to ignore the dysfunctional behaviours of the orchestra.

But in organisations where the leader is wellknown and has a formal position, it is of utmost importance to counteract negative group formations and characteristics in order to obtain a good cooperative working culture. Crucial for the well-being of an organisation mired in crises and chaos is that it tries to escape from a paralysing situation. Leadership may become particularly exposed – and crucial – in a critical situation. An absence of leadership is equally noticeable as it can complicate the everyday work of employees and result in a power struggle between individuals and groups. Being a manager and taking ultimate responsibility in ones leadership is a process intended to coordinate resources and actions on the basis of shared ideas and values (Bruzelius & Skärvad 2004). In this respect, the leader is a key player with a legitimate mandate to exercite influence, to the effect that power and leadership are deemed to be closely linked. Yet employees also have the power to exert influence on the basis of their professional roles, competencies, and ability to communicate. In the best-case scenario, a crisis will bring people and organisations together.

All the leaders profiled in these stories are in their mid to late middle ages and will have amassed considerable experience and knowledge. However, in a crisis situation, there are usually few relevant personal experiences or reference frameworks to draw upon that may be indicative of how best to handle the situation in question. Nor is it easy to follow a predetermined crisis management plan when different crisis follow another. One leader explained it like this: 'The situation itself determines your action', which suggests that there are no set ways in which a leader should act in crisis situations. You are bound to act according to your own experience, ability, ethics, and common sense, trying to identify what to reach and what action needs to be taken. However, no leaders consider themselves capable of doing everything on their own, so they rely on the assistance and efforts of their employees or subordinates to help them achieve satisfactory results.

CHAPTER 9

Reluctant leadership

Rebecka Arman and Östen Ohlsson

I'm the boss
There's no doubt of it
I'm the boss
And I'm proud of it

(Burl Ives 1963)

A common assumption is that being a leader is an advantage and that most people would like to be leaders if given the opportunity. Those who lead are amply rewarded in the form of tangible benefits, social status, and the opportunity to fulfil themselves. In addition, there is the expectation that those who truly aspire to become leaders are also the most suited for the task. According to Paul Lawrence (2010), we are all born to be leaders. As a result of biological evolution, 'leadership is what we as a species do well' (Lawrence 2010, p. 12). If the rewards are that great and we are designed for the task, why do not all of us endeavour to become leaders, and why do some of us turn down leadership offers while others are extremely reluctant to take on the task? Why is the initial reluctance followed by eventual acceptance? Please note that this is one question – not two. We have four tentative answers to this, all of which have their strong and weak points:

1. People are hypocritically lying when they say that they have no aspirations to become leaders.
2. The material rewards may not be worth the sacrifice. Even so, some people seem to be persuaded. Perhaps they are flattered, or have a sense of duty. Rewards might help.
3. We are not designed to lead, as Paul Lawrence claims. We may be designed to run (McDougall 2009), but leading does not seem

quite as natural. Perhaps we are instead meant to follow? This notion also offers the opportunity of earning rewards but of another kind. It is more about existential values – who do I want to be?

4. The rewards associated with leadership are counterbalanced by what use the leadership is to those who are led. If the proposed leader has no doubts about this, then maybe the rest ought to. It is not so much about what the potential leader wants, but what all the others want. They want him or her to be the leader for various reasons, one of which might be that he or she has enough self-awareness to hesitate. Rewards are of less importance. Instead, it is a matter of convincing the potential leader that he or she is the right person for the leadership role despite knowing that this is not the case. However, none of the other candidates would be any better.

These four answers to the mystery of reluctant leaders constitute hypotheses that will be tested in different ways. It is also possible to combine these four interrelated answers. The complexity makes it impossible to move forward without citing examples. Managers – or leaders – who do not seek or dream of elevated positions are our examples: people who either out of duty or by coercion take on the burdensome role of a leader, whether in politics or professional organisations. First, however, the benefits of being a leader merit more attention.

Biology or culture?

The benefits and functions of becoming a leader seem perfectly reasonable from a biological perspective. Those who run ahead of their herd will reap the benefits of easier living and reproduction. David Attenborough (2002) has in one nature programme after another illustrated how those who seek leadership push and shove for the desirable position.

The principle that the leader of a herd should reproduce the most applies not only to wild stallions and similar creatures. Genghis Khan, the great conqueror and tyrant, is said to have millions of direct descendants across the world (Zerjal *et al.* 2003). As many as 16 million men are believed to have exactly the same Y chromosome as Ghengis Khan. Here is a quotation from Genghis Khan himself, though we cannot guarantee its authenticity:

> The greatest pleasure is to vanquish your enemies and chase them
> before you, to rob them of their wealth and see those dear to them
> bathed in tears, to ride their horses and clasp to your bosom their
> wives and daughters. (upi.com/Odd_News)

It is rare to see such motives formulated in the management literature. The basic driving force for seeking power, which is presumably inherent in the creation of all life forms, is something that we will touch upon later in this chapter. However, let us first finish our discussion of the natural instinct to take the lead in order to facilitate reproduction.

Simple biological analogies present us with a few problems, though attempting to deny biological realities is equally problematic (see, *e.g.* Forsman 2009). Using animal behaviour as an excuse is taking things too far. There are always other analogies that lead to other conclusions. For example, the situation does not appear to be the same in a herd of elephants, in which the leader does not need to fight, push, or shove to secure the top position. Perhaps this is because the leader of an elephant herd is always a female. However, we are not going to analyse the difference between men and women as leaders in this chapter.

The main problem with biological analogies is that people are not just animals but are people too. Human beings seem to be able to organise their lives in a variety of ways and, compared with other animals, are less tied to biological necessities. According to some feminist theories, our biological gender does not tie us to any specific roles or behaviours, gender being socially constructed (Wittig 1985). We organise our society in many ways, none of which is 'natural'. If we have understood the semiotics of cultural criticism reasonably well, then the term 'natural' is in itself a problem, if not unnatural. Perhaps we should also be cautious when talking about the 'natural characteristics' of wild horses. We can always ask whether or not something ought to be the way it is. To the extent that it is meaningful to say that something is socially constructed, it is for the purpose of expressing critical aloofness (Hacking 1999). Living in a social world always gives us the opportunity to reflect upon a different and possibly better order. Gender relations, *i.e.* how we define and understand male and female, are a typical example. These could very well have developed in completely different directions, some of which would clearly have been an improvement. This might also be the case with our way of defining the relationship between leaders and followers. Perhaps the same reasoning should be applied to other creatures: having the position of a leading stallion might not be the best solution for horses despite its being based on millions of years of natural selection. And we would prefer to talk about human evolution with someone other than Genghis Khan.

One cannot help but wonder why it is so difficult to recruit managers and leaders when there seem to be so many advantages to being one. The most logical solution would be for everyone to announce their interest. Instead of the current fighting, pushing, and shoving, there would be qualification assessments, interviews, and tests – although with more or less the same end result: the strongest, best, and most suitable candidate would be chosen as leader. This is probably the ideal scenario for someone running an executive recruitment agency. However, the question is whether the executive recruiters would be able to guarantee any improvements. We recently talked to an executive recruiter who said that with the refined selection methods used nowadays, fewer mistakes are made when searching for and recruiting executives. We would like to think this is the case. Perhaps it is also the case that such successful recruitments are based on and reproduce certain perceptions of managers (or leaders) and cement a particular notion of what is natural, while the alternative could very well have been different – and possibly better.

There are plenty of stories about involuntary leadership. Ethnology, anthropology, and literature provide us with powerful, though not always entirely credible, examples and role models. In the world of films, leaders are either depicted as heroes or anti-heroes (Rombach & Solli 2006).

When Forrest Gump (1994) grows tired of his life, he runs across the entire North American continent and back again. He eventually gets noticed by the media. He is shown on TV and becomes a celebrity. Suddenly, there is a crowd of people behind him. What are they doing there? They are following Forrest Gump. He is their leader – at last, they have something to fight for. A kind of higher purpose, a purpose that is achieved by running after Forrest Gump. When he stops running – after all, the film cannot just be about running – his followers stop running too. The group simply dissolves in a rather undramatic manner. It was probably necessary to make it that way in order for the story to work. However, a portrayal of how these companions or disciples follow their master whatever he gets up to would have been just as believable and entertaining.

Then again, this would probably have made *Forrest Gump* a darker and less optimistic film, as in *Life of Brian* (1979), in which poor Brian, who looks suspiciously like Jesus, becomes the subject of intrusive worshipping from a persistent entourage of people wanting to be his disciples. Brian becomes filled with fear and revulsion at the thought of this type of forced leadership. He does not want to be a leader at all but cannot fend off the role of leadership that seems to cling to him. Finally, he is crucified as a last enforced sacrifice. His devout admirers express their affection for this magnificent sacrifice on behalf of them and their guilt. However, the sacrifice is merely a projection. While the admiring crowd swarm over their dying hero and saviour, the film audience and indeed, Brian himself, come to realise the depravity of people worshipping their leaders. And we cannot help but laugh.

With all due respect to film and fiction, the real-life stories gathered during field studies are even more compelling evidence. Claude Lévi-Strauss (1955/2000) explored Indian tribes in Brazil during the second half of the 1930s. The tribe of Nambikwara had a very loose social structure, leading a nomadic life in small groups and living off what nature had to offer. A group could dissolve if its members were not happy. Accordingly, the tribal chief could find himself without a tribe to lead. Formally, it was the responsibility of the tribal chief to appoint his successor; in practice, however, it was the tribal members who discussed and appointed the chief's successor. It was not uncommon for a prospective candidate to decline the offer of becoming the new tribal chief.

Becoming a chief admittedly brought certain privileges, but also burdensome duties. The chief was, for example, expected to share all his assets. If the chief received a gift from someone outside the tribe, that gift would almost immediately have to be distributed among the tribal members or there would soon be discontent. According to Lévi-Strauss, the members of this tribe were well aware of the function and responsibilities of their chief. The chief was not needed to lead and coordinate an already existing group; rather, the chief was needed to form a group in the first place – but not to lead it.

In the above examples, the leaders are depicted as victims rather than exploiters. We realise, of course, that there are many counter-examples, but perhaps the idea of leadership as a highly desirable position has still suffered a bit of a blow. Nor does a democratic or service-oriented leadership seem to constitute a modern and civilised form of leadership. We certainly agree that the Nambikwara had a civilised form of leadership but it was definitely not modern.

We could turn the question around by asking why anyone would lead voluntarily and happily when so many of us are such reluctant followers. Leadership is not always desirable or voluntary despite the benefits it may bring. However, this is a two-sided conundrum: Why do so many people follow voluntarily when it does not necessarily bring any distinct privileges? The definition of 'voluntarily' is, however, rather vague. We follow because of an inbuilt degree of compulsion. When a person moves in front of a bunch of newly hatched ducklings, the hatchlings immediately become imprinted on and follow that person as if he or she were their own mother (Lorentz 1969). After hatching, they get imprinted on the first moving object they see. You do not have to smell in a special way or quack or do anything else that resembles a duck. All you need to do is move in front of the ducklings. We imagine that the same thing would happen if you pulled an empty shoebox by a string in front of the ducklings, but cannot find any references to verify this. It would be an insult to compare adult humans to a bunch of newly hatched ducklings. However, the construction of social reality can take a variety of forms, which could imply that we are led in different ways. We construct something that we can follow, so in a way we are fairly similar to the ducklings.

We do not intend to look further into the concept of leadership being a characteristic projected by those who follow – that is for another publication. Otherwise, it would be exciting to radically disregard the characteristics and behaviour of leaders and simply look at leadership as the projection and behaviour of followers. The difficulty lies in trying to find sufficiently sophisticated empirical examples. While thinking about how to carry out such an empirical study, we endeavour to analyse the other side of the coin. Those who involuntarily end up in a leadership position – how do they function? What happens when a person unwillingly, reluctantly, or even under compulsion becomes a leader? What characterises these processes and what are their consequences? The above examples, from the cinema and the deepest jungle, are enlightening but we have several more in-depth examples to consider.

Party leader after some hesitation

In 2011, there was a frantic search for a new leader of the Social Democratic Party in Sweden. A nominating committee was given the task of finding a candidate for the party leadership before the next extraordinary party congress, to be held 25–27 March 2011 (social-demokraterna.se). Negotiations took place without the media having any direct insight, but it was pretty clear that most of the potential candidates approached either declined or tried to avoid being asked in the first place (svd.se/nyheter/inrikes/har-ar-de-hetaste-kandidaterna).

It has always been the tradition that people who would like to be considered for the role of the next party leader usually try to keep such aspirations secret for as long as possible. Furthermore, political parties have a tradition of scepticism regarding people with clear leadership ambitions. In 1996, the Social Democratic Finance Minister Göran Persson said again and again that he was not interested until suddenly he was put forward as the only candidate for party leader by the nominating committee. In his memoirs (Persson 2007), Göran Persson claims that he never had any aspirations to become party leader. He felt established in his role as Finance Minister and there was another very obvious candidate for party leadership, Mona Sahlin. However, after a media scandal (Esaiasson 1996), Sahlin was no longer conceived of as suitable and that is when Göran Persson started to officially decline the offer of candidateship in TV interviews. It is clear from his memoirs that there were other candidates apart from Persson, and that he doubted the appropriateness of moving from his post of Finance Minister to being party leader and, eventually, Prime Minister. What Persson says in his memoirs is not a matter of dispute, but he probably meant 'yes' when he said 'no' in public. Whether or not Sahlin disqualified herself from the party leadership by simply being too keen is, however, a matter of speculation. Perhaps it was this enthusiasm and not the debated affair that disqualified her as a candidate for the leadership post. The fact that she later became the party leader after all is another story.

This story of the top management of the Swedish Social Democratic Party provides a clear example of reluctant leadership. As a source, the memoirs of Göran Persson have their drawbacks. The book was written in hindsight and we do not have access to any first-hand information. We do, however, when it comes to another party leader: Tage Erlander was elected leader of the Social Democratic Party following the sudden death of Per Albin Hansson.

Tage Erlander kept a diary of everyday events and meetings, including lengthy analytical reflections (Erlander 2001). When Per Albin Hansson was leading the Government, Tage Erlander held the post of Minister of Education and was generally not deemed a potential future leader. On 22 October 1945, after speaking at Stockholm City Hall, he made the following comment in his diary about the media's image of him:

Yesterday, the university alumni reunion at the City Hall was really a great success for me. I must admit, however, that it is fairly easy to give everyone a pleasant surprise, bearing in mind the unanimous emphasising of my nullity by the media. Every trace of human life in such a doomed section must surely be met with a cheerful attitude. The media is by no means unfriendly – on the contrary – but it has decided that I am conscientious, diligent, and boring. Faced with the work that is now beginning to burden me, I sometimes wish that this characterisation was true but unfortunately, it is not. (Erlander 2001, p. 25)

Almost a year later, on 6 October 1946, the Prime Minister then in office, Per Albin Hansson, died unexpectedly. The days that followed were chaotic for the Social Democratic Government. The Social Democrats had to find a new leader and Prime Minister in a hurry. Gustaf Möller saw himself as the obvious choice, which is probably the reason why he was not elected. Putting himself forward as a possible candidate showed poor judgement, according to many of the people referred to in Erlander's (1973) memoirs. The National Executive Committee met on 9 October. At the meeting, Per Edvin Sköld among others put forward Erlander as the man for the future. A secret ballot was cast and when Möller did not get the support he expected, he withdrew his candidacy. That settled it. On 10 October, Erlander wrote in his diary:

I have never really dreamt of becoming a leader. Not until after the ballot in the executive committee did I begin to see where this might be heading. Möller had clearly been in the lead until Undén came into the picture. Thereby, the matter was decided. Incredible – how this is going to end, I do not know – I am not a man of big words and big decisions. I am afraid – I have always been afraid – and that I now accept is certainly not because of any ambition and will for power but more out of fear for the group. Loyalty towards the group and party. Does this loyalty to my surroundings as a main virtue make me a good leader for the country in these troublesome times? I doubt it, and if I fail – what happens then? Will everything be lost or can it be restored? (Erlander 2001, p. 142)

Perhaps striving for power and leadership is regarded as suspicious amongst the ranks of the Social Democrats. The Social Democrats have had quite a few leaders over the years – eight party leaders in 115 years.

Several of these leaders have held office for a long time and there are important examples of people having become party leaders without demonstrating any such ambition in advance. Tage Erlander became party leader in 1946, as a compromise candidate following the death of Per Albin Hansson. He was generally deemed a bit indecisive and without any real leadership talent. Yet he ended up leading the Social Democrats for 23 years, throughout its most successful period.

Ingvar Carlsson was another reluctant leader. Following the assassination of Prime Minister Olof Palme, there was no one else who could take over the job of party leader. The day after the murder, the executive committee of the party called a meeting during which everyone was unanimously in support of Ingvar Carlsson (Peterson 1999). There was little room for doubt in the crisis that prevailed at the time. As explained in his own words:

> I guess, in one way, I was well prepared for the role of party chairman. I had worked closely with Tage Erlander and Olof Palme. I had 11 years of experience as a minister and many years of working with the ssu [Social Democratic youth association, authors note] and the party.

> I was still unprepared, as I never had any ambitions of becoming the party chairman. On the contrary, I had actually planned on leaving political life around the same time as Olof Palme. (Carlsson 1999, p. 42)

There is something paradoxical about the way in which the Social Democrats view their leaders. On one hand, there is a traditional scepticism towards charismatic people while, on the other, the party remains faithful to its elected leaders. Or at least, that is how it was until the turn of the millennium.

The matter of charisma deserves further comment. We cannot say for sure, but it seems that charisma can emerge in new party leaders subsequent to their election. Per Albin Hansson was a convivial individual from a southern county who, once elected party leader and Prime Minister, was transformed into a national father figure. Tage Erlander was an analytical and intellectual person who scored nil in terms of popular appeal; very slowly, this cold analytical nature acquired more folksy and relatable qualities such as lucidity and humour.

There have, of course, been those who have willingly stood as candidates for the position of Social Democratic Party leader, but the same scenario has generally repeated itself over and over again. One can imagine that the same scenario of not standing for candidacy also occurred in conjunction with the election in 2011 (svd.se/nyheter/inrikes/har-ar-de-hetaste-kandidaterna). It was perhaps not exactly the same scenario. Once the nomination committee revealed its chosen candidate on 9 March 2011, it turned out to be a person who had featured rather sparingly in mass media speculations or, indeed, in the wish lists of various socialist debaters. Håkan Juholt had never spoken in the mass media of his lack of aspiration to become party leader, simply because no one had asked. Things did not go well, however, and less than a year later, there was a new party leader.

People with clear leadership ambitions tend to be viewed with suspicion. In the very first years of the Social Democratic Party in the 1890s, there was no party leader at all but a collective leadership. We do not know enough about Claes Tholin, the first Party chairman, but one can imagine that the transition from collective to individual leadership was accepted with reluctance by everyone concerned. Then again, Claes Tholin did not make a lot of fuss; instead, it is his successor Branting who emerged in history as an individual with a strong personality. The relatively reluctant leaders of the Social Democrats have often proved to work well.

The example of managers in health care

Swedish Social Democrats are certainly not unique, and likely have many parallels. Why then are their party leadership elections often associated with such anxiety? Another example can be found in the leadership of Swedish health-care services. Nurses often manage sizeable hospital departments, yet there is no sign of this in the public perception of nurses' training and the nursing profession. We cannot find any examples of managers in the health-care sector who are trying to hide from their longing subjects, like the hapless Brian in the Monty Python film. However, nurses and doctors seem to end up in management roles despite not having deliberately sought them.

It has proven difficult to recruit and retain middle managers in health care. During the 2009–2010 period, as many as 21 department managers (or unit managers) and operation managers ended their employment in Sahlgrenska Hospital in Gothenburg (VGREG 2009). Naturally, the HR department was asking itself what could possibly lie behind their reluctance to continue as managers. On closer examination, however, it turned out that most of these managers had been working at the hospital for a long time. Some of them were getting on a bit and were keen to do something else (Kjellberg & Samuelsson 2011). Nonetheless, the employer was worried about how best to recruit and retain people in their management capacity at the same time as they belong to professions with their own identities.

It is easy to see that doctors, nurses, midwives, assistant nurses, and social workers (the most common professionals among health-care managers) would rarely plan on becoming managers when choosing their future career. Such unwillingness to take on management responsibilities could be regarded as part of a professional ideology of altruism inspired by Florence Nightingale. Some would even say that there is something very fundamental about health-care ethics (Held 2006). There are other attractions of working in the health-care sector, such as having to deal with challenging problem solving. Few start their careers in nursing or medicine with a plan for how health-care services ought to be managed, developed, reformed, or improved – at least not from the top.

As evidence of this hypothesis, we would like to mention the following anecdote involving trainee nurses. As part of a doctoral course in higher education pedagogy, we had the privilege to observe a lesson about organisation and leadership for nursing students. The lack of interest and involvement on the part of the young students was obvious throughout the three-hour lecture. Some were talking, texting, or nodding off while others sat dreaming about other things, wishing for the lecture to be over. When the lecturer asked if there were any questions or thoughts, the intense silence that followed was almost palpable. The lecturer was making increasingly drastic attempts to try and explain the importance of her topic. She maintained that all aspiring nurses must, in their professional lives, be able to support and create organisations that benefit the patients. 'Everyone working in the health-care sector wants to do good', she reminded the students. Yet the students did not seem to agree that the best way in which to do good and help sick people was through managerial work.

The reader might wonder, however, if other professions are similar in this respect. It is often said that professional organisations find it difficult to recruit managers and that managers of professional organisations have a lower status and degree of influence than in other organisations (Mintzberg 1983). However, this situation probably varies from one professional organisation to another; it certainly varies from one profession to another. Let us consider a very different type of education, *i.e.* business economics. When asking students studying for a bachelor's or master's degree in organisation and management, most of them (around 60 per cent) confirmed, by a show of hands, that they had every intention of working as a manager at some point in the future. One group of just 20 students was more hesitant at first, with only four people raising their hands. However, when modifying the question to whether or not they could see themselves working as managers, given the chance, the number of raised hands increased significantly (to around 80 per cent). This time around, those reluctant to become managers were in the minority.

The everyday work of doctors has always been deemed to include elements of leadership, since doctors are ultimately accountable for the medical work carried out 'around' their patients by teams of various professions, and elements of leadership are now addressed in specialised training courses. However, existing nursing training programmes offer very little in the way of preparation for future management roles (based on reviewing a selection of course descriptions). It is unclear whether the inclusion of management training in existing training programmes would lead to better managers in the future. The point we are trying to make is that there is scepticism towards the role of managers in the health-care sector and that this scepticism also appears to permeate the training programmes.

According to our analysis, one can go as far as to say that a certain amount of candidate reluctance and persuasion is standard in recruiting managers in the health-care sector. Helena Öfverström (2008) interviewed more than 30 managers in the health-care service, most of whom were doctors, about their careers. These interviews indicated that most of the doctors had accepted their managerial roles 'for the good of the clinic' or because previous managers had nominated them as their 'heirs'. According to Öfverström, none of these interviewees had longed, planned, or strategised to become managers. One of the subcategories of 'for the good of the clinic' in her study was indeed entitled 'the reluctant', referring to those who had felt compelled to become managers when no other suitable candidate could be found. They missed their old jobs and saw their present role as a personal sacrifice. Two master's-level studies of a selection of managers in the health-care sector subsequently confirmed what Öfverström had found, *i.e.* that most of the managers had never planned on becoming managers; instead, they had been asked to apply for the job and none had any previous training in leadership (Kjellberg & Samuelsson 2011; Smith 2011).

A separate interview study of ten first- and second-line health-care managers gives insight into their reasons for becoming managers. In addition, the study examined many examples of discouraging dilemmas at work (Arman 2010). The following quotations illustrate the reluctance of the interviewees when faced with their new role as managers. The decision to become a manager was described by one interviewee as arising from a desire to help improve operations. This manager was perhaps not entirely reluctant and one senses a 'for the good of the clinic' attitude:

I: Why did you become a manager?

C1: Well, when working on the ward, I developed an interest in organisational psychology and then, when there was to be an organisational change ... I kind of felt that I had to do something. Then there was this opportunity to apply for the role of Unit Manager. And because I already had this interest in the organisation and had seen other managers who did not. ... well, then I thought that I could do that better.

Another manager, who had previously been active in the trade union, said that her decision to become a manager was also driven by a desire to exert influence and make changes. When we met her, she had worked as a manager for six months. She thought a lot about what she had got herself into, not to mention whether she ought to continue as a manager. In preparation for her new role or as a stepping stone, she had worked as an assistant manager for some time and therefore would probably fit into the 'heir' category:

I do not think that I have always been someone who likes to have influence. My involvement in the trade union showed me that instead of just sitting around complaining and having an opinion, you can actually do something about it. And once you have got a taste for it, I think it is very difficult to go back.

Another manager described how she had to undergo careful training before taking on her new role as manager. Her preparation for the new role is somewhat unusual, but is fully in accordance with the reluctant and unplanned nature of management roles in these professions. She agreed to the leadership training because of a combination of wanting to do something on her own initiative and having access to a new special programme offered in the region:

> I had decided that if, one day, I was going to have a managerial
> role, I would first do a course in leadership. ... After that, well ... I
> thought, okay, here we go then.

Once again, there is a sense of uncertainty, hesitance, and reluctance. Öfverström's study (2008) includes examples of 'heirs', *i.e.* people who had come close to being managers but who had been more discouraged than prepared and convinced. In our own study, the work descriptions given by the managers provide indications of what can be seen as deterrents to other potential managerial candidates. These and similar descriptions can be found in many other studies, so we have chosen merely to mention them without exploring their implications in depth. The managers included in these studies describe an indistinct organisation and limited responsibilities, a lack of leadership and management skills, a lack of confidence and trust from superiors in terms of financial decisions and budgets, as well as a feeling of loneliness and occasionally social exclusion at work. For many, the possibility of successfully resuming their clinical work seemed relatively remote or unattractive. The risk of getting stuck in the managerial role in this way may also act as a deterrent to other prospective managers in the health-care sector.

A lie or consequence?

All four hypotheses at the beginning of this chapter have been both confirmed and falsified in the above examples.

Lying is obviously one possibility. Göran Persson was probably very keen to become the new party leader. Some of the political interviewees seem, on the other hand, to have been speaking the truth about their reluctance to become leaders.

That the benefits of leadership are questionable is a notion that corresponds well with how things appear to work in the health-care sector. Once you become an administrator, the road to a nice specialist career is soon blocked. This entails another dilemma: Even if you were reluctant at the time of being recruited, this does not necessarily mean that you will later want to leave your position as a manager. There is essentially no way back. If you end up having to leave your position as manager, this can lead to crisis and frustration (Cregård 2004). The prospect of being affected by such crises must be considered one of the main disadvantages of leadership. The tribal chief in Nambikwara, on the other hand, was expected to give away everything he had; as a result, the relationship between the demands put on him and the few privileges he could enjoy as a chief seemed rather unbalanced.

The third hypothesis was that you might be happier to follow than to lead. This is a bit more difficult to verify. Some people are simply happy to lead while others are not. Whether or not leaders are happier individuals than others could be the subject of another study. It depends on what is meant by the term 'leader': Is someone who runs across the prairie followed by an entourage a leader?

Finally, it seems clear that what is good for the leader is not necessarily good for the rest of us: Better a hesitant and perhaps unsatisfied Tage Erlander than a nasty and satisfied Genghis Khan!

However, the above summary is far too simple. Let us explore the matter a bit deeper and consider the hypotheses one by one.

To want and to lie

Let us assume that people either want or do not want to become leaders and that they can be honest or dishonest about this. This assumption is illustrated in the examples given above.

The matrix in Figure 9.1 illustrates four standard types that can be distinguished based on our analysis. The first one (upper left-hand field) refers to what we often read about in the leadership and psychology literature, *i.e.* people who not only say that they want to become managers but who also, deep down, really and truly would like to. These people are usually found in a context in which it is permitted and appreciated to admit one's personal aspirations and ambitions.

The second type situation (upper right-hand field) refers to a fairly similar type, *i.e.* people who take a strategic and intentional approach to power but have ended up in or sought out an environment in which egalitarian ideologies prevail, such as in the health-care sector or the Social Democratic Party. Here, it is unacceptable to talk about power.

In the fourth field are those who really are reluctant but are persuaded to 'help out', as in the case of Tage Erlander or 'for the good of the clinic', as in the case of the health-care cases. The problem is that both Tage Erlander and other power players could just as well be lying and actually belong to type two instead. How can we know that? Many people do not want to be – nor do they become – managers or leaders.

Finally, in the third field are those who put themselves forward for promotion to a managerial role even though they would rather not be promoted. It can be devastating for a person to appear indolent and lethargic in an energetic and upwardly mobile circle of friends and acquaintances or in a workplace where hesitation and reflection are not among the valued criteria.

Table 9.1 Categories of willing and unwilling managerial candidates.

	Say that they want to	Say that they do not want to
Want to	(I) Power-conscious strategists operating in a power-glorifying and elitist context. Honest candidates.	(II) Power-conscious strategists operating in a power-sceptical and egalitarian context.
Do not want to	(III) People in elitist contexts who must be seen as ambitious, *e.g.* economics students subject to peer pressure.	(IV) The truly unwilling: Tage Erlander and others who sacrifice themselves for the cause. All those who do not want to be leaders.

One of the situations described in our four-field matrix merits further comment, *i.e.* those who honestly say they want to become leaders. In this situation, the ideal type of person would be a power-conscious strategist with at least one leadership qualification and working in an organisation in which it is acceptable to speak of one's desire for power. The leadership courses offered in conjunction with economics studies appear to be a type of boot camp for this and similar types of people, and such courses can be useful when applying for graduate studies in business and finance.

One possible objection is that the examples used in this chapter are not credible. Could it be that Tage Erlander actually wanted to become party leader? That he was lying in his memoirs and diaries and he was even lying to himself? Even those who find it strategically justified to hide their intentions may still be driven by a will to power.

We believe this to be false and that everyone mentioned in this chapter is speaking the truth – as far as this is possible. An analysis concluding that people are liars if they do not display a will to power would be far too one-sided and meagre. A more reasonable analysis would be that people are driven by multiple and sometimes conflicting motives and ideals. Complex movements in society together with multiple intersecting theories and ideologies lead us to understand and justify our choices and actions in varied and, at times, contradictory ways. Our empirical examples include situations in which ideologies intersect, creating intricate and socially constructed patterns. Most of the economics students simply assumed that they should want to become managers even though, deep down, they may not have been sure about their own desire or capacity for power. The nursing students, on the other hand, assumed that they should not be interested in leadership, despite being told by their tutor that their particular expertise was invaluable.

As to the stories told from the health-care managers' perspective, we see these as somewhat self-contradictory, which is exactly what they are. Even in the story of the Nambikwara, inconsistencies can be found in how the chiefs describe themselves. There is a web of complex systems of ideas in society to which we relate. It is simply impossible to describe the choices you make in life and your identity without contradicting yourself. This does not mean, however, that we are telling lies. The anxiety felt by Tage Erlander when facing the task of becoming the new party leader and Prime Minister was likely genuine and also fairly reasonable – you must be completely mad not to tremble with anxiety when facing such an important task. An aversion to wielding power and leadership is sometimes a necessity in certain contexts, such as professional health-care organisations and Social Democratic Party leadership elections, while in other contexts it must be concealed behind a façade of willingness. Consequently, conscious and unconscious lies as well as particular contexts compromise the analysis of people's desire for power and leadership.

This reluctance to assume leadership may not be evidence of an aversion to power, but could be explained by the fact that most people recognise that many managers have no real power to speak of. If this is the case, then it is consistent with studies of what managers actually do, the results of which indicate that managers mainly react and respond to requests and pressures from others, like powerless marionettes (Carlson 1951/1991; Mintzberg 1973).

Advantages and disadvantages

The second hypothesis is that the direct benefits of being a leader or manager are perhaps somewhat exaggerated. The examples that we have examined in detail seem to suggest that it is difficult to compensate for some of the disadvantages of being a leader. In other contexts, however, rewards seem to provide a clear incentive, and if you were to interpret the soaring salaries of CEOs in the private sector, you would not find the same reluctance to assume leadership.

The reluctance to assume leadership found in the health-care sector is clearly linked to professional role and status. There is a very one-dimensional elitism in the sector that allows for only one kind of excellence – the professional. According to an analysis by Andrew Abbott (1981), the status of a profession is based on a formal definition of professional duties in which all duties not defined as professional are considered of less importance and value. Abbott illustrates this with examples of managerial duties. The position of a manager might indicate high status to those outside the profession, but not necessarily to those within the profession. Here, only the most dedicated and specialised expert tasks, which the profession regards as its own territory, are rewarded. The more specialised the tasks, the higher the status attained in the same professional milieu. There is also a tangible side to expertise and specialist knowledge: as a specialist, you are paid a higher salary without having to become a manager.

A tentative explanation for the reluctance to assume leadership in the case of the Social Democratic Party is that it is an expression of egalitarianism. Striving or demonstrating willingness to become leaders would be too self-assertive given that 'for the good of the people and the Party' appears to be the leadership credo of the Party. Interestingly, similar leadership credos are invoked in the health-care sector, for example, by doctors who have reluctantly stepped into the role of unit manager: 'I did it for the good of the clinic – there was no one else who could or wanted to do the job.' At the same time, there is an ongoing power struggle between doctors and other medical professions, in particular nurses, as to who are actually the leaders (Nordin 2009). The deceptively self-effacing credo of doctors might as well be interpreted as: 'No one else could do the job – since all nurses, secretaries, physiotherapists, engineers, economists, and everyone else are all incompetent and ill-suited for the job.' It cannot be said about the health-care sector that its elitism is concealed behind a partially egalitarian discourse. At the same time, however, traces of egalitarian ideology can be found among health-care managers. It is surprising that the intersection of such different ideologies as egalitarianism and elitism can lead to the same consequence, that is, involuntary leadership.

The will to power

Hypothesis three focuses on what we want to do with our lives. We hypothesised that Paul Lawrence (2010) was wrong in saying that we are all meant to be leaders. However, according to some sources, the key factor is to have the will to power. In the field of psychology, research and theorisation to date have focused mainly on the characteristics, behaviours, and, to some extent, the depth psychology motives and disorders of leaders (*cf.* Jackson & Parry 2008). Consequently, personality and intelligence tests are now used to identify suitable candidates for managerial roles. The result of such tests is normally that those who want to become managers are seen as the most suitable for the job.

This was confirmed by the older model created by David McClelland and David Burnham (1976), which considers what drives people to become managers. According to this model, 'power is the great motivator'. The best managers are those driven by a will to power and success but who, at the same time, are driven to achieve operational targets and are mature enough to control their impulses. These managers delegate and create a strong sense of responsibility and 'team spirit' around them. In addition, they have no particular need to be liked and therefore are clear and to the point about what needs to be done. These managers have been promoted and therefore rewarded with a feeling of 'being liked', at least by senior managers (McClelland & Boyatzis 1982). A reluctance to assume leadership and power appears to be a major barrier for many managers, according to McClelland and Burnham (1976) and McClelland and Boyatzis (1982). 'Involuntary' managers are therefore almost a contradiction in terms, as they would eliminate themselves, according to this line of thinking. That is a theory that we can truly say is false! Some of the examples considered above display both genuine reluctance and high performance; even one such example would be enough to challenge the results and falsify the model of McClelland and Burnham (1976): Tage Erlander appears to have been a genuinely reluctant leader and yet he became one of the most successful politicians in 20th-century Sweden.

If the field of psychology fails to provide useful theories about what drives managers in situations of reluctance, perhaps philosophy can be of more help? The highly controversial philosopher Friedrich Nietzsche (1882/1987) claimed that he had deciphered the true destiny of mankind. One of his principal theses was the will to power (Spinks 2003). Nietzsche said, according to Spinks, that the will to power is the fundamental principle of life, with human consciousness and identity merely being products of this principle. The will to power is the cornerstone of the purpose of life and is devoid of survival, moral, and spiritual motives. At every level, 'truth' and 'value' in life are the product of a dominant life form, whose perspective is superior to all others. Constant conflict between interpretations and a striving for the domination of our own interpretation are fundamental to how we experience existence. Nietzsche said, according to Spinks, that many have been willing to sacrifice their lives for this dynamic. Philosophy therefore appears to offer a different approach to the concept of the unruly stallions, *i.e.* that everyone wants to have the interpretative prerogative to say what they think.

We could probably be accused of trivialising and demonising this great thinker. There is an ongoing debate about how Friedrich Nietzsche ought to be interpreted, whether as a philosopher of freedom or as a fascist (Fredriksson 2012). The will to power theory is about freedom, but for only some superhumans, which is difficult to reconcile with humanistic ideals. However, Nietzsche himself seemed to have realised the problematic nature of having power, even from a power perspective. In a biography of Nietzche's life and work, Rüdiger Safranski (2003) quoted a private letter that Nietzche wrote in 1889, before entering a period of mental darkness:

> When it comes right down to it, I would much rather have been a Basel professor than God; but I did not dare be selfish enough to forgo the creation of the world. You see, one must make sacrifices, no matter how and where one lives. (Nietzsche, quoted by Safranski 2003, p. 345)

Our examples of the will to power are unlikely to lead to anything good. In fact, most good and competent leaders have also been good followers, adhering to noble ideals and principles.

Who should we have as our leader?

Finally, there is the question of how bad it can get when the manager is a reluctant leader. In the management recruitment industry of today, a desire to lead is an imperative characteristic. You must wave your hand in the air, eagerly declaring your leadership skills, even to be considered. The usual talk and gossip about someone being an adequate candidate despite not displaying much interest feels very outdated these days. Just look at what happened to the Nambikwara people – or maybe not, since they no longer exist. We would have liked to say that reluctant leaders are better leaders than others, had we known for certain. The anxious Tage Erlander was a huge success. He also seems to have been good for those he led, though members of other political camps would probably say otherwise.

The reluctant leaders in the health-care sector lead out of a sense of duty and loyalty, and we can think of worse motives. Although there is a whole range of motives, our impression is that having doubts about one's leadership role and ability is a healthy sign rather than a problem. In fact, there may be something wrong with people who believe that they are chosen to lead. An unrealistic self-image should not constitute a criterion for recruitment. The reverse also applies: Those who completely lack self-confidence are as likely to be as useless as leaders as those with grand delusions. Regrettably, our conclusion is not much more than a homage to a balanced compromise. The right amount of modesty is not a bad thing: the will to power must not be completely unconstrained at the same time as there should be a moderate level of unwillingness.

Leadership as a problem

Björn Rombach and Östen Ohlsson

It is always a good idea, in the last chapter, to look at whether you have achieved the intended objective of your book. Are we any wiser? Have we got a better understanding of what leadership is? We are fairly certain that each of the above chapters has made many of our readers a little bit wiser. The authors of this book definitely became a lot wiser writing it. Exactly how much wiser and about what is for each author to decide. One starting point for this book was pluralism – which is never a problem as long as everybody thinks they understand one another. We have no intention of reviewing the contents of the chapters to explain how you ought to have understood and interpreted them. They are fairly self-explanatory.

The objective of the book was to prove two things by means of some extreme examples. First, the existing leadership discourse is too narrow. Deviating examples would make us see the need not only for a broader frame of reference but also to correct some key theses in the prevailing discourse. The existing discourse – or prevailing theories of leadership – needs to be problematised and corrected. That specific objective has already been achieved, though it was more or less expected since it was a planned result and very much the starting point of this book. At the same time, we acknowledge that we have only scratched the surface. The prevailing discourse will no doubt survive, though we have succeeded in questioning it.

Second, we tend to see leadership as a problem rather than a solution. The various case descriptions featured here include several examples of difficult and problematic leadership. However, the problems encountered are not the same. Some chapters relate to tangible and practical problems for everyone concerned. That leadership can be a problem for those who are exposed to it is perhaps most evident in the chapter about cold leadership. Even Bond finds it difficult to constantly have to deal with M. Many of the chapters depict leadership as a problem for those who lead. The disobedient leader, on the other hand, does the right thing and gets punished for it. The reluctant leader is exactly that, reluctant, in addition to being exposed, while the reality of the virtual leader intrudes most significantly on an otherwise exemplary form of leadership. The prevailing discourse is often challenged. The chapter on leadership in a convent challenges the assumed advantages of change leadership. The chapter about leadership and expertship describes the problematic relationship between formal and informal leadership, whereas the chapter about leadership in crises gives us insight into the various reactions that a crisis can conjure up, all of which, in their own way, result in fairly good outcomes.

The solution to the leadership problems described in this book, does not seem to lie in the actual imposition of leadership – whether from a democratic, transformative, or any other perspective. The objective of the book is therefore deemed to be almost achieved. We can confidently say that leadership, based on our cases, is more often a problem than a solution. This conclusion, however, is not worth much in itself. Repeating our starting points and designating them as our conclusions is certainly nothing unusual, but still seems impermissibly circular. What we have learned from this and which is worth passing on concerns the ways in which leadership constitutes a problem rather than a solution. However, we do not want to use this final chapter to repeat what has already been said or make a summary. Instead, we want to discuss and compare the findings of this work as a whole. The question raised in this final chapter is not what we can learn from the individual chapters but what we can learn from them combined. Here, we are presented with a range of different opinions and examples that are both contradictory and difficult to interpret and, in addition, do not point unequivocally in the same direction. However, something essential happens when we begin to think about the diversity they capture.

Learning from extreme cases

The word 'extreme' ought to be used with caution. Constant overuse of the word will desensitise us to it, after which it will need to be amplified. Having said that, let us still, in the next few paragraphs, revert to our discussion of the extreme as described at the beginning of this book.

The Swedish Adventurer of the Year in 2007 and 2010, Fredrik Sträng, is a believer in extreme leadership. In the case of extreme adventures, the leadership cannot be anything but extreme, regardless of whether it is good or bad. But in other circumstances? The extreme examples we chose for this book are not about extreme people in extreme environments.

There are also examples of extreme leadership in a religious context. Here, we find people who strongly believe and where incredibly strict obedience constitutes a form of extreme leadership. It is often the extreme followers of contrasting ideas and concepts who drag each other through the mud and accuse each other of extremism. Is it then not the followers who are extreme?

When using the word 'extreme', we refer only to such contexts in which the role of leadership has seldom or never been studied. This book includes stories about polar expeditions, blue light rescue operations, an abbey, consultants, secret agents, computer games, crises, and health-care services. Of course, not every extreme situation is covered in these stories and, conversely, some insufficiently extreme or overly moderate cases may have been included. However, extreme environments as such are not the point: rather, our focus is on learning from such extreme cases.

We do not claim that these cases are by any means sufficient. Leadership can obviously be varied in more ways than are treated here. We need to study many more variations of leadership and other pecu-liarities. However, we do not need to map all possible variants. Some variants are probably of no interest at all. So-called *gap-spotting* (Alvesson & Sandberg 2011) is only of value as an academic qualification. Instead, we need to stretch our imaginations and look for extremes that no one has yet realised as concerning leadership.

> A theory is tested not merely by applying it or by trying it out, but by applying it to very special cases – cases for which it yields results different from those we should have expected without that theory or in the light of other theories. *(Popper 1963, p. 156)*

We are at the beginning of an exciting journey. Extremes can clearly illustrate patterns that we would otherwise have overlooked.

A series of antitheses

When reading the chapters of this book, you realise the variety of things in the real world. This is exactly what we had hoped for, which is rather encouraging. Getting varied representations of the plurality of problems was indeed our purpose. All the chapters present different forms of leadership, the descriptions and interpretations of which are sometimes contradictory. We can compare these by asking questions and comparing answers.

We start with the easiest question, or perhaps it is the hardest question. What is leadership? The wisdom we gained from the chapters is essentially that nothing ever stays the same. Our futile attempts to define leadership end with the simple conclusion that those whom we refer to as leaders do not actually have much more in common other than the fact that they are called leaders. The same could be said about everyone called Michael. They do not have much more in common other than the name of Michael. Then again, most people called Michael tend to be men. Thirty years ago, we would probably have thought along the same lines in terms of our leaders. Nowadays, we do not take such a sexist approach, nor a gendered or origin-labelled one either, for that matter. To make the situation more equal, we replace the name 'Michael' with 'Alex'. As to a definition, we are back where we started, but with the difference that we are now steadier on our feet – though the significance of that difference is unclear. Maybe it is our own perceptions and descriptions of leadership that have changed rather than leadership itself. We have already dealt with the changing perceptions of leadership in another publication (Ohlsson & Rombach 2014), from which one might conclude that while some people think highly of leadership, others do not.

Despite looking at similar things, the perceptions and conclusions of the authors are very dissimilar, which is exactly what we had hoped for. In this final chapter, however, we bring forward a sort of high-level synthesis. We have chosen to let the various chapters actualise certain dichotomies concerning what leadership is all about in addition to highlighting certain types of problems. In this connection, a dichotomy often indicates an imbalance to which the leadership discourse takes a unvocal approach. Some of these issues, such as voluntary and involuntary leaders or experts and generalists, have already been analysed enough. However, there are others that we would like to discuss some more. We might think of this as a method for finding a coherent whole. We may occasionally refer to individual cases and chapters, but our observations are more often of a general nature, not referring to any specific chapter.

Change–preserve

The belief in an inherent need for change suffered a severe setback in Anna Cregård's chapter on monastic life, in which the focus of leadership was on eternal and inviolable values. We can imagine that such preservative leadership is important, even for leaders apparently completely committed to the rhetoric of change. When elected the first time around, President Obama used the word 'change' as a dominant slogan. It was less certain, however, what changes he could or indeed wanted to achieve. Some of these changes, however, others were keen to put a stop to, and as a result, no such changes occurred. When the rhetoric is about a change of system, being sceptical is probably not such a bad thing. One of the most important tasks of all politicians who do not want a revolution is to protect and consolidate basic principles. Democracy, the market economy, human rights, and national sovereignty were all matters that transformed Obama from a radical innovator to an ultra-conservative wall of concrete. Still, it is difficult (even in the USA) to win votes using slogans such as 'I plan to keep things the way they are except for a few minor changes'.

In her chapter on leadership in crises, Iréne Lind Nilsson looked at leadership from a different perspective. Leaders who are caught up in a crisis try to manage and mitigate the effects of change rather than driving the change forward. The winds of change are inevitable, even when you are more or less ready to face them. The same applies to cold: It is not what the thermometer says that determines whether or not we feel cold, but how we dress ourselves (all else being equal). It is also true as, it has been said (*e.g.* by Eriksson 2012), that 'there are no bad clothes – just dreadful weather'. However, when the weather is really warm then you are never cold, regardless of what you are wearing, and when there is a storm blowing in and around the organisation, you have to try to protect and preserve what is most important from being blown to pieces. The focus here is also on preservation rather than change, despite the leadership being exercised in the middle of a storm of impacts and problems.

We believe it is demanding and difficult to maintain things as they are and to preserve what is exposed to the erosive winds of change. For many leaders, whether in politics, business, or other organisations, the most important and difficult task is often to prevent what is already working well from being changed for the worse.

The modern change-oriented leadership can be reinterpreted. Transformative leadership is generally exercised when a leader endeavours to take his or her organisation to new heights by implementing a new development or change. Sometimes, this is probably the case. However, when completely different forces are brought into play, the aspirations of the organisation – and of its leader – have to adapt to the situation. When no one is buying from us any more, or our audience is booing us, or our students are no longer inspired to study, we must make changes in order to survive. The changes we make are then only the way we choose to handle these problems while the organisation itself, to the extent possible, remains intact and unchanged. Much of the pressure for change that an organisation faces derives from a lack of legitimacy and an image of the organisation that does not comply with the expectations of the surrounding world in terms of buying, applauding, and scoring points (DiMaggio & Powell 1983). When the image of an organisation is the problem, it is a completely misguided leadership that seeks to change structures and processes: If the façade is the problem, then surely it is the façade that needs to be altered and renovated.

Lead–follow

When writing the chapter on cold leadership, we felt that we had included most of what was worth saying about leaders and followers. Strong followers need strong leaders and sometimes there can be too much of a good thing. However, Staffan Furusten's chapter on leadership and expertship is a bit of a brain teaser, as it illustrates how the consultant leads his or her leader. According to the literature on professional organisations, this is not an uncommon phenomenon (*e.g.* Mintzberg 1983). It is not surprising that many doctors gladly refrain from becoming unit managers, as discussed in the chapter on reluctant leaders. Who wants to be the leader of those who are supposed to lead you?

The entire concept of a simple relationship between leaders and followers is meaningless, since relationships between people are generally never that simple other than in some exceptional cases. And it is not always the case that such exceptions constitute a desirable ideal. We are inclined to agree with Henri Fayol (1916/2008), who said that simplicity and ambiguity in an organisation create clarity and logic. For example, it is difficult to ask someone to take responsibility for something when there are others with exactly the same responsibility. While we are in favour of such things as the scalar chain and unit command principle, we must admit that it is sometimes unclear who decides, despite our best efforts to create clear structures. When we are all responsible, it might be prudent to tone down the romanticism that surrounds leadership.

As mentioned above, we do not wish to repeat what we have already mentioned in other publications but there is one, likely untrue, story of leaders and followers that we just cannot resist retelling:

> The bloodthirsty and dandyish revolutionary Maximilien de Robespierre was sitting at a café in Paris, as the worst of the Reign of Terror gripped the city. It might have been in 1793. We believe he was drinking cocoa. Brewed coffee was for barbarians (the espresso machine did not arrive until a hundred years later) and tea was simply too un-French. Also, chocolate would match the elegant attire he wore. While his mug of cocoa was cooling to a more drinkable temperature, a mob of angry Parisians passed outside the café, armed with whatever a mob arms itself with. Clubs, axes, knives, and any other weaponlike objects they could possibly get hold of. The mob had presumably got wind of some aristocrat, ineptly hiding in one of the underground cellars so commonly found in those days. As the mob passed by, Robespierre stood up and proclaimed: 'There go my people! I must follow at once, for I am their leader!' (Ohlsson & Rombach 2014)

The relationship between leaders and their followers is complex. The image that many of us have of leaders belongs to fairy tales, among nasty wolves, happy princesses, and noble knights. Leading could very well entail placing yourself in the front lines and asking the masses to show you the way. However, relationships can take many different forms. Much would be gained if we did not see these forms of relationships as deviations to be corrected (or funny things to be retold) but more as functional variations. However, this would make leadership theory too broad a category to discuss meaningfully, as 'human theory', so to speak.

Reality–'virtuality'

What is happening and affecting us does not always happen in what we call 'the real world'. Our civilisation has created fake worlds that sometimes seem more genuine and real than, well, the real world. Jean Baudrillard (1998) refers to this simulated and media-supported reality as 'hyperreality'. What we read about, believe in, and hope for can mean more to us than what lies at our feet.

Johan Berglund gives a clear example of this in his chapter on virtual leadership. Computer games, which all players and the rest of us know are pure fiction, are increasingly taking up players' time and energy. If this interest goes as far as to interfere with other interests, it is often referred to as video game addiction. For other hyperreality movements, there is no such label, maybe because such movements are so common as be considered more or less normal. Or maybe because the virtual is taking over in areas where we do not understand that the hyperreality is not real – a very good point made by Baudrillard.

Hyperreality creeps up on us and we do not always want to recognise that what feels so right and genuine is, in fact, fake, illusory, and sometimes pure humbug. We can distinguish the world of gaming from our true reality. However, this is more difficult in the case of, for example, a dream world made up of stories about leadership. How can we distinguish between the type of leadership that puts food on the table and the type that leads only to media coverage as modern and forward-thinking leadership? How do we know if the stories have gained the upper hand, and how do we get leaders wanting to know too? Perhaps it is not even worth trying.

'What about Bond!' we hear someone shouting, in front of their home cinema. As we see it, the Bond chapter is most interesting as a reflection of reality. In the films, we get a little closer to the subject matter, as reality is shown in an uncluttered and archetypical form, as in theory. The Bond films are particularly good at spreading myths about what leaders ought to do and how they ought to behave. At the same time, the world of Bond is and always will be a fictional world.

Hyperreality looks better than everyday reality. In it, you can make yourself seem very attractive by using grand titles and impressive leadership terms and become truly inspired in a triumphant emptiness (Alvesson 2006). Rather than actually leading, you just talk about it. As a result, well-known industry leaders and high-ranking politicians feature in colour pictures of glossy magazines. They pontificate on the future or on the importance of being dynamic and flexible, as if following a pre-rehearsed script. You sometimes get the impression that these publicly exposed leaders are symbolic reflections of many people's collective efforts. Instead of actually having or using it, they merely put power on display. This is nothing new, though the phenomenon may have intensified.

A favourite historical example of leadership being nothing but a chimera, a theatrical performance rather than powerful sovereignty, is the reign of Louis xiv of France, the Sun King. Louis xiv was decorated with every symbol of power available. Arraying himself with his often meticulously designed wigs, silk stockings, jewels, and varied accoutrements and parading himself before court must have taken up nearly all his energy, although he did reign for a considerable length of time, *i.e.* 1643–1715. Louis XIV can be described as a performance rather than a person (Burke 1996). He is a leader who never led. Or perhaps, once again, the situation is the complete opposite: that in fact his story exemplifies what leadership really is about.

When consultants come into a company, they play the same role as do all the tailors, portrait artists, and advisers of Louis XIV. They start as helpers, experts, and bureaucrats. As time passes, these anonymous public figures and *éminences grises* soon develop their own traits and tics. Sometimes, they even get the idea that it is they who are leading. This may indeed be so, though it is not the most common scenario: perhaps it is the consultants who style, direct, and lead these symbolic figures to the top of their game. However, it is difficult to be a backseat driver when the person in the driver's seat is not actually driving the car.

Perhaps well-functioning organisations do not need anyone at the top of the hierarchy. In the case of the required rate of return, *i.e.* the principle regulating quarterly capitalism, there is no need for a thinking individual making demands from the top of the pyramid. This has already been done: the followers provide their leaders with objectives while the rest of the world holds the leaders responsible for the results of such objectives, regardless of whether they devote most of their time to work or to silk stockings and portraits.

Totality–partiality

Characteristic of a modern bureaucracy is that its members have a regulated relationship with their organisation. The power and authority of the leader extend – at least formally – beyond the workplace, working hours, and contractual duties. The nuns in the Abbey are subject to a particularly extensive leadership. The Abbey is a total institution (Goffman 2004): there are no set working hours and there is no private life; membership is all-encompassing. In a sense, the leadership itself is also all-encompassing. We realise that the total institutions considered by Goffman – *i.e.* prisons and mental hospitals – can only partially be equated to the Abbey. However, the essential point here is that as a 'member' of such an institution, you have no other identity to escape to. The Abbey is a pre-modern organisation with its roots in the feudal society of medieval times. The contrast could not be greater between it and the virtual world of computer games. In that world, you are a member or leader of an environment that you can opt out of at any moment unless, of course, you are addicted to the game.

Before going any further, we would like to point out that 'total leadership' is not an established concept in the literature on leadership, particularly not as counterposed to 'partial leadership'. Still, some have tried to exploit the concept of total leadership. In *Total Leadership: Be a Better Leader, Have a Better Life* by Stewart Friedman (2008), we are advised on how to become better leaders. So as to become better leaders, Friedman recommends that we '*be real*', '*be whole*', and '*be innovative*'. We could not have said it any better ourselves! Trying to be a better person is a brilliant recommendation. Apart from becoming a better leader, there are plenty of other benefits of becoming a better person. One can wonder why no one else has thought of that? According to another source, total leadership is all about two principles:

> The first principle is that for organisations to succeed in the 21st century, they must develop leaders throughout the total organisation.

> The second principle is that for leadership development to be effective, it must utilize a complete, integrated, total leadership development process. (LMI-HR.com)

Here, you can also read that companies investing in this type of leadership are more successful than others. First, there seems to be empirical evidence for this conclusion and, second, it seems perfectly reasonable: organisations that involve their managers and other employees perform better than others. It would be unreasonable to think otherwise. It gets more complicated as we go on, however. Is the best solution a total involvement that excludes any understanding of other alternatives? This type of total involvement is only really found in fanatical cults. Certain successful companies such as IKEA and Apple are sometimes referred to as cults. However, that is probably a bit of an exaggeration. These companies operate in pluralistic environments in which they try to adapt to the conflicting demands of customers and society. The IKEA converts that we happen to know would hardly allow themselves to be burned at the stake for their faith in the Billy bookshelf.

The types of leadership described in the various chapters of this book ought to be positioned along a continuum, one extreme of which is total leadership and the other the mundane aspects of leadership found in the lives of followers. We do not know if there has ever been a perfect example of total leadership, though the Abbey, polar expeditions, and perhaps the UN colonel in war-torn Bosnia are as close as we can get. Bond's life is ruled by his superior, but he still manages to get up to all sort of mischief that his superior seems to disapprove of. Nor does he let his superior shoot him even when she believes that is the right thing to do. The consultants of Staffan Furusten and computer games of Johan Berglund are two examples at the partial leadership end of the spectrum.

In line with Max Weber (1925/1978), it is not difficult to see that the current trend is towards an increasingly partial leadership surrounded by restrictions and bureaucratic barriers. As a result, total leadership feels outdated, medieval, primitive, and inefficient. This is, for example, how Göran Ahrne and Apostolis Papakostas (2002) perceive it. According to them, as we become members of and increasingly rely on organisations, the organisations themselves become increasingly less dependent on us. As examples of this, they mention contemporary phenomena such as project appointments and recruitment agencies.

It may be true that dictators of the past were more totalitarian than are the leaders of modern democracies, though there are always counter-examples. The Nambikwara tribe in Brazil is the most traditional and 'outmoded' organisation mentioned in this book, and their somewhat reluctant tribal chiefs hardly constitute a good example of total leadership. The Abbey, on the other hand, described above as totalitarian, is so rigorously regulated, even down to the finer details of clothes washing, that its total leadership appears to dissolve in its own contradictions: at the end of the day, there is actually not that much for the Abbess to decide upon. The total institution does not automatically create a total leadership. The guild masters in Berglund's computer game can have their long-winded say only as long as the other guild members stay by their keyboards. The fact that the followers can leave their keyboards at any time and get a latte at the café around the corner only adds to the post-modern irony.

Charisma–bureaucracy

Whether or not leadership is total or partial depends largely on the complexity of the structures of which it is part. How could it be any other way? The leadership exercised in many institutions today is surely more partial than in the past. The diversity of the duties, products, and lifestyles that we associate with modern life are certainly significant, but let us not forget charisma. According to Max Weber (1925/1978), the distinction between bureaucratic and charismatic leadership is that bureaucratic leadership – or 'authority' as Weber called it – is a manifestation of modern rationality. Could not the same be said of charisma? Charisma is the effulgence that makes others follow a personal example. Whether such effulgence is among the characteristics of the leader or in the minds of the followers is an interesting topic for speculation. However, in this instance, it is neither here nor there. Some leaders are either blessed or cursed by a charismatic personality.

In the chapter on cold leadership, we adopt a sceptical stance towards charisma. There is a clear risk of charismatic people misleading easily led followers into doing stupid and dangerous things, sometimes with catastrophic outcomes. Eric Carlström disagrees in a healthy sort of way. Someone needs to take the initiative and do what needs to be done even if it falls outside the regulations; for example, in an emergency, there must be room for personal leadership. Iréne Lind Nilsson is thinking along the same lines in her examples from the Balkan war in the 1990s. Yet it is often considered an advantage for leaders to be uncharismatic. This appears to have been the case with the Social Democratic Party, as described by Rebecka Arman and Östen Ohlsson, at least in its early days.

Back then, charisma was kept in check by traditions. Leaders were expected to come from a particular family background or, if not, to fulfil certain conditions that did not necessarily have anything to do with charisma. Still, if the charisma is in the mind of the followers, then there might still be a disaster.

In more modern times, charismatic leaders have been able to act relatively independently of tradition. The engineer Salomon August Andrée appears to be an innocent lamb in this line of leaders, while Adolf Hitler and Josef Stalin spring to mind as more extreme cases. Once again, bureaucracy (or perhaps civilisation) is what can keep charisma within civilised limits. What makes us behave like decent people is not only a formal regulatory system but also the subtle disciplining instruments of our culture. Once again, we are facing a matter of balance. If we were to rely only on the provisos of the bureaucratic regulatory system, many crises would remain unsolved while precarious charisma would be left to run wild.

The leadership literature reviewed for this book treats the problem of balance much too lightly. People often express their approval of personal leadership, as even a cursory search on Google shows, which is likely to be the same as charismatic leadership. Some are more gifted than others. In the scientific literature, however, terms such as 'transformative leadership' are used instead, together with suggestions for learning to enact it (Yukl 2012). In any case, there are set instructions for how to lead and implement changes (Kotter 1996).

The role of charisma in leadership cannot be avoided. We could not eliminate the role of charisma even if we tried, so we must take a more analytical approach to the phenomenon. There are probably many types of charisma, each of which works differently in different situations. Our collection of examples offers no basis for an analysis, but if one compares the different types of leadership described as charismatic, one is sure to find both interesting and significant distinctions. Knowledge of the range of variation of a phenomenon is a prerequisite for any systematic knowledge; to that end, further studies of leadership in extreme contexts are clearly needed.

Leadership of the future

Let us now look to the future and how we can apply the antitheses discussed above. The future might well disturb the balances required in order to create dichotomies.

If you desire a moment of entertainment and fun at the expense of others, read about the visions of the future from a few decades ago. Not only are they nearly always completely wrong, but they are also based on what we now know to be totally unreasonable assumptions. More often than not, the purpose of such futuristic visions was not to offer a glimpse of what the future might hold, but rather to criticise the time when the vision was created. The critique of civilisation seems to gain momentum when looking ahead rather than backwards.

Although historical images of the future usually evoke smiles, it is the future nonetheless that we all wish to know something about. We guess that some of our readers might want to know what we think about the future after this study – as long as we keep to the question of future leadership. Should anyone poke fun at our projection for 30 years from now, we can console ourselves with the fact that we actually did not anticipate being remembered for that long.

We start with a few basic assumptions. Let us assume that technical and economic progress towards more advanced technologies and a global division of labour will continue for some time to come, perhaps around a hundred years. Naturally, there could be a trend reversal during this time: a comet might hit the Earth, a great war might break out, our preferences as to what constitutes a good life might change, or climate change might run completely amok. In our opinion, however, a more likely scenario is that whatever problems, crises, and shifts of perceptions there might be, they will not be of a magnitude that could put an end to the development of technology and the economy. Consequently, we can expect increasingly sophisticated technology operating in an increasingly globalised and elaborate division of labour. We believe this to be the foundation of our future. To believe anything else feels somewhat unwise to us. We do not know what countries will lead this development, what new innovations will be made, what people will choose to believe in, or what diseases will be cured – either way, it does not significantly affect our reasoning.

More about partially total leadership

Based on these simple assumptions, organisations like the Abbey will probably decline in number while the number of organisations with partial memberships and occasional contacts is likely to increase. The question is: where will this happen? To which we reply, in organisations with total leadership.

We can already detect a sense of anticipation for total leadership in which the leaders lead and the rest of us follow. The world images depicted in fantasy literature and computer games allow to us escape to a less complicated life in which this type of unambiguous social relationship is the norm. As if that was not enough, many of us yearn for such an existence in real life too. When the organisation we work for is not the answer, we join others until our life becomes complete. At the same time, there is a clear notion that computer games could be replaced and religions left for participation in multiple total leadership organisations. Thus, we are either individually or collectively creating our own totally led existence, away from constantly having to make individual choices and an outdated notion of freedom.

Emile Durkheim's (1893/1997) reasoning that an increasingly elaborate division of labour in society requires a new ideology – an organic solidarity – is a concept of renewed importance and depth. It is, after all, nearly one hundred years since Emile Durkheim presented this reasoning. The division of labour that Durkheim regarded as modern and elaborate has, in fact, surpassed all his expectations. It probably imposes new demands for trust and solidarity between different people and cultures. This explains the constantly growing interest in things such as trust and social capital (Putnam 1993).

Is this not an indication that future leadership will become increasingly total, but be exercised over smaller domains? In that case, one can imagine that, overall, our lives will be less and less under the command of total leaders and leadership. All of us would then be part of a web of influences that we either exert ourselves to resist or become subject to. As long as we continue sitting in front of our computers playing games, Johan will be the boss, while on other occasions, he will have to submit to our editorial work.

The difficulty lies in trying to create commitment in an otherwise fragmented existence. There is also a counter-trend to this. Our chapter on polar adventures tells of people who longed for something more substantial and complete in the fragmented existence of their days. In the days of Emile Durkheim, in fact. There will be the same longing in the future too, perhaps even more so. If that is the case, then there will still be room for total leaders like Scott or Andrée, leaders who take a holistic approach and do not allow for or enable selection of smaller parts. One can only hope that our fragmented civilisation can be kept together by solidarity and confidence, enough to prevent the emergence of another Hitler or Stalin.

More about bureaucratic leadership behind charismatic leaders

The question of bureaucracy versus charisma is an exciting issue for the future. On the surface, bureaucratic leadership is expected to continue to weaken to the advantage of charismatic leadership. As mentioned above, total leadership requires charisma in order for people to submit voluntarily. What does that say about the competence of the leadership?

According to Max Weber's analysis of the 'political unproductiveness of German social democracy', the problem and solution both lie in bureaucratisation, though the latter would require 'charismatic leader figures' (Borell 1987, pp. 9–10). Weber therefore dissolved the dichotomy he himself had created. Or perhaps one should distinguish between charismatic leadership and charismatic leader figures, as the latter could suggest a leader figure subject to bureaucratic control.

Future organisations are unlikely to be led by charismatic leadership. Organisation leaders who wish to exert influence by using their charisma can expect to encounter difficulties, as the level of required technical expertise and competence will keep increasing. There are two reasons for this. First, as a result of technical developments, the increasing number of available gadgets and services will require additional specialist skills and expertise. Second, globalisation will lead to economies of scale for speciality products and services that would never be lucrative on a national or regional market. Doctors, for example, could specialise in patients with a certain type of illness that, in a larger city, might only occur once a year, but on a global scale, would fill an entire hospital. Increasingly deep and narrow specialities will require the support of specially adapted instruments and technology. The leadership of this hyper-specialised world will require the support of a cadre of highly qualified officials with no desire to be either seen or heard.

This building of façades around leadership is something that we strongly believe will be part of the future. We do not want this phenomenon to be dismissed as yet another post-modern fad. This, we predict, is going to be a long-lasting trend that will come to be accepted as a reasonable norm. Why would something previously seen as reality take preference over a much better hyperreality? We believe that the next great revolution – or perhaps, the one after that – will consist of riots and acts of violence on the web against injustices perceived to exist there. All the while, our everyday life with all its injustices and inequalities will continue as usual, completely unaffected.

More about progressive preservative leadership

When it comes to change and preservation, it is quite difficult at first to see the bigger picture. After all, we are organisational researchers who lecture about leadership and who argue obstinately that change is an organisational characteristic, that organisations are inherently unstable and therefore changeable, and that it is important for the management of an organisation to help it continue along the same track and do what it is good at doing. This is what creates structures and stable processes. The fact that leaders talk so much about change has to do with two things: first, they say what their audiences want to hear, because if not, they will get booed; second, they run many projects that lead to organisational changes for the sole purpose of keeping things the way they are.

Contemporary times are often seen as more stable and less volatile than past times. The trends referred to above as basic assumptions, *i.e.* globalisation and the increasing division of labour, clearly have an overall stabilising effect. Globalisation creates a more homogeneous world where the effects of conflicts and other major events call for caution and, indeed, conservatism.

A complex world in which impulses come from far and near creates temptations that every leader should be able to resist. Making changes for their own sake is one such temptation. This suggests that preservative leadership is of growing importance. Business concepts, reputation, and sound internal work ethics need to be safeguarded from destructive forces. The concept of preservation is already an important aspect of today's leadership, though it is generally referred to as change leadership. Regardless, the doctrine of leadership ought to be developed to include preservation measures as well. After all, preservation is not about standing still; it is about applying skills and tools very different from those needed for chasing down employees who oppose all good and beneficial changes and about finding the right balance in a dynamic organisation. A future of progressive preservative leadership beckons.

Doctrine of leadership

Throughout this book we have questioned the useless theories and models of the dominant leadership discourse. The checklists and programmes of change that Harvard professors are so keen to promote seem to consist of a mixture of obvious predictability, a certain amount of actual experience, and an unreasonable degree of pious hope. In practice, however, this is probably better than nothing. John Kotter's (1996) '8-step process for leading change' creates a structure for those responsible for change processes. It provides order and predictability and incorporates a certain amount of experience, which should not be underestimated. However, it seems strange that there is no explanation as to why there are exactly eight steps. Why not six or twelve? At the same time as we are inclined to agree with certain aspects of the model, we still feel that there is something amiss about it.

Indeed, it seems as though many influential leaders have chosen not to embrace academic leadership doctrine to a significant degree. It appears that neither Steve Jobs nor Osama Bin Laden was a product of management training. This is something we all need to be grateful for. Perhaps the greatest problem for future leadership is devising a leadership doctrine that is actually useful. When such a doctrine is developed, anyone will be able to learn how to use effective behaviour management techniques to get their fellow human beings to do just about anything. For this reason alone, we do not wish fellow leadership researchers – our dear colleagues – any success whatsoever.

However, we are not quite certain that social sciences will ever be able to achieve such success. Social sciences – including the science of leadership – are inherently reflexive (Giddens 1996). We do not anticipate that the molecules we learn about in natural science will ever think about or act on the basis of what we know about them. They are completely oblivious to our knowledge and understanding of them. However, we – as leaders and followers – are acutely aware of the various theories about us. Our knowledge of these theories leads us to adapt in various but, for the theories, unpredictable ways. As a result, the doctrine of leadership will probably never be the practical toolkit that we sometimes hear requested in our management courses.

Maybe these lengthy formulas for how to become a true leaders of change and the problems caused by reflexive social sciences simply constitute a way to complicate something that would otherwise be simplicity itself for those who dare to face up to reality. One conclusion that can be drawn from Milgram's experiment (see Chapter 1) is that there is no need for complications. Making yourself look and sound authoritative is enough to lead people to do the most unlikely and disgusting things.

However, we do not want to end with such a dystopian perspective. Wishing for true progress is perfectly reasonable. Despite our criticisms, the study of leadership is about to become broader and deeper. The discourse has its limitations and the criticisms and alternative perspectives that exist will eventually have an effect on practice. We would like to see ourselves be part of the development of such alternative perspectives.

Whence and whither

This last chapter marks the end of this book; it also marks the end of the third part of our collective trilogy about organisation and leadership. Let us quickly recap.

First came *Res pyramiderna: Om frihetsskapande hierarkier och tillplattningens slaveri* (Raise the pyramids: hierarchical theories of freedom and slavery); first published in the summer of 1998, we had worked on *Res pyramiderna* since 1996. When the present book was submitted to the publishers in the autumn of 2018, nearly 23 years had passed since the overarching project started. Obviously, we have been busy doing other things too. We have taught, researched, spoken with practitioners, and produced other books and articles, sometimes together with other people; in addition, we have taken on more administrative tasks than was perhaps necessary and continued to live our lives.

It is often said that researchers and their research are driven by curiosity. The word 'curious' is undoubtedly one of the more frequent words that we have heard speakers use during our years in the academy. Thankfully, we do not ourselves suffer from this condition. Not at all. Nor do we believe it to be particularly common among other researchers either. The driving force behind this trilogy has instead been our despair at the current the state of things: How can so many incredibly stupid things be taken as the truth and then repeated again and again? No anger is allowed: research is not a military campaign but a duty. However, anyone who tries to contribute has a right to criticise or complain.

In *Res pyramiderna* (Raise the pyramids) we found ourselves looking at the flood of empty phrases and inadequate reasoning that characterises most solutions promoted in the management field. Our reasoning in this project was inspired by the endeavours of organisations to tear down pyramids and flatten organisations, something that almost became a national movement. As we see it, the problems that such measures are believed to have eradicated did not actually exist and, if they did, then flattening organisational structures was not the best solution. From a methodological perspective, one might say that this was a book about the art of reasoning that it could be the other way around. However, from an empirical perspective, we examined what there was to say on the matter.

Part two of the trilogy was published in 2014: *The Tyranny of Metaphors: Pathways to Freedom*. This book is also based on the assumption that much of what is being said in the field of management could well be said differently. That which is different is concealed by metaphors that control us and our thoughts and are therefore difficult to abandon. These metaphors are far more powerful than any member of an organisation can at first realise. We are all prisoners of metaphors. In *The Tyranny of Metaphors*, we present a variety of methods that can help us to break free from metaphors, allowing us to better understand organisations. The same methods can also be used to break free from those who lead with the help of metaphors. And it all ends with the exhortation: 'Think for yourself!'

Now, you have almost reached the end of the third part of this trilogy. There will be no more after this, not because we have tired of this emancipatory project and wish to fall into the abyss, clutching it in our arms (*cf.* Doyle 1905). No, simply because trilogies do not usually consist of more than three parts: our freedom is subject to certain limitations, which we know full well that others have overstepped (*e.g.* Adams 1979).

In this book we obstinately try to look beyond the obvious. This time, our collective knowledge of leadership is used as an example. It is an example that works well, as we all agree on what we know and how things stand. We also agree in other fields of knowledge, though more often than not this is because we realise the value of consensus and choose to highlight what we agree on. As for leadership, our search for knowledge seems to have come to a standstill, not because we have stopped searching but because there is nothing new to be found.

We are making a renewed attempt with this book. We asked ourselves: What will happen if we search for stories about the phenomenon of leadership in unusual contexts? What will we learn from studying leadership in extreme environments? What exactly have we learned, and what have we learned about this way of learning?

The time has come for us to bow out. We have made every contribution that we possibly could – a trilogy. We have written and you have read. Quite a few of our readers have already been in contact with us, but we would like to hear from newcomers too. Please feel free to send an e-mail at Bjorn.Rombach@.spa.gu.se. Questions and comments are welcome.

The continuation of this project is dependent on two possibilities. You may decide to write your own trilogy. That would be interesting, and if you do so, please send a copy. Or you may decide to practise what we preach. You are on your own there. Thinking outside the box is hard, but remember, at least some people will be hiding behind the pillar, cheering you on.

References

1. Is leadership really the solution?
Emma Ek Österberg, Björn Rombach and Östen Ohlsson

Books and articles

Adorno, Theodor, Else Frenkel-Brunswik, Daniel Levinson & Nevitt Sanford, 1950, *The Authoritarian Personality*. New York: Harper and Row.

Alvesson, Mats, 1996, 'Leadership Studies: From Procedure and Abstraction to Reflexivity and Situation'. *The Leadership Quarterly*, Vol. 4, pp. 455–485.

Alvesson, Mats and Andrée Spicer, 2011, *Metaphors we Lead By. Understanding Leadership in the Real World*. London and New York: Routledge.

Barker, Richard, 1997, 'How Can We Train Leaders If We Do Not Know What Leadership Is?' *Human Relations*, Vol. 50, No. 4, p. 343–362.

Bennis, Warren, 2003, *On Becoming a Leader*. New York: Basic Books.

Blake, Robert & Jane Mouton, 1964, *The Managerial Grid: The Key to Leadership Excellence*. Houston: Gulf publishing.

Brown, Michael E., Linda K. Treviño & David A. Harrison, 2005, 'Ethical Leadership: A Social Learning Perspective for Construct Development and Testing', *Organizational Behavior and Human Decision Processes,* Vol. 97, pp. 117–134.

Burns, James MacGregor, 1978, *Leadership*. New York: Harper Collins.

Bushe, Gervase, 2010, *Klart ledarskap* (Clear leadership), Stockholm: Ekerlids Förlag.

Carlson, Sune, 1991/1951, *Executive Behaviour*. Stockholm: Almqvist & Wiksell.

Carlzon, Jan, 1985, *Riv pyramiderna* (Tear the Pyramids Down). Stockholm: Bonniers.

Cohen, Michael, James March & Johan Olsen, 1972, 'A Garbage Can Model of Organizational Choice'. *Administrative Science Quarterly*, Vol. 17, No. 1, pp. 1–25.

Döös, Marianne & Kerstin Waldenström (red.), 2008, *Chefskapets former och resultat* (Forms and results of leadership). *Två kunskapsöversikter om arbetsplatsens ledarskap* (Two knowledge reviews of leadership in the workplace). Vinnova (Swedish Agency for Innovation Systems) Report VR 2008:15.

Fransson, Susanne (red.), 2007, *Marknaden – saklig grund för lönesättning?* (The labour market – a factual basis for pay?) Stockholm: Norstedts Juridik.

Greenberg, Jerald, 2011, *Behavior in Organizations*. Boston, MA: Pearson.

Hersey, Paul & Ken Blanchard, 1969, *Management of Organizational Behavior – Utilising Human Resources.* Englewood Cliffs, NJ: Prentice Hall.

Hesselbein, Frances, Marshall Goldsmith & Richard Beckhard (red.), 1996, *The Leader of the Future,* San Francisco: Jossey-Bass.

Holmblad Brunsson, Karin, 2007, *The Notion of General Management.* Malmö: Liber.

Kellerman, Barbara, 2004, *Bad Leadership*. Boston, MA: Harvard Business School Press.

Lange, Johan, 2011, *LUCK: Konceptet för hållbart ledarskap* (The concept of sustainable leadership). Älvsjö: Johan P. Lange.

Lewin, Kurt, Ronald Lippitt & Ralph White, 1939, Patterns of Aggressive Behavior in Experimentally Created 'Social Climates'. *The Journal of Social Psychology*, Vol. 10, No. 2, pp. 269–299.

Milgram, Stanley, 2009/1974, *Obedience to Authority*. New York: Harper Perennial.

Mintzberg, Henry, 1973, *The Nature of the Executive*. New York: Harper and Row.

Ohlsson, Östen & Björn Rombach 1998, *Res pyramiderna* (Raise the Pyramids) Stockholm: Svenska Förlaget.

Scott, Susan, 2011, *Fierce Leadership – A Bold Alternative to the Worst 'Best Practices' of Business Today*. London: Piatkus.

Sun, Peter & Marc Anderson, 2011, *Civic Capacity: Building on Transformational Leadership to Explain Successful Integrative Public Leadership. Proceedings on the 6th organization studies workshop*, Paris, 25–28 May 2011.

Sveningsson, Stefan & Mats Alvesson, 2010, *Ledarskap* (Leadership). Malmö: Liber.

Tengblad, Stefan, Freddy Hällstén, Christer Ackerman & Johan Velten, 2007, *Medarbetarskap – från ord till handling* (Employeeship – from words to action). Malmö: Liber.

Tunbrå, Lars-Olof, 2004, *Psykopatiska chefer – lika farliga som charmiga* (Psychopathic Managers – as dangerous as charming). Malmö: Liber Ekonomi.

Törnblom, Mia, 2011, *Du leder!* (You lead!). *Personligt ledarskap med Mia Törnblom* (Personal leadership with Mia Törnblom). Stockholm: Månpocket.

Velten, Johan, Stefan Tengblad & Runar Heggen, 2017, *Medarbetarskap: Så får du dina medarbetare att ta initiativ och känna ansvar* (Employeeship: How you get your employees to take initiative and feel responsible). Stockholm: Liber.

Weber, Max, 1998, *From Max Weber: Essays in Sociology* (excerpts from *Wirtschaft und Gesellschaft*, 1922). New York: Routledge.

Yukl, Gary, 2006, *Leadership in Organizations*. Englewood Cliffs, NJ: Pearson/Prentice Hall.

Internet

https://www.foretagande.se/
vagledande-principer-for-gott-
ledarskap-10-delar/, Företagande.se
(2017-06-22).

www.journals.elsevier.com/the-lead-
ership-quarterly/, The Leadership
Quarterly (2017-06-22).

2. Cold leadership
Östen Ohlsson and Björn Rombach

Books and articles

Ahlman, Axel, 1929, *Isviddernas hjältar*
(Heroes of the Icy Expanses). Lund:
Gleerups.

Allers Family Journal's 69th Manual
Kampen om polerna (Battle of the Poles).

Abersson, Gunnar, 1906, *S. A. Andrée,
hans följeslagare och hans polarfärd
1896–1897* (S. A. Andrée, his companions and his polar expedition
1896–1897). Stockholm: Norstedts.

Andersson, Johan, 1945, *Männen
kring Sydpolen* (The Men at the
South Pole). Stockholm: Saxon &
Lindströms.

Andrée, Salomon August, Nils
Strindberg & Knut Frænkel, 1930,
Med Örnen mot polen (With the Eagle
towards the Pole). Published by the
Swedish Society for Anthropology
and Geography. Stockholm:
Bonniers.

Andrist, Ralph, 1963/1962,
Polarforskningens hjältar (Heroes
of Polar Exploration). Malmö:
Allhems.

Aughton, Peter, 2001, *En legendarisk seg-
lats* (The Fatal Voyage). *With James
Cook and Endeavour towards Terra
Australis*. Lund: Historiska Media.

Babiak, Paul & Robert Hare, 2006,
*Snakes in Suits: When Psychopaths
Go to Work*. New York, NY: Regan
Books.

Bennis, Warren, 1970, *American
Bureaucracy*. New Brunswick NJ:
Transaction Publishers.

Bergquist, Lars, 1981, *Isvandring med
Nordenskiöld* (A Walk on the Ice
with Nordenskiöld). Stockholm:
Norstedts.

Brögger, Waldemar Christopher &
Nordahl Rolfsen, 1896, *Fridtjof
Nansen 1861–1893*. Stockholm:
Norstedts.

Byström, Dan & Jon Sörensen, 1940,
'Fridtjof Nansen'. In: *Dåd och bragd
7* (Deeds and feats 7). Stockholm:
Hugo Gebers Publishers.

Clegg, Stewart, Martin Harris &
Harro Höpfl (red.), 2011, *Managing
Modernity. Beyond Bureaucracy?*
Oxford: Oxford University Press.

Cook, James, 1982/1768–1780, *Kapten
James Cooks resor* (The Voyages of
Captain James Cook). A selection
of Cook's own diaries edited by
Christopher Lloyd. Uddevalla:
International Books Automation.

Danielsson, Bengt & Göran Burenhult,
1991, *I James Cooks kölvatten* (In the
Wake of Captain James Cook).
Höganäs: Bra Böcker.

Diski, Jenny, 2004/1997, *På tunn is*
(On Thin Ice). *En resa till Antarktis
(Journey to Antarctica)*. Stockholm:
Alfabeta.

Disney, Walt, 1959, *Kalle Anka på
Sydpolen* (Donald Duck at the South
Pole). Stockholm: Folket i Bild
(FIB's GoldenBooks 150).

Duncan, Joyce, 2002, *Ahead of Their
Time. A Biographical Index of Risk-*

Taking Women. London: Greenwood Press.

Edberg, Rolf, 1961, *Nansen – europén* (Nansen – the European). Stockholm: Tiden

Fiennes, Ranulph, 2003, *Captain Scott*. London: Hodder & Stoughton.

Fogg, Gordon & David Smith, 1990, *The Explorations of Antarctica*. London: Cassell.

du Gay, Paul, 2000, *In Praise of Bureaucracy*. London: Sage.

du Gay, Paul (red.), 2009/2005, *The Values of Bureaucracy*. Oxford: Oxford University Press.

Goodsell, Charles, 2004, *The Case for Bureaucracy. A Public Administration Polemic*. Washington, D.C.: CQ Press.

Grafton, Anthony, 1999/1997, *The Footnote. A Curious History*. Cambridge, MA: Harvard University Press.

Grenna Local Folklore Society, 1931, *S. A. Andrée. Minnen och anteckningar från polarfararens barndoms- och ungdomstid* (Memories and notes from the childhood and young adult life of a polar explorer).

Hacking, Ian, 1999, *The Social Construction of What?* Cambridge, MA: Harvard University Press.

Havemose, Karin, 2008, *I ljuset av Andrée* (In the light of Andrée). *Ingenjörskonst, gränser och vetenskapens praktik* (Engineering, borders and scientific practices). Stockholm: Santérus.

Hector David, 1894, *James Cook eller Jorden runt tre gånger* (James Cook or Around the world three times). Stockholm: Norstedts.

Hedin, Sven, 1926, *Adolf Erik Nordenskiöld*. Stockholm: Bonniers.

Hempleman-Adams, David, 2002/2001, *I vindarnas våld* (At the Mercy of the Winds). *Med sikte mot Nordpolen* (Aiming for the North Pole). *En modern äventyrare i Andrée-expeditionens spår* (A modern adventurer in the tracks of the Andrée Expedition). Stockholm: Wahlströms.

Holt, Kåre, 1977/1975, *Kapplöpningen* (The Race). *Amundsen och Scott mot Sydpolen* (Amundsen and Scott towards the South Pole). Höganäs: Bra Böcker.

Huntford, Roland, 2003, *Scott and Amundsen. Their Race to the South Pole*. London: Abacus. (CD recording by Tim Pigott-Smith).

Hällsten, Freddy & Stefan Tengblad, 2006, 'Employeeship in practice'. In: Hällsten, Freddy & Tengblad, Stefan (red.), *Employeeship in practice*, pp. 29–32. Lund: Studentlitteratur.

Imbert, Bertrand, 1998/1987, *Polarforskningens pionjärer* (The pioneers of polar research). Stockholm: Berghs.

Kjellström, Rolf, 1995, *Polaräventyr* (Polar Adventure). Stockholm: Carlssons.

Kjellström, Rolf, 1999, 'Andrée-expeditionen och dess undergång – tolkning nu och då' (The Andrée Expedition and its downfall – interpretation now and then). In: Wråkberg, Urban (red.), *The Centennial of S. A. Andrée's North Pole Expedition*, pp. 44–55. Stockholm: The Royal Swedish Academy of Science.

Kristensen, Monica, 1988/1987, *Mot 90° syd.* (To 90° South). Stockholm: Trevi.

Laktionov, Aleksander, 1960, *Nordpolen.* (The North Pole). *Ur polarfärdernas historia (From the history of polar expeditions)*. Moscow: Publishers of literature in foreign languages.

Liljevalch's Art Gallery, Catalogue No. 90 (Axel Edström), 1931, *Fynden på Vitön* (White Island Findings).

Exhibition in memory of S. A. Andrée,
Nils Strindberg and Knut Frænkel.
Stockholm.

Lundström, Sven, 1997, 'Vår position
är ej synnerligen god' (Our situation
is not particularly good). *Andrée-
expeditionen i svart och vitt* (The
Andrée Expedition in black and
white). Stockholm: Carlssons.

Melville, Herman, 1851, *Moby Dick
or the Whale*. https://genius.com/
Herman-melville-moby-dick-chap-
1-loomings-annotated (2017-09-15)

Milne, Alan, 2003/1926, *Winnie-the-
Pooh*. Stockholm: Bonnier Carlsen.

Minnesalbum S. A. Andrée (Chronicle
of S.A. Andrée), 1930. Malmö:
Världslitteraturens förlag *(World
Literature Publishers)*.

Mitford, Nancy, 2010/1949, *Love in a Cold
Climate*. London: Penguin Books.

Moorehead, Alan, 1967/1966,
Ödesdigert möte (The Fatal Impact).
*Kapten Cooks resor till Tahiti,
Australien, Antarktis* (Captain
Cook's travels to Tahiti, Australia
and the Antarctic). Stockholm:
Bonniers.

Nansen, Fridtjof, 1897a, *Fram öfver
polarhafvet I* (Across the Arctic
Ocean I). Stockholm: Bonniers.

Nansen, Fridtjof, 1897b, *Fram öfver
polarhafvet II* (Across the Arctic
Ocean II). Stockholm: Stockholm:
Bonniers.

Nansen Høyer, Liv, 1958, *Fridtjof
Nansen. En historia om kärlek* (A story
about love). Stockholm: Bonniers.

Nielsen, Jerri & Maryanne Vollers,
2001, *Ice Bound. A Doctor's Incredible
Battle for Survival at the South Pole*.
New York: Miramax.

Nickerson, Sheila, 2002, *Midnight
to the North. The Untold Story of the
Inuit Woman Who Saved the Polaris
Expedition*. New York, NY: Penguin
Putnam.

Nilson, Carl Gustaf, 1997, *Vill Nilson
följa med Andrées polarexpedition
till Spetsbergen?* (Does Nilson want
to join Andrée's polar expedition
to Spitsbergen?). *En timmermans
dagboksanteckningar* (A carpenter's
diary). Gothenburg: Typografia
Olsén.

Nilsson, Gustaf-Adolf, 1957, *Sjöfarare*
(Seafarers) *Kåserier om sjöskildrare
genom tiderna* (Anecdotes about
depictions of the sea throughout
time). Malmö: Allhems Publishers.

Obeyesekere, Gananath, 1992a,
*The Apotheosis of Captain Cook:
European Myth-Making in the Pacific*.
Princeton: Princeton University
Press.

—, 1992b, British Cannibals:
Contemplation of an Event in the
Death and Resurrection of James
Cook. *Critical Inquiry*, Vol. 18, pp.
630–654.

Swedish Polar Research
Secretariat,1993, *Swedish Polar
Bibliography. A Guide to Swedish
Literature on Polar Research 1945–
1988. With supplement 1989–1992*.
Stockholm: Swedish Polar Research
Secretariat.

—, 1994, *Swedish Polar Bibliography. A
Guide to Swedish Literature on Polar
Research Supplement 1993–1995*.
Stockholm: Swedish Polar Research
Secretariat.

Raleigh, Duane, 1995, *Ice: Tools and
Technique*. Cabondale, CO: Elk
Mountain Press.

Rydén, Per, 2003, *Den svenske Ikaros*
(The Swedish Ikaros*). Berättelserna
om Andrée* (The stories about
Andrée). Stockholm: Carlssons.

Rönnbäck, Oscar, 1944, *Polarisens
hjältar* (Heroes of the Arctic Ice).
En berättelse om Andrée och hans män
Stockholm: Harrier.

Samwell, David, 1786, *A Narrative of the Death of Captain James Cook*. London: Printed for G. C. J. and J. Robinson, Pater-Noster-Row (excerpt from the Gutenberg Project).

Sannes, John, 1942, 'Fridtjof Nansen'. In: *Radiotjänst, Radiobiblioteket 4. Nordiska gestalter* (Nordic characters), pp. 65–78. Uppsala: Almqvist & Wiksell.

Shackleton, Ernest, 1909, *Antarktis hjärta* (The Heart of the Antarctic). *Berättelsen om den engelska sydpolsexpeditionen* (Being the Story of the British Antarctic Expedition) *1907–1909*. Stockholm: P.A. Norstedts & Söner.

Shackleton, Edward, 1960, *Fridtjof Nansen polarforskeren*. Copenhagen: Steen Hasselbalch Publishers.

Skinnarmo, Ola & Johan Tell, 1999, *Ensam mot Sydpolen* (Alone towards the South Pole). Stockholm: Forum.

Solstad, Dag, 2006, *Armand V: fotnoter til en uutgravd roman*. Oslo: Forlaget Oktober (Publishing House).

Styhre, Alexander, 2009, *Byråkrati – teoretiker, kritiker och försvarare* (Bureaucracy – theorists, critics and defenders). Malmö: Liber.

Sundman, Per Olof, 1968, *Ingen fruktan, intet hopp* (No fear, no hope). *Ett collage kring S. A. Andrée, hans följeslagare och hans polarexpedition* (A collage of S. A. Andrée, his companions and polar expedition). Stockholm: Bonniers

Thayer, Helen, 1994/1993, *Ensam kvinna mot Nordpolen* (The First Solo Expedition by a Woman and Her Dog to the Magnetic North Pole). Stockholm: Forum.

Weber, Max, 1998, *From Max Weber: Essays in Sociology* (excerpts from *Wirtschaft und Gesellschaft*, 1922). New York: Routledge.

Wetterfors, Paul, 1932, second edition, *Fridtjof Nansen. Polarforskaren och människovännen* (The Polar Researcher and Philanthropist). Uppsala: J.A. Lindblad Publishers.

Wood, Martin, 2005, 'The Fallacy of Misplaced Leadership'. *The Journal of Management Studies*, Vol. 42, No. 6, pp. 1101–1121.

Wråkberg, Urban, 2004, 'Historia och kunskapsarkeologi i polartrakterna' (History and archaeology of knowledge in the polar regions). *Tvärsnitt* (Cross-section), No. 3.

Films (by title)

Bare et liv – historien om Fridtjof Nansen (Only one life – The story about Fridtjof Nansen), 1968. Sergej Mikaeljan.

En frusen dröm (A frozen dream),1997. Jan Troell.

Ingenjör Andrées luftfärd (The Flight of the Eagle),1982. Jan Troell.

The Pool, 2001. Boris von Sydowski

Scott of the Antarctic (De fria viddernas män), 1948. Charles Frend.

Internet

www.coolleaders.co.za/ (2017-09-15).

http://evergreen.loyola.edu/~rcrews/sl/archives/feb97/0074.html (2017-09-15).

https://www.hurtigruten.com (2017-09-15).

www.news.cornell.edu/Chronicle/97/11.13.97/COOL.html (2007-09-25).

https://www.nobelpeaceprize.org (2017-09-15).
www.popularhistoria.se (2017-09-15).
www.skolverket.se (2017-09-15).

www.south-pole.com (2017-09-15).
www.sr.se (2017-09-15).
www.vujer.com (2017-09-15).
www.w5internet.com (2017-09-15).

3. Disobedient leadership at the accident site
Eric Carlström

Books and articles

Andersson, Sten, 2004, *Om vetenskapens gränser (About the limits of science). Socialfilosofiska betraktelser* (Social philosophical reflections). Gothenburg: Daidalos.

Anthony, Robert & Vijay Govindarajan, 1995, *Management Control System*. Boston: Irwin McGraw-Hill.

Auf der Heide, Erik, 1989, *Disaster Response: Principles of Preparation and Coordination*. Toronto: The C.V. Mosby Company.

Balaban, Oded, 1990, 'Praxis and Poesis in Aristotle's Practical Philosophy'. *The Journal of Value Inquire*, No. 24, pp. 185–198.

Berlin, Johan & Eric Carlström, 2008, 'The 90 Second Collaboration: A Critical Study of Collaboration Exercises at Extensive Accident Sites'. *Journal of Contingencies and Crisis Management*, Vol. 16, No. 4, pp. 173–181.

Berlin, Johan & Eric Carlström, 2009, *Samverkan på olycksplatsen* (Collaboration at the accident site). *Om organisatoriska barriäreffekter* (About organisational barrier effects). Trollhättan: University West.

Berlin, Johan & Eric Carlström, 2015, 'Collaboration Exercises: What Do They Contribute? – A Study of Learning and Usefulness'. *Journal of Contingencies and Crisis Management*, Vol. 23, No. 1, pp. 11–23.

Boin, Arjen, Paul 't Hart, Eric Stern, & Bengt Sundelius, 2007 *The Politics of Crisis Management: Public Leadership under Pressure*. Cambridge: Cambridge University Press.

Carlström, Eric, 2009, *Vårdchefer* (Healthcare Managers). *Konsten att leda* (The art of leading). Lund: Studentlitteratur.

Carlström, Eric, 2012, 'Middle Managers on the slide'. *Leadership in Health Services*. Vol. 25, No. 2, p. 90–125.

Cooke, Matthew, 1999, 'How Much to do at the Accident Scene? Spend Time on the Essentials, Save Lives'. *British Medical Journal*, Vol. 3, No. 19, pp. 1150–1152.

Corbacioglu, Sitki & Naim Kapucu, 2006, 'Organisational Learning and Selfadaption in Dynamic Disaster Environment'. *Disasters*, Vol. 30, No. 2, pp. 212–233.

Dreyfus, Hubert & Stewart Dreyfus, 1986, *Mind over Machine*. New York: Free Press.

Eriksson, Tore, 2004, *Terroristattackerna i Madrid den 11 mars 2004* (Terrorist attacks in Madrid on 11 March 2004). Karlstad: Swedish Rescue Services Agency.

Hall, Pippa & Lynda Weaver, 2001, 'Interdisciplinary Education and teamwork: A long and winding road'. *Medical Education*, Vol. 35, No. 9, pp. 867–875.

Kendra, James & Tricia Wachtendorf, 2003, 'Elements of Resilience after the World Trade Center Disaster: Reconstituting New York City's Emergency Operations Centre'. *Disaster,* Vol. 27, No. 1, pp. 37–53.

Kiel, Douglas, 1994, *Managing Chaos and Complexity in Government.* San Francisco: Jossey-Bass.

Lagen (2003:778) om skydd mot olyckor (Act (2203:778) on the protection against accidents).

Lewis, Malcolm 2006, 'Nurse Bullying: Organizational Considerations in the Maintenance and Perpetration of Health Care Bullying Cultures'. *The Journal of Nursing Management,* No. 14, pp. 52–58.

Lindblad, Christina & Björn Sjöström, 2005, 'Battlefield Emergency Care: A Study of Nurses Perspectives'. *Accident and Emergency Nursing,* No. 13, pp. 29–35.

County Administrative Board of Västra Götaland, 2007, *Risk och sårbarhetsanalys* (Risk and vulnerability analysis). Report 2008:22.

Morgan, Gareth, 2006. *Images of Organization.* New York: Sage.

Noji, Eric, & Michael Toole, 1997, 'The Historical Development of Public Health Responses to Disasters'. *Disaster,* Vol. 21, No. 4, pp. 366–376.

Poncelet, Jean Luc, 1997, 'Disaster Management in the Caribbean'. *Disaster,* Vol. 21, No. 3, pp. 267–279.

Rickards, Tudor & Susan Moger, 2000, 'Creative Leadership Processes in Project Team Development: An Alternative to Tuckman's Stage Model'. *British Journal of Management,* Vol. 11 No. 4, pp. 273–83.

Rüter, Anders, Helene Nilsson & Tore Wikström, 2007, *Sjukvårdsledning vid olycka och katastrof* (Medical command and control at incidents and disaster). *Från skadeplats till olycksplats* (Major incidents and disasters) Lund: Studentlitteratur.

Scholtens, Astrid, 2008, 'Controlled Collaboration in Disaster and Crisis Management in the Netherlands, History and Practice of an Overestimated and Underestimated Concept'. *Journal of Contingency and Management,* Vol. 16, No. 4, p. 195–207.

Suserud, Björn-Ove, 2001, 'How Do Ambulance Personnel Experience Work at a Disaster Site?' *Accident and Emergency Nursing,* No. 9, p. 56–66.

Swedish Accident Investigation Authority, 2009, *Jordskred vid vägbygge E6 i Småröd, O län, den 20 december 2006* (Landslide by road construction along E6 in Småröd, O county, on 20 December 2006). Report RO 2009:01.

Tsoukas, Haridimos & Christian Knudsen, 2003, 'Introduction: The Need for Meta-Theoretical Reflection in Organization Theory'. In: Tsoukas, Haridimos & Christian Knudsen (ed.), *The Oxford Handbook of Organization Theory. Meta-Theoretical Perspectives.* Oxford: University Press.

The Lancet, editorial, 2010, 'Growth of Aid and the Decline of Humanitarianism', *The Lancet,* Vol. 374, No. 9711, pp. 253.

Weick, Karl, 1990, 'The Vulnerable System: An Analysis of the Tenerife Air Disaster'. *Journal of Management,* Vol. 16, No. 3, pp. 571–593.

—, 1993, 'The Collapse of Sensemaking in Organizations: The Mann Gulch Disaster'. *Administrative Science Quarterly,* No. 38, pp. 628–652.

—, 1995, *Sensemaking in Organizations.* Thousand Oaks, London and New Delhi: Sage.

—, 1996), 'Drop your tools: an allegory for organizational studies'. *Administrative Science Quarterly*, Vol. 41, pp. 301–13.

—, 2001, *Making Sense of the Organization*. Oxford: Blackwell Publishers.

—, 2002, 'Puzzles in Organizational Learning: An Exercise in Disciplined imagination'. *British Journal of Management*, Vol. 13, No. 2, pp. 7–15.

4. Preservative leadership
Anna Cregård

Books and articles

Blackaby, Henry & Richard Blackaby, 2001, *Spiritual Leadership: Moving People on to God's Agenda*. Nashville, TN: Broadman & Holman Publishers.

CIC *Codex Iuris Canonici* (Code of Canon Law) 697–703§

Cregård, Anna, 2017, 'Investigating the Risks of Spiritual Leadership'. *Nonprofit Management and Leadership*, Vol. 27, 533–547.

Ducey, Ariel, 2007, 'More Than a Job: Meaning, Affect, and Training Health Care Workers'. In: Clough, Patricia Ticineco, *The Affective Turn – Theorizing the Social*. Durham, NC: Duke University Press.

Fairholm, Gilbert, 1996, 'Spiritual Leadership: Fulfilling Whole-self Needs at Work'. *Leadership & Organization Development Journal*, Vol. 17, No. 5, 11–17.

Foucault, Michel, 1998/1974, *Discipline and Punish: The Birth of the Prison*. Lund: Arkiv Academic Press

Fry, Louis, 2005, 'Toward a Paradigm of Spiritual Leadership'. Introduction to *The Leadership Quarterly*, Vol. 16, pp. 619–622.

Fry, Louis & Melanie Cohen, 2009, 'Spiritual Leadership as a Paradigm for Organizational Transformation and Recovery from Extended Work Hours Cultures'. *The Journal of Business Ethics*, Vol. 84, pp. 265–278.

Goffman, Erving, 1983, *Totala institutioner: fyra essäer om anstaltslivets sociala villkor* (Total institutions: four essays on the social situation of mental patients). Stockholm: Rabén & Sjögren.

Grint, Keith, 2010, 'The Sacred in Leadership: Separation, Sacrifice and Silence'. *Organization Studies*, Vol. 31, No. 1, pp. 89–107.

von Heidenstam, Verner, 1989/1901, *Heliga Birgittas pilgrimsfärd* (Saint Birgitta's Pilgrimage). Stockholm: Bonniers.

Lagercrantz, Agneta, 2003, 'Figuren som balanserar där mellan himmel och jord vid skorstenen – hon är nunna' (The figure next to the chimney, balancing between heaven and earth – she is a nun), 18 May, *Svenska Dagbladet*.

Long, B.S., and J.H. Mills. 2010, 'Workplace Spirituality, Contested Meaning, and the Organization: A Critical Sensemaking Account,' *Journal of Organizational Change Management*, Vol. 23, Issue 3, 325–341.

Lundén, Tryggve, 1957–59, *Den heliga Birgitta: Himmelska uppenbarelser 1–4* (Saint Birgitta: Heavenly

Revelations 1–4). Malmö: Allhem. First edition was compiled by Alfonso Pecha de Vadaterra in 1377.

Nordberg, Michael, 2003, *I kung Magnus tid. Norden under Magnus Eriksson 1317–1374* (In the times of King Magnus: The Nordic countries under the reign of Magnus Eriksson 1317–1374). Stockholm: Norstedts.

Reave, Laura, 2005, 'Spiritual values and Practices Related to Leadership Effectiveness', *The Leadership Quarterly,* Vol. 16, 655–687.

Todnem, Rune By, 2005, 'Organisational Change Management: A Critical Review'. *Journal of Change Management*, Vol. 5, 369–380.

Vadstena klosters minnesbok: Diarivm Vazstenense (Memorial Book of Vadstena Abbey: Diarivm Vazstenense), 1918/1984, Swedish translation by A W Lundberg, Birgittamuseiföreningen i Vadstena. Stockholm: P.A. Norstedts & Sons Publishers.

Yukl, Gary, 1981/2004, *Leadership in Organizations*. Englewood Cliffs, NJ: Pearson Prentice Hall.

Films on DVD

S:ta Birgittas abbedi Pax Mariae, *Birgittasystrarna i Vadstena* (The Birgittine Sisters in Vadstena).

S:ta Birgittas abbedi Pax Mariae, *Sätta i rullning. Den heliga Birgittas liv och orden* (To put in motion. The life and Order of Saint Birgitta).

S:ta Birgittas abbedi Pax Mariae, *Våga gå på vatten* (Courage to walk on water).

Internet

www.vatican.va/archive/ENG1104/_ INDEX.HTM, Den Heliga Stolen (The Holy Chair) (2011-09-01).

www.medeltidshandskrifter.se, Medeltidshandskrifter i Sverige (Medieval manuscripts in Sweden) (2011-09-15).

www.birgittaskloster.se, St. Birgitta's Abbey Pax Mariae (2015-10-05).

www.svenskakyrkan.se, The Swedish Church. (2011-08-10).

http://ia600504.us.archive.org/11/ items/MN5063ucmf_4/MN5063uc- mf_4.pdf, The Chicago university library, *Vadstena klosters minnesbok* (The Memorial Book of Vadstena Abbey).

www.ecornell.com (2015-10-02).

www.inc.com (2015-10-02).

www.executiveeducation.wharton. upenn.edu (2015-10-02).

www.bbc.com (2015-10-19).

5. Leadership and expertship
Staffan Furusten

Books and articles

Abbott, Andrew, 1988, *The System of Professions. An Essay on the Division of Expert Labor*. Chicago, IL.: Chicago University Press.

Alexius, Susanna, 2007, *Regelmotståndarna: om konsten att undkomma regler* (Rule resisters: The art of escaping rules). Stockholm: Stockholm School of Economics/ EFI.

—, 2017, 'Experts without Rules – Scrutinizing the Unregulated Free Zone of the Management Consultants', In: Furusten, Staffan & Andreas Werr (eds.), 2017, *The Organization of the Expert Society*. London: Routledge. pp. 22–37

Armbrüster, Thomas & Johannes Glückler, 2003, 'Bridging Uncertainty in Management Consulting: The Mechanisms of Trust and Networked Reputation'. *Organization Studies,* Vol. 24, No. 2, pp. 269–297.

Brante, Thomas, 2014, *Den professionella logiken – hur vetenskap och praktik förenas i det moderna kunskapssamhället.* (The professional logic: how science and practice unite in the modern knowledge society) Stockholm: Liber.

Freidson, Eliot, 2001, *Professionalism – the third logic*. Oxford, Blackwell Publishers.

Furusten, Staffan, 1999, *Popular Management Books – How they are Made and What they Mean for Organizations*. London: Routledge.

—, 2003, *God managementkonsultation – reglerad expertis eller improviserat artisteri?* (Good management consultancy – regulated expertise or improvised artistry?). Lund: Studentlitteratur.

—, 2009, 'Management Consultants as Improvising Agents of Stability,' *Scandinavian Journal of Management,* Vol. 25, No. 3, pp. 264–274.

—, 2013, 'Commercialized professionalism on the field of management consulting', *Journal of Organizational Change Management*, Vol. 26 pp. 265–285.

Furusten, Staffan & Andreas Werr (red.), 2005, *Dealing with Confidence: The Construction of Need and Trust in Management Advisory Services*. Copenhagen: CBS Press

—, 2009, 'The Need for Management Advisory Services: A Consequence of Institutionalization, Organization, and Trust'. In: Buono, Anthony & Flemming Poulfelt (red.) *Client-Consultant Collaboration: Coping with Complexity and Change*. Charlotte: Information Age Publishing.

— (eds.), 2012, *Expertsamhällets organisering* (Organisation of the expert society) Lund: Studentlitteratur.

— (eds.), 2017, *The Organization of the Expert Society,* London: Routledge.

—, 2017a, 'The Contemporary Expert Society', In: Furusten, Staffan & Andreas Werr (eds.), 2017, *The Organization of the Expert Society,* London: Routledge. pp 1–21.

Giddens, Anthony, 1991, *The Consequences of Modernity*. Cambridge: Polity Press.

Kubr, Milan, 2005, *Management Consulting – a guide to the profession*. New Dehli, Bookwell Publications.

MacDonald, Keith, 1995, *The Sociology of Professions*, Sage: London.
Weber, Max, 1949, *The Methodology of* *the Social Sciences*. New York: Free Press.

Internet

www.ne.se/konsult/229341, Nationalencyklopedin.
www.mathlein.se/Besser/besser1. htlm/2012-02-14.

www.chef.se (2010-05-11).

Interviews

MK1–7, Interviews with experienced senior management consultants (MK) during the period of 1998–2003.

K1–11, Interviews with buyers (K) of management consultancy services during the period of 1997–2003.

6. *To lead secret agents*
Björn Rombach and Rolf Solli

Books and articles

Balderson, Bo, 1980/1978, *Statsrådet sitter kvar* (The Cabinet Minister remains in office). Stockholm: Bonniers.
Brech, Edward, Andrew Thomson & John Wilson, 2010, *Lyndall Urwick. Management Pioneer. A Biography.* Oxford: Oxford University Press.
Carlson, Sune, 1991/1951, *Executive Behaviour. Reprinted with Contributions by Henry Mintzberg and Rosemary Stewart.* Uppsala: Acta Universitatis Upsaliensis.
Chapman, James, 2000, *License to Thrill. A Cultural History of the James Bond Films.* New York: Columbia University Press.
Comte-Sponville, André, 1996/2001, *A Short Treatise on the Great Virtues.* New York: Holt.
Cork, John & Collin Stutz 2009 (revision of the 2007 ed.), *James Bond encyclopedia.* London: Dorling Kindersley.
Danilov Anastasia, Torsten Biemann, Thorn Kring & Dirk Sliwka, 2013.

'The dark side of team incentives: Experimental evidence on advice quality from financial service professionals'. *Journal of Economic Behavior & Organization*, Vol. 93, pp. 266–272.
Drago, Robert & Gerald Garvey, 1998, 'Incentives for Helping on the Job: Theory and Evidence'. *The Journal of Labor Economics*, Vol. 16, No. 1, pp. 1–25.
Fayol, Henri, 1916, *Administration industrielle et générale.* Paris: Dunod.
—, 1916/2008, *Industriell och allmän administration* (Industrial and general administration). Stockholm: Santérus.
Felé, Lena Anderson, 2008, *Leda lagom många.* (To lead the right No.). *Om struktur, kontrollspann och organisationsideal* (About structures, spans of control and organisational ideals). School of Public Administration, University of Gothenburg.

Forsberg, Tore, 2006 (3rd revised ed.), *Spioner och spioner som spionerar på spioner* (Spies and spies who spy on spies). *Spioner och kontraspionage i Sverige* (Spies and counter-espionage in Sweden). Stockholm: Hjalmarsson & Högberg.

—, 2009, *Spioneri* (Espionage). *En förbjuden nödvändighet* (A prohibited necessity). Stockholm: Hjalmarsson & Högberg.

Gifford, Clive, 2006/2003, *Spioner* (Spies). *Fascinerande fakta* (Fascinating facts). Stockholm: Berghs.

Glassy, Mark, 2001, *The Biology of Science Fiction Cinema*. Jefferson, NC: McFarland & Company.

Grigorjev, Boris, 2009/2007, *Illegalister (The illegal)*. *KGB:s hemligaste spioner* (KGB's secret spies). Nacka: Efron & Dotter.

Gulick, Luther, 2003/1937, Notes on the Theory of Organization. In: Gulick, Luther & Urwick Lyndall (red.), *The Early Sociology of Management and Organizations*. Vol. IV. Papers on the Science of Administration, pp. 1–45. London: Routledge.

Hales, Colin, 1986, 'What Do Managers Do? A Critical Review of the Evidence'. *Journal of Management Studies*, Vol. 23, No. 1, pp. 88–115.

Howard, Michael, David LeBlanc & John Viega, 2010, *24 Deadly Sins of Software Security*. New York: McGraw Hill.

Johnsén, Henrik Rydell, 2010, 'Dödssyndernas genealogi' (The genealogy of the deadly sins). In: Stenquist, Catharina & Lindstedt Cronberg Marie (red.), *Dygder och laster* (Virtues and vices). *Förmoderna perspektiv på tillvaron* (Premodern perspectives on life), pp. 23–38. Lund: Nordic Academic Press.

Kotler, Philip, 2004, *Marknadsföringens tio dödssynder* (The Ten Deadly Marketing Sins). Sundbyberg: Optimal.

Krauss, Lawrence, 1997/1995, *The Physics of Star Trek*. London: HarperCollins.

Lampers, Lars Olof, 2002, *Det grå brödraskapet: en berättelse om IB: forskarrapport till Säkerhetstjänstkommissionen* (The grey brotherhood: A tale about IB: A research report to the Security Service Commission). Stockholm: Fritze's official publications.

Management Concepts, 2009, *The 77 Deadly Sins of Project Management*. Vienna, VA: Management Concepts.

Mintzberg, Henry, 1973, *The Nature of Managerial Work*. New York: HarperCollins.

—, 1991, 'Managerial work: forty years later'. In: Carlson, Sune, *Executive Behaviour. Reprinted with contributions by Henry Mintzberg and Rosemary Stewart*, pp. 97–119. Uppsala: Acta Universitatis Upsaliensis.

Nordberg, Jenny, 2007, Spionernas dilemma – dåliga chefer (The dilemma of secret agents – bad bosses). *Svenska Dagbladet* 2007-12-24.

Pryser, Tore, 2009/2007, *Kvinnliga spioner* (Female spies). *Agenter i Norden under andra världskriget* (Agents in the Nordic countries during World War II). Stockholm: Natur & Kultur.

Raine, George, 2010, *The Seven Deadly Sins. A Factional Account*. New York: iUniverse

Rogers, Frederick, 2011/1907, *The Seven Deadly Sins*. LaVergne, TN: Nabu public domain reprints.

Rombach, Björn & Rolf Solli, 2006, *Constructing Leadership. Reflections on Film Heroes as Leaders*. Stockholm: Santérus Academic Press.

—, 2009, 'Perceiving Snow, Ice and Cold'. In: Lindahl, Marcus & Alf Rehn (red.), *Feelings and Business*, pp. 109–150. Stockholm: Santérus Academic Press.

—, (2010). 'Imparare la leadership nell'università del cinema'. *Sviluppo & Organizzazione*. 238, pp. 92–96.

Schimmel, Solomon, 1997, *The Seven Deadly Sins. Jewish, Christian, and Classical Reflections on Human Psychology*. Oxford: Oxford University Press.

Schmier, David, 2009, *The 7 Deadly Job Search Sins*. Breinigsville, PA: Gethired.

Strohmenger, Sebastian, 2010, *The Seven Deadly Sins. Anger, Greed and Envy as Managerial Challenges*. Saarbrücken: Verlag Dr. Müller.

Töllborg, Dennis, 1999, *Medborgerligt pålitlig?* (Civil reliability?). *Svenskt säkerhetsskydd i förändring* (Swedish security in transition). Stockholm: Norstedts Juridik.

Westbrook, Kate, 2005, *The Moneypenny Diaries – Guardian Angel*. London: John Murray.

—, 2007. *The Moneypenny Diaries – Secret Servant*. London: John Murray.

—, 2008. *The Moneypenny Diaries – Final Fling*. London: John Murray.

Ian Fleming's Bond books
(listed according to year of publication of English editions)

– 1965 (1955). *Casino Royale*. Stockholm: Bonniers, Zebra special 5. (Casino Royale, 1953).

– 1956. *Live and Let Die*. Stockholm: Bonniers. (Live and Let Die, 1954).

– 1957. *Moonraker*. Stockholm: Bonniers, Zebra 47. (Moonraker, 1955).

– 1956. *Diamonds are forever*. Stockholm: Bonniers, Zebra 37. (Diamonds Are Forever, 1956).

– 1965 (1958). *From Russia, With Love*. Stockholm: Bonniers, Zebra special 1. (From Russia, With Love, 1957).

– 1965 (1958). *Dr. No*. Stockholm: Bonniers, Zebra special 2. also titled: 1979, *Dr No*. Stockholm: Bonniers. (Doctor No, 1958).

– 1965 (1960). *Goldfinger*. Stockholm: Bonniers, Zebra special 3. (Goldfinger, 1959).

– 1965 (1962). *For Your Eyes Only*. Stockholm: Bonniers, Zebra special 9. (For Your Eyes Only, 1960, including the adventures: 'Risico', 'Quantum of Solace', 'The Hildebrand Rarity', 'From a View to a Kill', 'For Your Eyes Only').

– 1962. *Thunderball*. Stockholm: Bonniers. (Thunderball, 1961).

– 1962. *007 – The Spy Who Loved Me*. Stockholm: Bonniers, Zebra 189. (The Spy Who Loved Me, 1962).

– 1964. *On Her Majesty's Secret Service*. Stockholm: Bonniers, Zebra 178. (On Her Majesty's Secret Service, 1963).

– 1964. *You Only Live Twice*. Stockholm: Bonniers. (You Only Live Twice, 1964).

– 1965. *The Man with the Golden Gun*. Stockholm: Bonniers. (The Man with the Golden Gun, 1965).

– 1966. *Octopussy*. Stockholm: Bonniers. (Octopussy, 1966, two adventures: 'Octopussy', 'The Living Daylights'. Note that later English editions may, according to James Chapman (2000, p. 308) include a third adventure titled 'The Property of a Lady'. (We do not know if the same applies to the Swedish editions.).

Ian Fleming's James Bond Short Stories (MP3)

Quantum of Solace: The Complete James Bond Short Stories. Read by Simon Vance. Blackstone Audio 2008. ('From a View to a Kill'; 'For Your Eyes Only'; 'Quantum of Solace'; 'Risico'; 'The Hildebrand Rarity'; 'Octopussy'; 'The Property of a Lady'; 'The Living Daylights'; '007 in New York').

James Bond films

(A well-made filmography up to *Tomorrow Never Dies* can be found in Chapman 2000, pp. 292–307. The same information is, however, available from many other sources such as Cork and Stutz 2009 and then up to and including *Quantum of Solace*).

Bond films for the study of M

1. 1962 – *Dr. No*
– Sean Connery (Bond) and Bernard Lee (M).
2. 1963 – *From Russia, with Love*
– Sean Connery (Bond) and Bernard Lee (M).
3. 1964 – *Goldfinger*
– Sean Connery (Bond) and Bernard Lee (M).
4. 1965 – *Thunderball*
– Sean Connery (Bond) and Bernard Lee (M).
5. 1967 – *You Only Live Twice*
– Sean Connery (Bond) and Bernard Lee (M).
6. 1969 – *Her Majesty's Secret Service*
– George Lazenby (Bond) and Bernard Lee (M).
7. 1971 – *Diamonds Are Forever*
– Sean Connery (Bond) and Bernard Lee (M).
8. 1973 – *Live and Let Die*
– Roger Moore (Bond) and Bernard Lee (M).
9. 1974 – *The Man with the Golden Gun*
– Roger Moore (Bond) and Bernard Lee (M).
10. 1977 – *The Spy Who Loved Me*
– Roger Moore (Bond) and Bernard Lee (M).
11. 1979 – *Moonraker*
– Roger Moore (Bond) and Bernard Lee (M).
12. 1981 – *For Your Eyes Only*
– Roger Moore (Bond), M is absent from this film
13. 1983 – *Octopussy*
– Roger Moore (Bond) and Robert Brown (M).
14. 1985 – *A View To A Kill*
– Roger Moore (Bond) and Robert Brown (M).
15. 1987 – *The Living Daylights*
– Roger Moore (Bond) and Robert Brown (M).
16. 1989 – *Licence To Kill*
– Timothy Dalton (Bond) and Robert Brown (M).
17. 1995 – *GoldenEye*
– Pierce Brosnan (Bond) and Judi Dench (M).
18. 1997 – *Tomorrow Never Dies*
– Pierce Brosnan (as Bond) and Judi Dench (as M).
19. 1999 – *The World Is Not Enough*
– Pierce Brosnan (Bond) and Judi Dench (M).
20. 2002 – *Die Another Day*
– Pierce Brosnan (Bond) and Judi Dench (M).

21. 2006 – *Casino Royale*
– Daniel Craig (Bond) and Judi Dench
   (M).
22. 2008 – *Quantum of Solace*
– Daniel Craig (Bond) & Judi Dench
   (M).

23. 2012 – *Skyfall*
– Daniel Craig (Bond) & Judi Dench
   (M).
24. 2015 – *Spectre*
– Daniel Craig (Bond) & Ralph
   Fiennes (M).

Other Bond films

Casino Royale, 1954 (TV-series, not
   included in our analysis).
Casino Royale, 1967 (production accompanying TV-series, not included in
   our analysis).

Never Say Never Again, 1983 (production accompanying TV-series, not
   included in our analysis).

DVD films about the Seven Deadly Sins

The Seven Deadly Sins (8 discs), directed
   by Richard Hobert, 1993–2000.
Seven, directed by David Fincher, 1995.

Seven Deadly Sins, directed by Jeff
   Renfroe, 2010.

Internet

www.agent007.nu/bondmusiken.htm,
   James Bond music (2011-08-16).

www.sis.gov.uk, Secret Intelligence
   Service MI6 (2012-06-01).

7. *Virtual leadership*
Johan Berglund

Books and articles

Asplund, Johan, 1987, *Det sociala livets
   elementära former* (The Elementary
   Forms of Social Life). Gothenburg:
   Korpen.
Grimes, Sara, 2006, 'Online Multi-
   player Games: A Virtual Space for
   Intellectual Property Debates?'
   New Media & Society, Vol. 8, No. 6,
   pp. 969–990.
Grimes, Sara, & Andrew Feenberg,
   2009, 'Rationalizing Play: A
   Critical Theory of Digital Gaming'.
   The Information Society, Vol. 25, No.
   2, pp. 105–118.
Gustafsson, Claes, 1994, *Produktion
   av allvar: om det ekonomiska förnuf-
tets metafysik* (The Production of
   Seriousness: The Metaphysics of
   Economic Reason). Stockholm:
   Nerenius & Santérus.
Hjarvard, Stig, 2008, 'The Mediatization
   of Society: A Theory of the Media
   as Agents of Social and Cultural
   Change'. *Nordicom Review*, Vol. 29,
   No. 2, pp. 105–134.
Kücklich, Julian, 2005, 'Precarious
   Playbour: Modders and the Digital
   Games Industry'. *The Fibreculture
   journal:* 5www.fibreculture.org/jour-
   nal/issue5/Kucklich_print.html.
Rombach, Björn (red.), 2005, *Den
   framgångsrika ekonomiskan* (The

Successful Economic Language).
Stockholm: Santérus.

Rowlands, Timothy, 2012, *Video Games Worlds – Working at Play in the Culture of EverQuest*, Walnut Creek, CA: Left Coast Press.

Steinkuehler, Constance, 2006, 'The Mangle of Play'. *Games and Culture*, Vol. 1, No. 3, pp. 199–213.

Taylor, T.L., 2002, '"Whose Game Is This Anyway": Negotiating Corporate Ownership in a Virtual World'. In: Mäyrä, Frans (red.), *Proceedings of Computer Games and Digital Cultures Conference*. Tampere: Tampere University Press.

—, 2006a, 'Beyond Management: Considering Participatory Design and Governance in Player Culture'. *First Monday*: 7.http://firtmon-day.org/htbin/cgiwrap/bin/ojs/index.php/fm/rt/printerfriend-ly/1611/1526.

—, 2006b, 'Does WoW Change Everything? How a PvP Server, Multinational Player Base, and Surveillance Mod Scene Caused Me Pause'. *Games and Culture*, Vol. 1,No. 4, pp. 318–337.

—, 2006c, *Play Between Worlds – Exploring Online Game Culture*. Cambridge, MA: MIT Press.

Thente, Jonas, *Dagens Nyheter,* 2010-08-30

Vesa, Mikko; Hamari, Juho; Harviainen, J Tuomas & Warmelink, Harald (2017) 'Computer Games and Organization Studies'. *Organization Studies*, Vol. 38(2), 273–284.

Internet

http://firstmonday.org/htbin/cgiwrap/bin/ojs/index.php/fm/rt/ printerFriend-ly1611/1526.

8. *Leading in crisis*
Iréne Lind Nilsson

Books and articles

Adorno, Theodor, Else Frenkel-Brunswik, Daniel Levinson & Nevitt Sanford, 1950, *The Authoritarian Personality*. New York: Harper & Brothers.

Alvesson, Mats & Stefan Sveningsson, (eds.), 2007, *Organisation, ledning och processer* (Organisation, leadership, and processes). Lund: Studentlitteratur.

Bruzelius, Lars & Per-Hugo Skärvad, 2004. *Integrerad organisationslära* (Integrated organisation theory). Lund: Studentlitteratur.

Cullberg, Johan, 1992, *Kris och utveck-ling* (Crisis and Development). Stockholm: Natur & Kultur.

Ericson, Bengt, 2007, *Antonias revansch – Hur hon räddade sitt imperium och kom tillbaka som en vinnare* (Antonia's revenge – How she saved her empire and made a comeback). Stockholm: Fischer & Co.

Granström, Kjell, 2000, *Dynamik i arbetsgrupper. Om grupprocesser på arbetet* (Workgroup dynamics. About group processes in work). Lund: Studentlitteratur.

Kotter, John, 1988, *The Leadership Factor*. New York: Free Press.

Lind Nilsson, Iréne, 2001, *Ledarskap i kris, kaos och omställning* (Leadership in crisis, chaos, and change). *En empirisk studie av chefer i företag och förvaltning* (An empirical study of leaders in enterprise and administration). Uppsala Studies in Education 98. Acta Universitatis Upsaliensis.

—, 2010, *Maktens fallgropar* (The pitfalls of power). Lund: Studentlitteratur.

—, 2015, *Söker du makt? Fundera på dina drivkrafter!* (Are you striving for power? Reflect upon your driving forces!) Stockholm: 33 sidor.

Lind Nilsson, Iréne & Lisbeth Gustafsson, 2006, *Ledarskapets inre och yttre resa* (The inner and outer journey of leadership). Lund: Studentlitteratur

Maltén, Arne, 1992, *Grupputveckling inom skola och andra arbetsplatser* (Group development in schools and other workplaces). Lund: Studentlitteratur

Polsky, Howard, 1967. *From Claques to Factions – Subgroups in Organisations*. National Association of Social Workers.

Stogdill, Ralph, 1948, 'Personal Factors associated with Leadership. A Survey of the Literature'. *Journal of Psychology*. Vol. 25, pp. 35–71.

Weber, Max, 1964, *The Theory of Social and Economic Organization*. New York: The Free Press.

Wieland-Burston, Joanne, 1991, *Att möta kaos: när själen söker ordning* (Chaos and Order in the World of the Psyche). Stockholm: Berghs.

Zaleznik, Abraham, 1977, 'Managers and Leaders – Are They Different?' *Nordicom Review*, Vol. 55, No. 5, pp. 67–68.

Internet

www.redbull.se, Red Bull, X-Alps (2012-01-11).

9. Reluctant leadership
Rebecka Arman and Östen Ohlsson

Books and articles

Abbot, Andrew, 1981, 'Status and strain in the professions'. *American Journal of Sociology*, Vol. 86, No. 4, pp. 819–835.

Arman, Rebecka, 2010, *Fragmentation and power in managerial work in health care*. University of Gothenburg

Carlson, Sune, 1991/1951, *Executive Behaviour*. Stockholm: Almqvist & Wiksell.

Carlsson, Ingvar, 1999, *Ur skuggan av Olof Palme* (Out of the shadow of Olof Palme). Stockholm: Hjalmarsson & Högberg.

Cregård, Anna, 2004, *Abruption: uppsägning som översättning och improvisation* (Abruption: Dismissal as translation and improvisation). Gothenburg: Kfi Report No. 71

Erlander, Tage, 1973, *1940–1949*, (Memoirs). Stockholm: Tidens förlag.

—, 2001, *Dagböcker 1945–1949* (Diaries). Hedemora: Gidlund Publisher.

Esaiasson, Peter, 1996, 'Mona Sahlins förlorade popularitet'

(Mona Sahlin's Lost Popularity) In: Holmberg, Sören& Weibull, Lennart (red.), *Mitt i 90-talet* (In the mid 1990s). Gothenburg: The SOM Institute

Forsman, Birgitta, 2009, *Arvet från Darwin* (Darwin's legacy). Stockholm: Fri Tanke.

Fredriksson, Göran, 2012, 'Drabbad av Nietzsche, fängslad av Deleuze' (Afflicted by Nietzsche, imprisoned by Deleuze). 'Svensk nynietzscheanism rekonstruerad' (Swedish Newnietzscheanism reconstructed). *Häften för kritiska studier* (Booklets for critical studies), No. 200–201, pp. 52–73.

Hacking, Ian, 1999, *The Social Construction of What?* Cambridge, MA: Harvard University Press.

Held, Virginia, 2006, *The Ethics of Care – Personal, Political and Global*. New York: Oxford University Press.

Jackson, Brad & Ken Parry, 2008, *A Very Short, Fairly Interesting and Reasonably Cheap Book about Studying Leadership*. London: Sage.

Kjellberg, Fanny & Tina Samuelsson, 2011, *Leader retention – At a Hospital in Sweden* (thesis). University of Gothenburg

Lawrence, Paul, 2010, *Driven to Lead*. San Francisco: Jossey-Bass.

Lévi-Strauss, Claude, 2000/1955, *Spillror av paradiset* (Paradise Lost). Lund: Arkiv

Lorentz, Konrad, 1969, *Djuriskt och mänskligt* (Studies in animal and human behaviour). Stockholm: Norstedts.

McDougall, Christopher, 2009, *Born to run – jakten på löpningens själ* (In pursuit of the soul of running). Stockholm: Månpocket.

McClelland, David & Richard Boyatzis, 1982, 'Leadership Motive Pattern and Long-Term Success in Management'. *Journal of Management Studies*, Vol. 67, No. 6, pp. 737–743.

McClelland, David & David Burnham, 2003, 'Power is the great motivator'. *Harvard Business Review*, "Best of 1976", January, pp. 117–126.

Mintzberg, Henry, 1973, *The Nature of Managerial Work*. New York: Harper & Row.

—, 1983, *Structure in Fives*. New York: Prentice Hall.

Nietzsche, Friedrich, 1987/1882, *Den glada vetenskapen* (The Happy Science). Gothenburg: Korpen.

Nordin, Eva, 2009, 'Sjukhuset som tagits över av sjuksköterskor' (The hospital taken over by nurses). sjukhuslakaren.se 2009-10-27.

Persson, Göran, 2007. *Min väg, mina val* (My Path, My Choices). Stockholm: Bonniers.

Peterson, Tage, 1999, *Resan mot Mars* (The Journey to Mars). Stockholm: Bonniers.

Rombach, Björn & Rolf Solli, 2006, *Constructing Leadership*. Stockholm: Santérus Academic Press.

Ross, William, 1981, *Syster Anns hemlighet* (Nurse Ann's Secret). Copenhagen: Wennerbergs Publisher.

Safranski, Rüdiger, 2003, *Nietzsche: Tankarnas biografi* (A Philosophical Biography). Stockholm: Natur & Kultur.

Smith, Anders, 2011, *An Investigation into the Process and Consequences of ambiguous Goals in Swedish Primary Healthcare* (thesis). University of Gothenburg.

Spinks, Lee, 2003, *Friedrich Nietzsche*. London: Routledge.

VGREG, 2009, *Västra Götalandsregionens budget 2009* (Västra Götaland County Budget). Gothenburg: VGR

Wittig, Monique, 1985, 'The Mark of Gender'. *Feminist issues*, Fall 1985.

Zerjal, Tatiana *et al.* (22 co-authors),
    2003, 'The Genetic Legacy of
    the Mongols'. *American Journal of
    Human Ethics,* Vol. 72, pp. 717–721.

Internet

www.socialdemokraterna.se/Vart-parti/
    Var-historia/ (2012-04-04).
www.svd.se/nyheter/inrikes/har-ar-de-
    hetaste-kandidaterna (2017-09-20).
www.upi.com/Odd_News/2003/02/06/

Öfverström, Helena, 2008, *Steget till
    chefskap* (The Step to Management).
    Gothenburg: BAS.

Genes-of-historys-
    greatest-lover-found/UPI-
    15661044569919/#ixzz1xm7IFG4W
    (2017-09-20).

Films

Forrest Gump, 1994, Robert Zemeckis
Life of Brian, 1979, Terry Jones.

The Life of Mammals, 2002, David
    Attenborough.

Recordings

Ives, Burl, 1963, *I'm the Boss/The Moon Is High*: Decca 31504.

10. *Leadership as a problem*
Björn Rombach and Östen Ohlsson

Books and articles

Adams, Douglas, 2002/1979–1984, *The
    Hitchhikers Guide to the Galaxy. The
    Trilogy of Four.* London: Picador.
Ahrne, Göran & Apostolis Papakostas,
    2002, *Organisationer, samhälle
    och globalisering* (Organisations,
    society, and globalisation). Lund:
    Studentlitteratur.
Alvesson, Mats, 2006, *Tomhetens tri-
    umf* (The Triumph of Emptiness),
    Stockholm: Atlas.
Alvesson, Mats & Jörgen Sandberg,
    2011, 'Ways of constructing research
    questions: gap-spotting or prob-
    lematization?' *Organization*, Vol. 18,
    No. 1, pp. 23–44.
Baudrillard, Jean, 1998, *Selected
    Writings.* Cambridge: Polity Press.
Borell, Klas, 1987, *Byråkrati och karisma,
    lejon och rävar* (Bureaucracy and

charisma, lions and foxes). Research
    reports from the department of
    sociology, Uppsala University.
Burke, Peter, 1996, *En kung blir till* (The
    Fabrication of Louis XIV). *Myter och
    propaganda kring Ludvig XIV* (Myths
    and propaganda surrounding Louis
    XIV). Stockholm: Tiden Athena.
DiMaggio, Paul & Walter Powell,
    1983, 'The Iron Cage Revisited:
    Institutional Isomorphism
    and Collective Rationality in
    Organizational Fields'. *American
    Sociological Review,* Vol. 48, No. 2,
    pp. 147–160.
Doyle, Arthur Conan, 2005/1905,
    'Det sista problemet' (The final
    problem). In: Doyle, Arthur Conan,
    *Sherlock Holmes versus Professor
    Moriarty,* pp. 75–93. Lund: Bakhåll.

Durkheim, Emile, 1997/1893, *The Division of Labor in Society*, (De la division du travail social). New York: Free Press.

Eriksson, Henrik, 2012, 'Vedervärdiga kläder ... '(Hideous clothing...). *Nya CykelTidningen*, No. 3, p. 31.

Fayol, Henri, 1916/2008, *Industriell och allmän administration* (Industrial and general administration). Stockholm: Santérus.

Friedman, Stewart, 2008, *Total Leadership. Be a better leader, have a better life.* Boston, MA: Harvard Business Press.

Giddens, Anthony, 1996, *Modernitetens följder* (The consequences of modernity). Lund: Studentlitteratur.

Goffman, Erving, 2004, *Totala institutioner: Fyra essäer om anstaltslivets sociala villkor* (Total institutions: four essays on the social situation of mental patients). Stockholm: Norstedts.

Kotter, John, 1996, *Leading Change.* Boston, MA: Harvard Business School Press.

Mintzberg, Henry, 1983, *Structure in Fives*. Englewood Cliffs: Prentice Hall.

Ohlsson, Östen & Björn Rombach, 2014, *The tyranny of metaphors.* Stockholm: Santérus Academic Press

Popper, Karl, 1963, *Conjectures and Refutations: The Growth of Scientific Knowledge.* London: Routledge.

Putnam, Robert, 1993, *Making Democracy Work: Civic Traditions in Modern Italy.* Princeton: Princeton University Press.

Varga von Kibéd, Matthias & Insa Sparrer, 2011, *Ganz im Gegenteil.* Heidelberg: Carl-Auer.

Weber, Max, 1978/1925, *Economy and Society.* Vol. 2 (Wirtschaft und Gesellschaft). Berkeley, CA: University of California Press.

Yukl, Gary, 2012, *Ledarskap i organisationer* (Leadership in organisations). Harlow: Pearson Education.

Internet

www.lmi-hr.com/~lmihr/index.php?option=com_content&view=article&id=110&Itemid=192 (2012-09-27).